Table of Contents

Foreword

Over the years, quite a few soccer officiating "textbooks" have been published. Each new book contributed to the overall purpose of making each of us better at what we do. Most were text-heavy with a smattering of graphics to depict what the text was telling us. The introduction of *Soccer Officials Guidebook For a Crew of Three Officials (Diagonal System of Control)* raises the bar substantially in defining what a soccer textbook should be. Without question, there is no other book now available that so effectively combines instructional text with graphics that support and enhance the written word.

The staff at *Referee* magazine, "the magazine of sports officiating," has been developing this text-and-graphic concept for a number of years. Similar manuals for baseball, football and basketball officials have preceded this effort. For this book, *Referee* contributing editor, U.S. Soccer State Referee, state instructor and state assessor Carl P. Schwartz and publication design manager Matt Bowen prepared 400 superb graphics that describe and illustrate countless teaching points. This is especially important for those of you who are responsible for training officials. Other than actual game experience, there is no better resource for learning how to become a better soccer official.

More than just a book published by *Referee* magazine, this book has been reviewed and endorsed by the U.S. Soccer Referee Department and U.S. Soccer manager of referee development and education Alfred Kleinaitis. With U.S. Soccer national instructor trainer Dan Heldman serving as project leader, a group of State and emeritus National Referees and experienced instructors contributed their input to help shape this final product. Those individuals are Mike Goblet, Ulrich Strom, Gil Weber and Tim Zich. The result: a clear, concise text that mirrors and executes the teaching principles of the U.S. Soccer. Additionally, since we know many of you work under other codes and mechanics, those differences are clearly pointed out when they deviate from U.S. Soccer mechanics.

Whether you're a new official or a veteran, you will benefit from this book. If you're just beginning, you're getting the best information available to help you improve. If you're a veteran, you'll be able to refine your skills and learn what it takes to move to the next level. If you're an instructor, you now have a U.S. Soccer-endorsed textbook with enough strong material to cover new topics at every meeting or clinic.

The U.S. Soccer Referee Department is excited to be a part of this groundbreaking publication. In the years to come, you will see this book become the definitive resource for better soccer officiating. Enjoy the journey to becoming a better official.

Esse Baharmast

Esse Baharmast
U.S. Soccer Director of Advanced and International Referee Development

Acknowledgments

This book is a product of teamwork. Special thanks to Matt Bowen, *Referee* publication design manager, for his efforts and talents. The visual effects that set this book apart are the result of his dedication, hard work and ability.

The NCAA secretary-soccer rules editor, C. Cliff McCrath, continues to provide insightful comments and a source of renewed enthusiasm toward the game. Dr. Raymond Bernabei, NISOA executive director, granted his kind permission to use extracts from the NISOA instructional manual, *Diagonal System of Control*, and clarified technical interpretations on current mechanics. Alfred Kleinaitis, USSF manager of referee development and education, and his staff were instrumental in making this book possible. The culmination of their efforts in publishing *Advice to Referees on the Laws of the Game* and *Guide to Procedures for Referees, Assistant Referees and Fourth Officials* allowed a quantum leap in standardizing referee mechanics. Their timely efforts are greatly appreciated.

The following people provided invaluable input and editing prowess: local referee John Oberst, my friend and electronic wizard Josef Zeevi and longtime *Referee* contributor Dan Heldman. Heldman consolidated the input from four others who make enormous contributions to this work: Mike Goblet, Ulrich Strom, Gil Weber and Tim Zich. Their commentary and attention to detail made this book much better.

Very little about soccer refereeing originated with me. I've had the pleasure to come in contact with some special people during my years in the game, people who taught me a great deal about the sport I love and how to appreciate it: USSF national instructor and national assessor Pat Smith, former national director of assessment Don Creswell, former teaching and traveling partner Lyle Gisi, current national assessor from northern California John Kennedy, and my first NISOA assignor and recent inductee into the NISOA Hall of Fame, Derk Zylker. Many of their ideas and teachings are reflected in this work.

Thanks to the rest of the *Referee* team for their understanding and encouragement during the entire process. It was a team effort.

Carl P. Schwartz
Contributing Editor
Referee magazine

Introduction

Older readers may remember the association training officer reading the *Laws of the Game* directly from the book. In recent years, the NISOA and USSF instructional systems have made great strides with trained and certified instructors and standardized lesson plans. But those 16-hour USSF courses aren't enough to completely convey what the instructor has learned in a 20-year career.

Part of our job is teaching. When *Referee's* editors brainstormed for new product ideas, the one thing that stood out was the need for a visually enhanced, diagram-based mechanics manual: *Soccer Officials Guidebook* was born.

This book gives you the intricate knowledge normally found at a camp and combines it with advanced visual effects. We've added *Referee's* real-world philosophy written by officials, for officials.

We've created game-specific play diagrams and added the officials' proper positioning. You'll learn how to recognize plays and officiate them correctly.

Perhaps most important, we present a variety of ideas. Soccer officiating is not about the black-and-white words found on a page. It's not about the dots spread across a field layout. It's about capturing the spirit of the game. It's about managing the people and the environment to create an atmosphere where the wonderful game can be enjoyed to its fullest. Soccer officiating is about three things: safety, equality and enjoyment.

We've created computer-enhanced graphics showing you an official's view of onfield action. You look over the referee's shoulder and see what the referee sees. It's as if you were on the field yourself.

If you are confronted with a game situation that resembles the PlayPics on these pages, remember that our suggestions are based on the USSF, Federation and NCAA manuals currently in use. But if taking the prescribed actions will lead to a loss of game control or introduce an element of unfairness not intended by the laws and rules, you must act as your own game manager. You must make the courageous decisions to keep the balance between the competing teams.

Of course, *Soccer Officials Guidebook* is just that — a guide. Some concepts within these pages will not completely agree with the National Federation, NCAA or USSF manuals, or coincide with state or local association practices. We've included what we think is the best way to do things based on years of discussions with referees all over the world. Since most of my referee experience comes from my 11 years in Europe, the basis or foundation of the book is closely allied with FIFA/USSF philosophy. Where appropriate, we've included the proper rulings and terminology from the other codes.

The variations and deviations from the Federation, NCAA and USSF manuals will, at worst, show you some things you don't want (or aren't allowed) to try. At best, it opens up a new way of thinking for you. Like any guidebook, you won't embrace it all; but what you do like will make you better.

Drop me a note and let me know what you think.

Carl P. Schwartz
Contributing Editor
Referee magazine

Chapter 1

Definition Of Terms

The following terms are used throughout the book. Although many of the terms will seem self-explanatory, a brief review will insure complete understanding.

A-League — Within North America, the second level of professional soccer with Second Division status.

AYSO — American Youth Soccer Organization. Headquartered in Hawthorne, Calif., with more than 600,000 registered players and 56,000 referees, their game is based on these philosophies: everyone plays, balanced teams, open registration, positive coaching and good sportsmanship.

Advantage — Taken from a concept in law 5 that "allows play to continue when the team against which an offense has been committed will benefit from such an advantage and penalizes the original offense if the anticipated advantage does not ensue at that time." Other sports know that philosophy as "no harm, no foul" or advantage/disadvantage. That authority allows the referee to keep the game flowing.

Blocking the passing lanes — Standing between the attacker with the ball and a teammate who could receive a pass; what a good defender tries to do and what a referee must avoid doing during open play.

Bridging — Also known as backing under or tripping, a player remains on the ground while an opponent goes airborne to play the ball. Often there is minute backward movement to create contact.

Careless — A lack of attention to the impact of an action. That is the lowest level of force needed for a referee to judge an action to be an offense.

Caution — A formal disciplinary action by the referee with the aim of stopping further misconduct by a player or substitute. Sometimes known as "booking," the referee displays a yellow card for all to see.

Center forward — The target player in the attacking zone. Teammates usually try to play the ball into the center forward for scoring opportunities. Often a tall player with capable heading skills. In this text, the center forward wears jersey number ❽.

Center half — The attacking, offensive midfield player who often collects the ball from defenders and distributes it to other attacking players, either in the mixer or on the wings. In this text, the center half wears jersey number ❺.

Cha-cha — A style of playing with short passing, hip movement and misdirecting opponents via body fakes. The Brazilian style of play is a primary example.

Clearance — A long, clearing kick from a defender in the defensive zone. Distance is a greater consideration than accuracy. See "Whack."

Club linesmen — Parents, friends or substitutes who "run the line" to assist the referee with balls that pass wholly over the lines. Often untrained, those individuals are not neutral as they are supporters of one team or the other.

CONCACAF — Confederacion Norte-Centroamericana y del Caribe de Futbol. The former name of the continental governing body over the USSF that reports directly to FIFA. See "The Football Confederation."

Corner arc — The quarter circle in each corner of the field to mark the area where corner kicks originate.

Counterattack — the rapid movement of the ball from one team's defensive end into their attacking zone.

Cross — When a wing player has the ball and sends a pass into the central attacking zone. Usually a cross is a high arching ball so a teammate can time a run onto the ball and head it into the net.

Crossover steps — One method for the assistant referee to run parallel to the touchline. It is not advised; it is easy to trip using that method.

Cutting off the passing lanes — See "Blocking the passing lanes."

Dead-ball officiating — Activity during the time immediately after the ball becomes dead. Good dead-ball officials don't stop officiating when the ball is dead; they continue to watch the players and prevent problems.

Diagonal System of Control — See "DSC."

Directly — Used in several places in the laws, that critically important concept implies that no other player touches the ball following a restart. For example, if an awarded indirect free kick enters the goal directly from the restart, no goal is awarded. Likewise, if the same player is the first to touch a ball directly after a corner kick (or restart other than dropped ball) it is an offense. That word has vital implications for offside infractions.

Dismissal — When the referee requests a team member, other than a player or substitute, to depart the field area. That is the same as a red card, but the red card is not displayed to a team member other than a player or substitute under FIFA laws.

Disqualify — The term used by Federation (see "Federation") to denote a send off. Unique rules allow disqualified players to be replaced under certain limited circumstances.

Dribbler — A player who makes multiple, successive touches on the ball while running.

Dropping zone — The approximate area where the referee expects the ball to land after a goalkeeper's punt, a goalkick or a free kick.

DSC — Diagonal System of Control. Three-referee system with a referee and two assistant referees. Only the referee has a whistle. That system is named DSC for the diagonal path the referee follows across the field to keep the lead assistant referee in view.

Dual diagonal system — Also known as the three-whistle system, it is one method of game control.

Dual system — Two onfield referees, each with a whistle, have shared responsibility for determining fouls and game control.

Dummy — To intentionally let the ball pass near your body without playing it. Usually a player lets the ball go through the legs to a teammate. The advantage of that technique is that it causes the defender to hesitate, creating space.

Ejection — The NCAA term used for a send off.

Excessive force — Use of intentional violence. A foul committed with that level of force is misconduct. Referees should send the offender off (red card).

Extra time — Law 7 allows for two further equal periods to be played if the competition rules provide for that in case of a draw. Under collegiate rules, that is called overtime. See "overtime."

Extreme position — That is actually a good position in many circumstances. Examples of extreme positions include being off the field of play during a throw-in down the touchline, ahead of play on a direct free kick. The benefits of an extreme position need to be weighed against the additional fitness demands if the referee must recover quickly. Some referees call that an "aggressive position."

Far post — See "Visual definition," p. 22.

Federation — Short for the National Federation of State High School Associations. The Federation is the governing body for high school athletics and produces the official soccer manual for the Federation. The Federation manual is used throughout high school soccer and is referred to often in this book.

FIFA — Federation Internationale de Football Association. Headquartered in Zurich, Switzerland that international governing body has worldwide responsibility for soccer (commonly known in other nations as "football").

Flat — Also known as I-formation or straightlined, the referee is directly in line with a series of players and the vision of events is obscured by bodies.

Flatback — A defensive set used by many teams. The three or four defensive players have little depth across the field; essentially they are lined up, or flat.

Flick on — An intended grazing of the ball with the head or leg to pass the ball to a teammate. Often the ball's direction is changed only slightly.

Fourth official — A reserve official who may be appointed under competition rules and officiates if any of the three match officials is unable to continue. The fourth official has many administrative responsibilities.

Freeze your eyes, not your feet — Refers to the responsibility and technique for the referee when a foul is called. "Freeze your eyes" means it's your responsibility to watch all the players during the dead ball (the eyes actually should scan the player area, so they're not actually "frozen" on one player). "Not your feet" means you can begin moving to your new position and prepare players for the ensuing play while watching them carefully. There are times when you must run to the spot of the foul to prevent retaliation.

Goal area — Mistakenly referred to as the "goal box," that 6- by 20-yard area at both ends of the field marks the area where goalkicks originate and marks the closest point an indirect free kick can be taken by the attacking team.

Golden goal — The first, game-deciding goal scored in extra time, if the competition rules allow for it. Also known as a "sudden-death goal."

Header — To intentionally play the ball with the head. A player tries to direct the ball to a teammate, into the goal or away from a trouble area.

I-formation — See "Visual definition," p. 23. Also referred to as "straightlining."

Inside-out look — See "Visual definition," p. 20.

In the opinion of the referee — The decision-making ability vested in the referee. Under the diagonal system of control, the referee is the sole person responsible for the conduct of the match. Referees are to use their training, experience and judgement — along with a good dose of law 0 and law 18 — to make their choices.

IFAB — International Football Association Board. The rules-making body of international soccer. FIFA is given four rotating votes on that eight-member board and the associations of England, Ireland, Scotland and Wales are each given one vote. It takes six votes to approve an alteration to the law. Law changes go into effect on July 1 in the same year they are approved. The *Laws of the Game* are supplemented by Decisions of the International Football Association Board to clarify points made within the laws. The decisions of the IFAB are considered binding.

Inswinger — A specialized type of cross where the kick, usually a corner kick, curves inward toward the goalkeeper as it nears the goal mouth. A left-footed kicker kicking from the right side would deliver an inswinger.

Into touch — When the ball wholly passes over either of the touchlines (the longer of the two lines on the "sides" of the field), it goes "into touch." The team awarded the throw-in may then touch the ball, pick it up and execute a throw-in to get the ball back into play. Commonly referred to as "out of bounds" in other sports.

Kicks from the penalty mark — A method to determine a winning team after a draw or tie. The rules of the competition will specify if there is to be extra time before the kicks from the penalty mark. Those are not to be confused with a penalty kick or an MLS-style shootout where the kicks start from 35 yards from the goalline.

Law 0 — Law zero. That unwritten law contains the spirit of the game.

Law 18 — Common reference for common sense, as in applying the fair thing to do for a situation not covered in the *Laws of the Game*. See a more complete definition for law 18 in *Advice to Referees*.

Lead — The lead official in a dual (two-person) system is normally positioned near the second-to-last defender and is primarily responsible for play in the attacking zone and offside decisions.

Lead assistant — The assistant referee towards whom play is moving. Normally the referee is facing that individual.

Look-back — A technique where the referee glances over the shoulder while running away from where the ball has just been played. Players often tangle after the ball is away and sometimes referees incorrectly do not observe that action because they are following the flight of the ball. An occasional look-back will keep the players honest.

MLS — Major League Soccer. The highest level of professional soccer in North America, it has First Division status with FIFA.

Mixer — The area in and around the penalty area. Due to the critical importance of even one goal, that area is heavily defended while the attacking team tries to attack in numbers. That mass of bodies creates havoc as they each pursue their own success — attacking or defending. Kicked balls, rebounds, diving saves, perhaps even illegal actions by attackers and defenders heighten the simile to the mixer.

NCAA — National Collegiate Athletic Association. One of three major rule codes within the United States, NCAA is the rulemaking body for the National Collegiate Athletic Association, National Christian College Athletic Association, National Junior College Athletic Association and National Association of Intercollegiate Athletics.

Near post — See "Visual definition," p. 22.

No-call — A referee who observes an action may make a conscious decision to not whistle a foul or infraction. See "Advantage." Some offenses may also be considered trifling or too minor to stop the flow of play and award a free kick. See "Trifling." The referee may use discretion on some decisions covered in law 12, such as a minor push where the player maintains control and executes an intended pass; other facets, such as a ball into touch, must be decided as spelled out in the law.

Obvious goal-scoring opportunity — In the opinion of the referee, when an attacking player is moving toward the opponent's goal with the ball and has no defender, or only one defender, to beat before scoring a goal.

Offside — The offense of interfering with play, interfering with an opponent or gaining an advantage while being in an offside position. Since the offense is only called against a single player, offside is generally referred to in the singular.

Offside position — A place on the field where players are ahead of the ball, without at least two opponents who are nearer the opponent's goalline. Players are not in an offside position in their own half of the field. It is not an offense to be in an offside position.

Offside trap — A tactical maneuver by the defense to move forward just prior to the opposing team making a pass, with the intent of placing the attackers in an offside position and hoping to gain an offside decision.

One-touch — To receive a pass and distribute the ball all in a single touch. The advantage of that technique is that the defensive players must rapidly adjust to the changing angle of the ball.

Outswinger — A specialized type of cross where the kick, usually a corner kick, curves outward, away from the goalkeeper as it nears the goal mouth. A left-footed kicker kicking from the left side would deliver an outswinger.

Overlapping run — A teammate without the ball runs past a teammate with the ball, either to draw a defender away from the ball or with the hope of receiving a pass with space to work and a running head start.

Overtime — The term used under college rules for extra time, used to determine a winner in a match that is tied at the end of regulation play.

Own half — When players are in the same half of the field of play they are defending.

Peeking — Squatting or leaning to see a play. The better technique is to move the feet and run to a position to gain the proper angle to see the play.

Penalty arc — A curved line above the top of the penalty area that marks the 10-yard radius from the penalty mark. The territory bounded by the penalty arc is not part of the penalty area.

Penalty area — Mistakenly referred to as the "penalty box," that 18- by 44-yard area at both ends of the field marks the area where direct free kick fouls become penalty kicks as well as marks the area where a goalkeeper may handle the ball legally.

Penalty kick — It is a free kick taken by an attacker from a point 12 yards from the goalline with only the goalkeeper to defend against the kick. All other players must be outside the penalty area and penalty arc.

Plane of the line — An important concept for the position of the ball relative to the lines on the field. If any portion of the ball is above the plane of the line, it is still within that area. An example is when a throw-in breaks the plane of the line, it is in play.

Plant leg — The supporting leg as a player shifts the weight in preparation to shoot or pass.

Player — A team member in a numbered jersey who is eligible to play and is legally on the field. Other team members wearing numbered jerseys are substitutes.

Playing distance — The distance players can cover in two strides at the speed they are moving at the time.

Player designations — The *Laws of the Game* do not require jersey numbers, but many national associations and leagues do require numbers. Players are those listed on the game roster and legally on the field.

For the MechaniGrams, player designations are assigned: ⑰ is the goalkeeper; ②,③ and ④ are defenders; ⑤ is the center half; ⑥ and ⑦ are midfielders; ⑧ is the center forward; ⑨ is the playmaker; ⑩ and ⑪ are the strikers. Collectively ⑨, ⑩ and ⑪ are called attackers. Numbers ⑫, ⑬ and ⑭ are substitutes. That numbering system goes back to the origins of the game when players didn't own their own jerseys, instead using the team's jersey for whichever position they played that day. See "Visual Definitions," p. 19.

Preventive officiating — Refers to actions by officials who prevent problems from occurring by talking to players and coaches. Preventive officiating is often related to dead-ball officiating.

Q&A — FIFA's questions and answers. A series of questions about the laws posed by the national associations and confederations which are not clearly spelled out in the *Laws of the Game*. Definitive guidance is given in the Q&A. Published periodically, the current version is available at www.fifa.com.

Qualifiers — World Cup qualifying matches played within the confederations to earn automatic berths to the World Cup final tournament.

Reckless — An action by a player despite the awareness of its impact; unnatural, designed to intimidate. A foul committed with that level of force is misconduct and should lead to a caution (yellow card).

Re-entry — When a player becomes a substitute and wishes to come back into the game as a player. Various codes have different limitations on re-entry, from none to unlimited. It is incumbent on the referee to know the re-entry rules in that league or competition.

Referee the defense — A strategy and philosophy that has the official focusing on the defensive player's movements to correctly judge contact situations.

Screen — A legal action by a player who delays or prevents an opponent from reaching the ball (also referred to as "shielding"). The ball must be within playing distance. See "Playing distance."

Second-to-last defender — Commonly known as the last defender because it is assumed the goalkeeper will also be near the goalmouth, that is the key player in making a determination of offside position. Referees must be particularly attentive to that player when there is an active goalkeeper who moves forward often.

Selling the call — Placing emphasis on a call with louder voice and whistle, and slightly more demonstrative signals. Selling only occurs on close calls and should be used sparingly. It is designed to help the call gain acceptance and show the official's decisiveness.

Send off — Under the *Laws of the Game*, that is the term used when a player may no longer participate in the game and may not be replaced. A red card is displayed.

Sidestep — A method for the assistant referee to run parallel to the touchline. The preferred method as there is less chance of tripping and provides a better look.

Slow build-up — When the attacking team brings the ball up the field in a controlled fashion, stringing together a series of passes between teammates, waiting for space, hoping to exploit a weakness by the defense.

SAY — Soccer for American Youth. Headquartered in Cincinnati, with more than 6,600 teams for players ages 4-18.

SITS — Soccer in the Streets. Headquartered in Jonesboro, Ga., that inner city soccer program has 24 chapters in major metropolitan areas.

SOG — Spirit of the game. An unwritten code that players, coaches and spectators bring to playing and viewing the game. FIFA is trying to keep the positive spirit alive with its "Fair Play, Please" campaign.

Spacing — See "Visual definitions," p. 21.

Spirit of the game — See "SOG."

Square pass — A pass to a teammate roughly parallel with the goalline, across the field of play. The advantage of that technique is that the receiver can take the ball while moving forward.

Stationary — Before a free kick may be put into play, the ball must be "stationary", i.e., not moving. Historically, referees have ruled that if the ball will not complete one circumference under its own power, it is considered stationary.

Stay wide — Refers to an official's position on the field away from the play, usually in a slow build-up setting. When the referee stays wide, the referee stays out of the passing lanes and avoids interfering with the play and still has a view of the players, the ball and assistant referees.

Straightlining — See "Visual definition," p. 23.

Strikers — Offensive players who attack the goal. Perhaps smaller, more agile with capable foot skills, those players look for opportunities to put the ball in the net.

Substitute — A team member wearing a numbered jersey who is eligible to play but has not been given permission to enter the field.

Sudden victory — The first, game-deciding goal scored in extra time, if the competition rules allow for it. Also known as a sudden-death goal or golden goal.

Suspend — A temporary stoppage in play caused by the elements, spectators or other events outside the referee's control. Suspensions can lead to resumption of play, termination or continued suspension. A suspension must be noted on the referee's game report. A suspension may lead to an abandonment, a cessation of play because of problems with the field or equipment.

Sweep the field — Looking over the entire field (players, bench areas, scorer's table, assistants) before restarting play after a stoppage.

Sweeper/stopper — A defensive set used by many teams that has one defender playing behind the others to give depth to the defense.

Switch play — Moving the ball from one side of the field to the other. The advantage of that technique is that the defense is momentarily exposed as it repositions to defend against new angles. Also known as "switching fields."

Technical area — Primarily for matches played in stadiums, that seating area holds the technical staff (coaches, trainers, physician) and substitutes. Based on space limitations that area varies, but it should be marked and should stop at least one yard outside of the touchline. Occupants of the technical area must behave in a responsible manner.

Terminate — To stop playing. The game is over because of dangerous weather situations, unruly crowds or a game participant who is dismissed but does not leave the playing area.

The Football Confederation — The name of the continental governing body over the USSF that reports directly to FIFA. Formerly known as CONCACAF.

Three-whistle system — Also known as the dual diagonal system, it is one method of game control that has three referees on the field, each with a whistle.

Top of the area — The curved area at the top of the penalty area (technically, that is the "penalty arc" but it is commonly referred to as "the D").

Touchlines — The longer of the boundary lines on both sides of the field, the sides without the goals.

Trail — In a halffield setting the trail official is positioned near the touchline opposite the lead and is responsible for perimeter play. The trail is also primarily responsible for fouls away from the ball.

Trail assistant — The assistant referee that play is moving away from. Normally the referee's back is to that individual.

Trifling — Essentially trivial or minor, that term was in the *Laws of the Game* before the 1997 rewrite of the laws.

Two-touch — A system of play in which the player uses the first touch on the ball to control the ball's motion and uses the second touch to distribute the ball or shoot.

USASA — United States Amateur Soccer Association. Headquartered in North Bergen, N.J., under the present USSF configuration, that association controls all play for players older than U-19 who are not playing professionally.

USSF — United States Soccer Federation. Headquartered in Chicago, that is the national governing body for soccer in the United States.

USYSA — United States Youth Soccer Association. Headquartered in Richardson, Texas, under the present USSF configuration, that association controls all play for players U-19 and younger.

USL — United Soccer Leagues. Headquartered in Tampa, Fla., USL controls the second and third tier of professional soccer, including A-League, D3 Pro League, Premier Development Leagues and two women's leagues.

Wall — Oddly, for as common as that defensive tactic occurs during games, a wall is not mentioned in the *Laws of the Game*. As few as one player, but typically four or five players, form a human barrier between the location of a free kick and the goal. Ideally, defenders will be at the minimum distance of 9.15 meters (10 yards) when setting their wall.

Wall pass — A player with the ball passes to a teammate with the hopes of receiving the ball back directly, as if the pass had been bounced off a wall. The advantage of that technique is that it causes defenders to lose their balance while the player who originally had the ball now has a running start after collecting the wall pass.

Warning — The referee speaks with or gestures to the players. The two common types are: the *quiet word*, where the referee speaks with the player as they both move around the field while the ball is in play; and the more serious *public word*, where the referee halts play and confronts the player in a one-on-one lecture. A sample gesture may be a finger to the lips to quell dissenting comments.

Wave down — The referee motions the assistant referee to move to the corner flag. Usually done on free kick situations just outside the penalty area, the referee assumes responsibility for offside decisions while the assistant is positioned to act as a goal judge. Some referees also use the terminology that they will wave down an assistant referee's flag if they will not be acting on that signal.

Whack — Common usage for two times when something is kicked rather indiscriminately. A player whacks a ball out of the defensive half, more concerned with distance than accuracy, or an opponent whacks the legs of the player with the ball. Throughout this text, if a player whacks the opponent, consider it to be done in a reckless manner. See "Reckless." The original codification of the *Laws of the Game* in 1863 referred to that as "hacking."

Whole — Completely or entirely. Those terms designate the location of the ball in relation to the line, whether in the air or on the ground. Examples are: a throw-in is awarded "when the whole of the ball passes over the touchline;" a goal is scored "when the whole of the ball passes over the goalline, between the goalposts and under the crossbar."

Wingers — Offensive players who play on the flanks of the field, near the touchlines. They tend to be speedy players with enough leg force to cross the ball to center forwards and strikers.

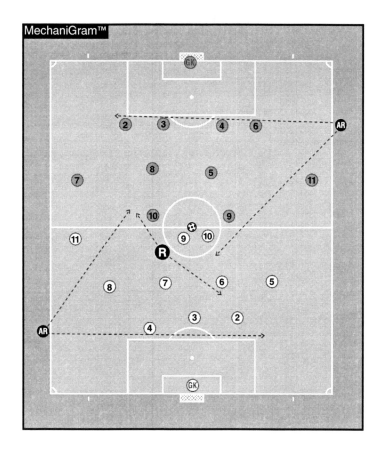

Visual definition: player designations

Action on the field:

At the start of the game, opposing teams are lined up in different tactical formations. The dark team is in the 4-4-2, while the white team is in the more offensive 3-4-3 formation. Starting from the back, the formation numbers tell you the number of defenders, the number of midfielders and the number of strikers. Of course, the positions are not static so defenders may make runs forward and participate in the attack.

In addition, the dark-shirted team is in a flat-back four defense while the white team has a sweeper-stopper formation.

Referee Responsibilities

As a referee, if you are able to spot the team's formation, you gain valuable insight into their orientation and mindset. Carefully watch substitutions. That is a strong clue to you to vary your positioning.

Assistant Referee Responsibilities

Assistant referees should determine a team's defensive posture and note which defender is leading the offside strategy. If a team is playing a flat-back four, look for them to constantly challenge the offside positioning.

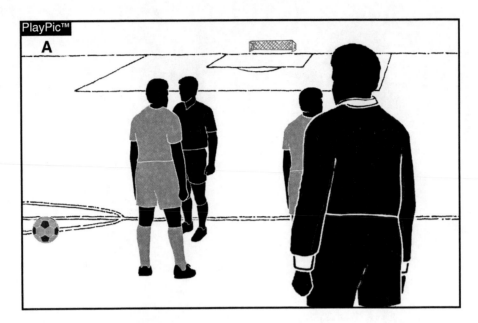

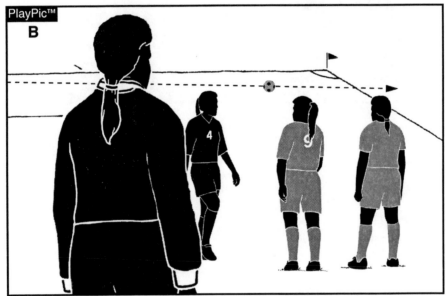

Visual definition: 'inside-out' look

Avoid straightlining, or being caught flat, on plays in the wing. A simple two- to four-step adjustment *toward the center of the field* gives you the proper angle.

In PlayPic A, the referee is straightlined on the play and must move to see potential contact on or by the defender. In PlayPic B, the referee moves two to four steps toward the center of the field. From there, the referee has a great look at the defensive player.

You must fight the urge to run around the entire play toward the touchline, using 10 steps or more and wasting precious time. By the time you run around the play, the offensive player could take a shot, foul or have been fouled, and you may not have seen it.

After adjusting two or three steps toward the center of the field to improve your angle, watch the rest of the action from there, including the follow-through after a shot. After you've taken care of that responsibility, you can start moving, working for your next good angle on the ensuing action.

Visual definition: spacing for the referee

Officials need to back off the play to give proper visual perception. You must create "spacing" on each play. Spacing is the distance between you and the play. If you're too close or too far, you can't see the play clearly.

When you get too close to a play, your view of the play is distorted. Your depth perception is off and your field of vision is narrow.

On most small fields, the referee's spacing ability is limited. When players are close behind you, back up as far as you can without interfering. If you still feel there's not enough room, adjust toward the touchline to create more spacing. You might be giving up a great angle, but you're seeing the whole play better.

What's the right distance? It depends on your field of vision needs on a particular play. If the play is directly in front of you, move about eight-10 feet away. If the players are away from you, position yourself about 20-30 feet back. Ultimately, you want to be close enough to give the perception you can see the play from where you are and far enough to keep the proper perspective.

In PlayPic A, the referee is too close. In PlayPic B, the referee is much too far from play.

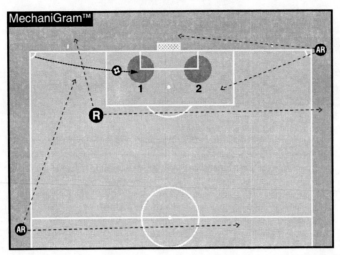

Visual definition: near post and far post

Players use those terms relative to the position of the ball. They refer to how far the ball is expected to be played. Referees should be atuned to those terms when you hear players or coaches shouting. While the player with the ball may not make the shot or pass called for by a teammate, the term gives you valuable clues as to the likely next significant action. In turn, that helps you make positioning decisions.

While near post and far post also apply to general play, they are mostly used during set plays (restarts) and shots on goal. In a typical example, the MechaniGram shows a corner kick from the referee's side. Circular area 1 shows a ball being delivered to the near post while any ball landing in circular area 2 would be delivered to the far post.

In the PlayPic, attacker ⑩ has a couple of options. The goalkeeper has moved over to cover the expected near post shot (path A) leaving ⑩ the option of taking the more difficult far post shot. Those tactical decisions by the keeper and shooter are part of the joy and excitement of the game. ⑩ may choose the near post shot, hoping to cross up standard tactics and surprise the goalkeeper.

Your awareness of those distances, angles and area of next significant action leads to wise positioning decisions. Better positioning leads to better match control.

Referees have a different reference point for similar terms. The corner closest to where the assistant referee is standing is the "near corner," while the other corner is known as the "referee's near corner" or "far corner."

Visual definition: straightlining, I-formation

"Straightlining" occurs when your view of a play is obstructed by the players themselves. In effect, you are in a straight line with the players and have no angle to see between them. Some referees call that being flat or in the I-formation with play.

A one- or two-step move left or right eliminates straightlining. Keep your head up and continually watch the play when moving.

The most common straightlining concerns:

1. Offensive player with the ball with defensive pressure. You must avoid straightlining to see between the players and correctly judge the play. Did the offensive player push?

2. Free kicks near goal. To correctly officiate action around the goal, you must avoid straightlining. Coupled with proper spacing, you can judge whether or not the offensive player pushed to receive the pass, the defender pushed the offensive player in the lower back or if the offensive player hooked the defender on the spin move to the goal.

3. Corner kicks. Get good angles to see screens. Avoid straightlining and you'll see if the defender fouled by pushing through the attacker or if the attacker fouled by extending a leg, hip or elbow.

Those decisions and others are nearly impossible if you're straightlined.

In PlayPic A, the referee is straightlined. In PlayPic B, the referee moves one or two steps to get a better angle.

Definition of terms

• Soccer officiating is about three things: safety, equality and enjoyment.

• The normal position for the referee and assistant referee is referred to as "balancing the field" or "being on the diagonal."

• The trailing assistant referee in a halffield setting is positioned on the opposite half of the field and is responsible for perimeter play behind the referee's field of vision and counterattacks.

• The International Board has emphasized the importance of carrying out its mandate to show the red card and send off the field any player who endangers the safety of an opponent by the use of a tackle from behind. Referees are reminded that, although that does *not* mean every tackle from behind must be punished by a send off, their discretion in this area is strictly limited to deciding if such action has endangered an opponent's safety. If it has, the player *must* be shown the red card. USSF joins the International Board in warning referees that their performance in that area will be monitored closely, with appropriate action taken for a failure to follow IFAB's mandate.

Quiz

Without referring back, you should be able to answer the following true-false questions.

1. Only the diagonal system of control (DSC) is authorized when working USSF matches.

2. You should sell every call so every call is accepted.

3. A termination or a suspension must be noted on the referee's game report.

4. Whether you are the referee or assistant referee, proper spacing is essential to see plays correctly.

1 - True, 2 - False, 3 - True, 4 - True

Chapter 2

Officiating Philosophy

Safety, equality and enjoyment. Those three tenets are the foundation of the *Laws of the Game*. Referees must uphold those three principles above all else.

Let's analyze recent law changes. Assistant referees are instructed to withhold doubtful offside flags so the play flows, making it more enjoyable. Referees who witness a tackle from behind which endangers the safety of an opponent are warned that a red card must be shown. More scoring is possible directly from restarts such as kickoffs and goalkicks because of recent changes.

This book is a mechanics and techniques manual. You must work with instructors, mentors, assessors, trusted fellow referees and constant learning to hone your spirit of the game. Some of it is based on history and tradition. Whether you see the game through the eyes of a cha-cha style Latin player or the rough-and-tumble play of the English parks leagues, you have a limitation on your appreciation of the game from your playing days. Now, as referees, you hold the golden thread that weaves the fabric of the spirit of the game.

To carry on the fine tradition of officiating this sport, you must constantly study its history. You must learn more about the game constantly and work with instructors, mentors, assessors and trusted fellow referees to hone your sense of the spirit of the game. The USSF has made that easier via the publication of the *Advice to Referees on the Laws of the Game*. That booklet compiles into a single source much of the historical documentation that determines fair play.

See both sides

You must internalize the FIFA Fair Play campaign. Too often, referees see a whack on the shin. They feel bad for player A4 who committed the foul, knowing they should caution A4 for the unsporting behavior. The referee has read up on the teams and knows that, if A4 gets one more yellow card, A4 will have to serve a one-game suspension. Plus, their next game is the big rivalry.

See both sides. B8 is doubled over in pain due to that whack in the shins. It hurts. Your sympathy is misplaced. Start to feel sorry for B8. Card A4 so that a sense of caution creeps into the playing style and opponents do not go away bruised and battered. Safety. Equality. Enjoyment.

Know your own character

What type of referee are you? What is your fundamental style of managing players? Do you use humor well? Are you a likeable salesman, who explains the fouls and decisions to the satisfaction of those involved? Are you a strict disciplinarian that rules the game with a heavy fist? Is your work rate so high that you are so close to every

play your decisions are not questioned? Knowing that about yourself yields important clues as to how you can best use the material in this guidebook.

Adherence to the law

There are those referees who, quite correctly, are proud of the fact that they make every decision based on the black-and-white as printed on the page. There is no doubt, there is no margin for error. If it's printed that way on page 19, that's what those referees will call.

No one will advocate that you break the law. But there are also top officials who advocate that you bend the law to fit the circumstances you find on the field. You must predetermine which style fits your officiating best and blend that into your philosophy. Fit those concepts into the manner in which you manage the game and the contestants. It will aid your consistency.

Think about aspects of the game

Many decisions can be made in the comfort of your living room. If an attacker gets whacked in the back of the leg and swings an arm that contacts an opponent, for me, that's a gray-area decision. If a player balls up a fist and hits an opponent three times, I already know what I'll do. I've thought that process through. I know what I'll do when I hear a player, coach or spectator use a racial slur. There won't be any confusion on my part when that takes place on the field.

I've seen it enough times and spoken with enough senior referees to know what undercutting looks like; I've felt it from the player's perspective. Even though the leaping player may wind up on top of the undercutting player, I know who gets the free kick. Think about aspects of the game. Here are a few affirmations: *"Referee the defense but think like the offense."*

While no single sentence can really summarize officiating, that one gives you the framework for success. To do that effectively, you've got some homework to do.

The greatest single thing you can do to help improve your officiating is gain a better understanding of the game itself. Anticipation is critical in officiating. You give yourself a much better chance of getting in proper position and making the correct call if you anticipate what is going to happen. That doesn't mean anticipate *the call*, a major error. It means knowing what's likely to happen and adjusting accordingly. The only way you can get better at anticipating is by becoming a student of the game.

To elevate your officiating, you must learn about offensive and defensive strategies. If you know what each team is trying to do (well beyond "score more goals than the other team"), your game awareness, communication, field coverage and judgment will improve.

This book places great emphasis on recognizing plays and adjusting accordingly. In order to "referee the defense and think like the offense," you must first understand each element of the sentence.

Referee the defense

When officiating a game, you must recognize, understand and react to what the defense is doing. Defensive coverages often dictate offensive plays; they also greatly impact your field coverage. Watch where defenders are positioned on the field and what they're doing from those positions. Are they in a man-to-man? A zone? What type? By recognizing the defense, you can adjust your coverage and positioning accordingly.

Referee the defense also means primarily watching the defender's movements. You must watch the defense before judging whether the offensive player or defensive player committed a foul. You can now call that play correctly. The simple philosophy is a crucial part of good judgment.

Obviously, referee the defense doesn't mean you can watch only the defender. You must also watch the offensive player for violations and fouls. By maintaining good angles and establishing proper spacing, you can watch both players. Refereeing the defense is as much an attitude as a visual command.

Think like the offense

Students of the game usually make good referees. Why? They learned as players to recognize defenses and they know what to do to beat those defenses. Good officials do the same thing. Once you've learned to recognize defenses and understand defensive tendencies, you must think about what the offense is likely to do and adjust accordingly. Gaining that knowledge allows you to anticipate correctly and move to get proper angles and spacing.

The more you know about the game, the less chance you have of getting surprised. Studying the rules and mechanics isn't enough. A complete official knows what's going on from the players', coaches' and officials' perspectives.

This book helps you understand what players are trying to do so you can be prepared on the field to make the proper adjustments.

Trust

When it comes down to it, trust is a vital element in officiating. You must trust yourself and the knowledge you've obtained to see you through game situations. You must also trust your partners not only to handle situations properly but to implement proper field coverage.

You must develop trust with your partners to establish good on-ball, off-ball coverage. In almost every instance, only one official should be watching the player with the ball. The other officials must watch players off-ball. Think about it: Usually there are only a couple of players around the ball. That leaves the majority of the players in other areas. If all officials were glued to the ball, the majority of the players would be unattended. That's when problems occur, like rough play or trash-talking. If one official is on-ball and the others are off-ball, all the players are watched and the game stays under control.

You must trust your partners to handle things correctly when on-ball so you can watch off-ball and vice versa. We have a tendency to want to watch the ball even when we're not supposed to. Maybe that stems from watching games on TV, which always focuses on the ball. Maybe it comes from the belief that more exciting things happen with the ball. Perhaps you are an active player as well as a referee. Whatever the reason, you must trust your partners to handle it. If you don't, off-ball coverage is non-existent and the game suffers.

Three officials who trust each other in handling situations and field coverage responsibilities form the building blocks to successful officiating. Fight the urge to watch the ball all the time. Trust your partners to handle it. Your game will stay under control, your judgment will improve and you will become a better official.

Communication

Effective communication rounds out the successful official. It makes sense: If you've got a lot of knowledge and make good decisions but can't effectively communicate with others, no one can tell that you've got a lot of knowledge and make good decisions. Good communicators make good officials.

Communication goes well beyond words. It includes body language and signals. There is a great deal of emphasis on proper, clear signals throughout this book. Why? Signals are our language. They're our way of telling others what's going on. Bad signals mean poor communication. Good signals show decisiveness, clearly indicate what's going on and even help calls become accepted.

Learn how to referee the defense, think like the offense, trust yourself and your partners and communicate effectively. You'll find yourself improving every time you step onto the field.

Eye contact

Perhaps the most critical aspect of three referees working together is eye contact. The referee can sprint from goal area to goal area and never be more than 15 yards from the ball, but that same referee will be more effective using input from both partners.

The *Guide to Procedures* says "Referees should take every opportunity of less activity on the field to make eye contact with each of the assistant referees, to confirm the location of players relative to the officials and to observe portions of the field which may not have received recent attention."

What to look for

What are you looking for when you look at your partners? Make sure they are paying attention. It can get lonely and boring if the assistant goes 10-15 minutes without eye contact from the referee. Looking at them keeps their head in the game.

Make sure they aren't taking any heat. Does the bench-side assistant have a coach bending his ear with some nonsense about a play that happened 12 minutes ago? If so, go put a stop to it. Does the other assistant have a parent following her up and down the touchline? You won't know unless you look, will you?

Are they looking up the touchline to make certain they have enough space to run during a breakaway? If so, stop the game and clear a path for their safety. Move the coaches and substitutes into the technical area (at least one yard from the touchline). Move spectators, coolers and umbrellas at least 10 feet from the touchlines. You want your assistants and all the players to have a safe environment.

Look to compliment them. If their last call was a very close goalkick/corner kick decision and they rendered a sharp signal, give them a thumbs up. If they hustled to stay with the second-to-last defender on that 40-yard breakaway, give them a nod that means well done. If they are relaxed and having a good game, do something unexpected. One trick I've pulled on partners when the game allows: With 25 minutes or more left in the half, ceremoniously look at your watch and then give them the "one-minute-left" signal on your pants. They'll look at their watch, look back at you, look at the watch again and finally back at you with a quizzical look. It breaks the routine just enough. It's fun. Use your imagination to have some fun if the game allows.

Are your partners struggling? Is this their sixth game of the day? Do they need some water on a 100-degree day? If they do, perhaps the players do also. In extreme heat, some competitions are scheduling water breaks. While there is nothing specific in the *Laws of the Game* allowing such a water break, you have to use your common sense — if it's the right thing to do for the athletes, take the time needed for their health and safety.

Get into the habit of establishing eye contact with both assistants each time the ball goes out of play. You will get more effort from your assistants, they will work harder for you than for other referees and they will enjoy themselves more. Your game control will improve and you will be more at ease.

No limits

Don't just limit your eye contact to situations when the ball is out of play. You can also use eye contact to get additional information about potential fouls or misconduct.

The *NISOA Assistant Referee Duties & Responsibilities* properly defines "when asked" as "when the referee looks to the assistant referees for information. There is no verbal exchange. It is done entirely through eye contact."

If you have used eye contact regularly throughout the early portion of the match, the trio will be attuned to each other and be very comfortable passing information via eye contact. That leads to better game control and higher confidence.

Philosophy of signals

Clear and concise communication is a necessary ingredient for any successful person, regardless of the profession. The same is true for officials. When people hear the word "communication," most think of how a person speaks to an individual or group. A sometimes overlooked yet critically important communication method is body language.

In many ways, an official's body language is just as important as any verbal communication. Just like profanity to a player or coach can get an official in trouble, poor body language can escalate a negative situation. Conversely, positive body language can help ease and control a potential conflict.

Think about this: Why do we bother to give signals? It's because we need to tell others (players, coaches, fans, etc.) what happened on the field and it's impossible to yell loud enough for everyone to hear. Sounds condescendingly simple, but keeping that basic principle in mind will make you more aware of what signals you use and how you give them.

Signaling
When you call a foul or violation, your body language sends a message to everyone watching. Raise your hand high and straight above your head or 90 degrees to your shoulder. A bent arm looks weak and shows people you're unsure of your call.

If there is confusion, verbalize what you've called while giving the proper signal at the spot.

Selling a call is like raising your voice. Sometimes it is necessary and effective. Do it too often and people get angry or turned off. Sell a call only when necessary. Obvious calls need good signals too, but close calls need a little extra emphasis to communicate to everyone clearly. Don't over-sell; you don't want to embarrass a player or appear that you're caught up in the emotion of the game.

Follow the prescribed signals in the manuals. It's important because people have come to accept and understand them. Again, think about signals as words. If two English-speaking people were talking and one briefly switched to a foreign language, confusion would set in. The same is true for signals. By using your own, unauthorized signals, you're speaking a "foreign" language and confusion reigns.

There are, however, some commonly accepted signals that are not included in the USSF, Federation or NCAA manuals. Listed as "other signals" in the "Signals chart," consider using them if your governing bodies allow.

Slow down and think about your signals as a language. If you "speak" slowly and clearly and use the right "words," the correct message and tone will get across.

Guide to Procedures for Referees, Assistant Referees and Fourth Officials
The standard USSF mechanics are clearly spelled out in a 16-page pamphlet. The pamphlet was most recently updated in 1998 and was reprinted with two thick green stripes across the front cover. Following those procedures allows referees to work together. How important is that?

When 120-130 referees gather at youth regionals, they are coming together from 14 states. If each locale had their own procedures, it would be chaotic — just at the time when the players need the best refereeing to decide regional winners. When teams and referees gather in warmer climates for holiday tournaments over the Christmas holidays, there may be referees from 25 states taking part in those huge tournaments. Can you imagine 25 different sets of mechanics? Can you imagine a USL referee traveling 200 miles to work a game, only to find out that she can't understand her partners because they are using different mechanics during a professional-division contest. There has to be a national standard. USSF has set the standard for all 100,000 plus referees to follow.

Unless you are told otherwise, the mechanics and positioning recommendations in this book follow the USSF *Guide to Procedures*. If the Federation or NISOA have different mechanics, we've pointed those out. We try to offer the rationale behind the signals, to give you the reason the standard mechanic or positioning will work. There are some non-standard situations that call for non-standard mechanics. Above all else, use common sense in your signals. You have an obligation to be understood by your partners.

The 1998 edition of the *Guide to Procedures* says under the general mechanics section, "While every official must develop his or her own style of conduct, it is the objective of this procedures guide to keep such individual styles within a common boundary of standard practices.

"An official's style should not interfere with the flow of the game, result in unclear communication of information to players or fellow officials, or cause undue attention to be drawn to the official and away from the match itself."

Officiating philosophy

• Safety, equality and enjoyment. Those three tenets are the foundation of the *Laws of the Game.* Referees must uphold those three principles above all else.

• You must work with instructors, mentors, assessors, trusted fellow referees and constant learning to hone your spirit of the game.

• The more you know about the game, the less chance you have of getting surprised. Studying the rules and mechanics isn't enough. A complete official knows what's going on from the players', coaches' and officials' perspectives.

• Communication goes well beyond words. It includes body language and signals. There is a great deal of emphasis on proper, clear signals throughout this book. Why? Signals are our language. They're our way of telling others what's going on.

Quiz

Without referring back, you should be able to answer the following true-false questions.

1. Assistant referees are instructed to withhold doubtful offside flags so the play flows.

2. Many decisions can be made in the comfort of your living room.

3. To elevate your officiating, you must learn about offensive and defensive strategies. If you know what each team is trying to do, your game awareness, communication, field coverage and judgment will improve.

4. Referees should not get into the habit of establishing eye contact with both assistants each time the ball goes out of play.

1 - True, 2 - True, 3 - True, 4 - False

Chapter 3

Soccer Basics

Good officials project professionalism on and off the field. Among the areas where you can stand out:

Accepting games
Before even getting on the field, you've obviously got to get assigned games. There are many different assigning methods that vary from state to state, level to level and association to association.

Learn what the process is from other local officials and association leaders. Then, follow the system. Do not compromise your principles to get games. In some areas, it's wrong to contact coaches directly for games. If that's the case, don't do it. You'd be sacrificing your integrity just for an assignment. It's not worth it.

In other areas, officials must get games from coaches or athletic directors. While that practice often gives the appearance of favoritism and impropriety, follow the procedures that are accepted and don't deviate. Be careful.

Once you've figured out the procedure and accepted an assignment, keep it. Few things upset assignors more than turned back games. Some assignors are plagued by so many turned back games, they are charging officials who accept a game and weeks later turn it back. Obviously emergencies do happen, but they should be few in number.

The USSF *Referee Administrative Handbook* lists the game priorities in referee appointments. Allow your various assignors to handle those matters of resolving conflicts.

When you receive a contract in the mail, return it in a timely fashion. Think of your officiating as a business. As the business owner, realize how important contracts are to your business. If they are returned late or incomplete your business will suffer because you're less likely to get other contracts.

Conditioning
Soccer officiating requires you to be in good physical condition. Consider taking a physical examination before each season. *Stay* in shape rather than *get* in shape. Being physically fit is a lifestyle. If you never get out of shape, it won't be such a chore getting ready for the season.

Arriving at game site
Arrive at the game site well in advance of the scheduled start time. Allow enough time to get stuck in traffic and still make it in plenty of time.

The proper amount of time varies by level and by local practice. General rule: Arrive at least 30 minutes before kickoff. Allow enough time to stretch out, get

dressed, have a pregame with your partners and conduct pregame duties without rushing.

If possible, drive with your partners. That gives you time for idle chit-chat and possibly a pregame conference on the way to the game.

Dress
At some levels, officials have private lockerrooms. When that's the case, do not go to the game dressed in any part of your uniform. It just looks unprofessional. Make a good first impression on game management by arriving nicely dressed.

Many officials at the high school and college levels use all black, wheeled, airline-travel type luggage. That luggage keeps your clothes clean and pressed and, because of the wheels, is easy to transport.

Your uniform should be clean and well kept.

Jacket
Black or NISOA/USSF approved. All officials should wear the same color or not wear them at all. Check with other officials to make sure you're buying the right style and color.

Shirt
Standard black, fuchsia or gold are worn. The officials should match styles. An undershirt should be plain white or black, but white tends to work better. The shirts should always be tucked in. At press time for this book, the USSF had approved several new shirts for wear by USSF referees. Make sure you buy the correct style.

Pants
All black shorts. Make certain they are not too short. When you see the first sign of them turning grey due to washings, replace them. The fabric should match the fabric of the shirt, i.e., satin finish and satin finish.

Shoes
Entirely black shoes are most acceptable, however, some state associations and college conferences allow black with minimal white markings (like shoe logos). Black laces are always worn.

Socks
Black with three white stripes unless a professional league specifies otherwise.

Whistle
Carry a spare in your shorts pocket. A wrist lanyard is the preferred method by most officials. Have several

different whistles, with different tones, available for use.

Meeting with game management

Once at the game site, inform someone from game management that you have arrived. At the youth level, the game manager is likely a league supervisor. In high school and college, it's probably the host athletic director or representative.

The game manager likely will show you to your lockerroom. With the game manager:
• Confirm kickoff time.
• Ask if there's going to be an extended halftime for parent's night, special presentations, etc. Make sure the game manager informs both teams before the game.
• Find out where the game manager will be located during the game. You may need to find the game manager quickly during the game to take care of crowd control or other administrative duties.
• Make sure your lockerroom is locked after you leave and someone is there to open it when needed.

By taking care of duties with game management before the game, you won't have to worry about those details during the game.

After the game

If facilities are available, shower and change back into the same clothes you arrived in. Don't leave with your uniform on. You want to leave with a professional appearance, just like you arrived.

Leave the game site with your partners. There's safety in numbers. In cold weather climates, make sure all cars start properly before anyone leaves.

Communicating with the governing body

If conduct or game reports are necessary, they should be sent promptly to the proper authorities. Send all reports within 24 hours of the game.

If there was a problem during the game that warrants a report to your supervisor, consider calling the supervisor as soon as possible before mailing the report. Supervisors usually like to hear about problems first from the officials so they don't get surprised when the angry coach or administrator calls.

Report all items that are supposed to be reported. Most governing bodies require all send offs and dismissals to be reported. If you don't report yours, the governing body can't discipline the offender. You may think the send off or ejection was "minor" and doesn't warrant suspension, etc. *That's not your call!* Report all send offs and dismissals and let the governing bodies make their decisions. Sometimes, officials don't report

because they think they're doing the offender a favor. What if the offender has been ejected four or five times throughout the season but only one has been reported? The authorities won't be aware of the continuing problem. You are hurting yourself and other officials by not reporting properly.

Frequent study

Learning is an on-going process. A complete knowledge of the rules and mechanics is essential. Study the laws year round, with special emphasis on new laws at the beginning of the season. Test taking and small group discussion are effective educational tools. Read periodicals. Attend monthly referee meetings. Write articles for local or national publications.

Know the restarts

I've heard it said that soccer refereeing is very easy. There are only three things you have to remember. First is to protect the players. Second is to enforce the rules. And third is to not take any static for doing either of the first two. While your task is a bit more complex than that, it becomes much easier if you are certain of a few key elements.

As an instructor for entry-level classes, I've tried to make it easy for new referees to understand a few fundamental concepts. What are the eight restarts? Can you score directly from the restart? When is the ball in play? Where do the opponents have to be? A more comprehensive version of that restart chart is in *Advice to Referees* 8.6.

If you are absolutely certain of the information on the restart chart, your confidence goes sky high. A player or coach tries to shake you with a comment about a restart. If you are certain, you can ignore the comment. If you have a doubt, that doubt lingers. While you are focused on figuring out if you ruled correctly on the last play, a contact situation occurs in front of you and no call is made. Your focus was diverted by your uncertainty, and now the same coach has a legitimate beef about the no-call on the contact situation.

Know the restart chart on page 344. Your annual test scores will improve. Your application on the field will improve. You will begin to see the larger aspects of game control once you do not have to focus on the restarts — your decisions on them will come automatically.

Soccer basics

• Learn what the assignment process is from other local officials and association leaders. Then, follow the system. Do not compromise your principles to get games.

• Consider taking a physical examination before each season. *Stay* in shape rather than *get* in shape. Being physically fit is a lifestyle.

• Leave the game site with your partners. There's safety in numbers. In cold weather climates, make sure all cars start properly before anyone leaves.

• Learning is an on-going process. A complete knowledge of the rules and mechanics is essential. Test taking and small group discussion are effective educational tools. Read periodicals. Attend monthly referee meetings. Write articles for local or national publications.

Quiz

Without referring back, you should be able to answer the following true-false questions.

1. You may turn back a game when a better one comes along.

2. As a general rule, arrive at least 10 minutes before kickoff.

3. Upon arrival at the game site, inform someone from game management that you have arrived. At the youth level, the game manager is likely a league supervisor. In high school and college, it's probably the host athletic director or representative.

1 - False, 2 - False, 3 - True

Chapter 4

MechaniGrams
How To Understand Them

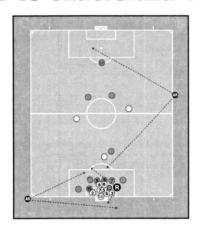

One of the things that makes a great official is a complete understanding of the game. That goes beyond rules and mechanics. Great referees anticipate plays. They always seem to be in the right place at the right time. It's not an accident or just luck. It's preparation and an understanding of the game that puts them in the right spot at the right moment.

Studying the game
Part of that preparation is studying the game itself. Just what are the teams trying to do on the field? The novice or unprepared referee doesn't think beyond, "This team is trying to score more goals than the other team."

There are some teams where that is their tactical understanding of the game. Coed recreational games with many first-year players is one example. Youth bumblebee-style games where the children are just kicking the ball and giggling does not take much introspective thought. If you are in your first couple of years with a whistle and still waiting to whistle your 100th game, do not over-analyze the game. Enjoy it.

The great referees think about offensive styles, defensive schemes, tempo and tendencies. For example, they'll know or recognize that team A likes to push the ball up the right side and establish a fast-paced tempo. They run multiple overlapping midfielders to free up players with some space. They like to whack the ball to the corner flagpost then cross it back into the mixer for driving headers. They will crash the mixer, then apply immediate re-attack all over the field. They play an aggressive, man-to-man defense. They will switch to a zone defense only for defending against corner kicks.

The different approaches are obvious: The more you know about the game and a team's tendencies, the better prepared you are.

Recognizing and knowing what coaches and players are trying to do elevates your game. When you have that knowledge, you can adjust your field coverage accordingly. The obvious question is, how do you get better at anticipating plays? You study the game and the specific plays.

As soccer becomes more complex, officials must be more aware of specific plays and team tendencies. When officials recognize offensive plays and defensive strategies, they make better field coverage adjustments.

Gaining the knowledge
How do you gain the knowledge about specific plays and teams? One way is to talk to other officials. If you know referees that have had a team you're about to officiate, ask them questions about style and tempo. Another way is to watch the players during the pregame warmup.

The most common: Learning and adjusting while the game is in progress. You must develop the ability to see what's happening on the field and adjust accordingly. Whether the referee or the assistant, you're not just watching a bunch of players move. Learn to watch specific, orchestrated offensive and defensive plays while on the field. Then, make the necessary adjustments.

Always read the defense first. Why? Defensive schemes are easier to recognize. Plus, offensive plays are based on defensive strategies, not vice versa. Once you've read the defense, think about the offensive plays that are likely to be used against that specific defense. Adjust accordingly.

For most referees that don't have an extensive playing or coaching background, it takes time to develop those skills. Practice while watching other games (on television or in person). See what's happening on the field and recognize the plays and defensive schemes. Think about what is likely to happen once you've recognized the play.

Here's an example of how a well-schooled official thinks on the field. Team A is down two goals with 6:40 remaining in the tournament semifinal game. They haven't applied an offside trap all game; they've stayed in a loose zone. A team A player nails a 22-yard shot and team A cuts the gap in half. What's likely to happen when play resumes? Since team A is now down one goal with little time left, they obviously need more players in attack to get an opportunity to score again. Is that likely to happen if team A sits back in their loose zone? Obviously not! Instead, team A is likely to apply pressure after the goal. Team A is likely to push players up and shift to an offside trap to allow fewer defenders to stay back for the counterattack.

Anticipating that action, a referee adjusts the field coverage accordingly. A referee who doesn't understand the game or recognize specific plays will be caught by surprise; a well-schooled referee is prepared. If you're the referee, a subtle let's-bear-down signal to the assistant might be useful.

Reading the MechaniGrams
Remember the old "chalk talk" when you were a player? The coach frantically drew circles and lines and pounded the chalk until it became a fine white dust, all while yelling, "Remember on defense, it's ball-you-man!" MechaniGrams take the chalk talk a giant step forward.

The result: *Soccer Officials' Guidebook* teaches referees to recognize restart plays, helps them adjust basic field positioning to properly officiate each play, and shows exactly where each official should be looking. It's a modern-day referee chalk talk!

MechaniGrams and PlayPics are separated into categories: each of the eight restarts, misconduct, foul recognition, no-calls. Each includes actual game situations showing the movements of players and officials. Text accompanies each frame, describing the action so officials can learn to recognize those plays in their games, and referee movement, so officials know where to go and what they're trying to see. In many cases, there are several options — decide which option is most appropriate given your game circumstances.

Use the illustrations to learn what plays look like and what you're supposed to do once you recognize them. As you become a student of the game, your officiating will dramatically improve.

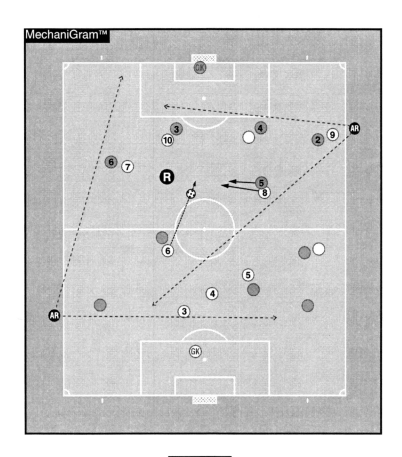

KEY

R Referee	**AR** Assistant Referee	**4th** Fourth Referee	**CL** Club Linesman

→ Movement   Initial Position **AR** ——————→ **AR** Current Position

A Optional Position   ●◁⋯ Coverage Area   ○ Offense   ● Defense

⊛ Ball   ⋯⋯⊛▶ Ball Movement   ▨ Goal

MechaniGrams

• One of the things that makes a great official is a complete understanding of the game.

• Great referees anticipate plays. They always seem to be in the right place at the right time. It's preparation and an understanding of the game.

• Recognizing and knowing what coaches and players are trying to do elevates your game. When you have that knowledge, you can adjust your field coverage accordingly.

• Use the illustrations to learn what plays look like and what you're supposed to do once you recognize them. As you become a student of the game, your officiating will dramatically improve.

Quiz

Without referring back, you should be able to answer the following true-false questions.

1. The great referees think about offensive styles, defensive schemes, tempo and tendencies.

2. A way to know more about a team's style of play is to carefully watch the players during the pregame warmup.

3. Defensive schemes are easier to recognize.

1 - True, 2 - True, 3 - True

Chapter 5

Duties

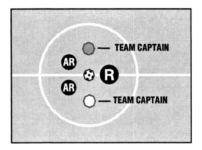

Field positioning and duties during dead-ball times, such as the pregame warmup, halftime and injuries are important.

Pregame: don't linger with the coaches

During the pregame warmup, start with your walk around the field, looking for unsafe field conditions. Verify important distances, such as the penalty mark and penalty arc. For Federation and most USSF youth games, enter the field no later than the 15-minute mark; for NCAA games, enter no later than the 30-minute mark. Some professional division games require even longer lead times — know your requirements.

Avoid lengthy discussions with one coach, while the other wonders what you are talking about for so long. Many coaches view the pregame as an invitation to chit-chat or ask questions. Don't give the coaches the chance to "shmooze" you by telling you how great it is to see you, etc. Don't give a coach the chance to ask questions that the coach can later use against you. For example, if a coach before the game asks you about impeding, then doesn't like your impeding call in the game, the coach could bring up the pregame conversation by saying something like, "That's not how you said you were going to call it." Don't give them the opportunity.

Many of the pregame conversations with coaches are unnecessary and usually are designed to test you. They may even try to use your words against another official. How often have you heard the rules question from a coach start with, "Last week, we had a ref call … that's not right, is it?" The coach either knows the rule and is testing you or is likely not relaying the play to you accurately. Don't give them the chance; stay away from lengthy discussion with coaches before the game. Introductions and a simple request for their lineup card is sufficient. Under Federation rules, you have an obligation to ask the coach if the players are properly equipped. (4-3-1 and 5-2-2d)

Even if the coach's questions and concerns are legitimate and not as sinister as previously described, think about the perception. If you have an extended, friendly conversation going on with one coach, what's the other coach to think? Even if that official wouldn't think of calling a game one-sided, that perception is now in the front of the offended coach's mind.

It's preferable to do your stretching exercises before entering the field. There are too many other things to be doing and watching while on the field to conduct a workout session.

Watch the teams

Though there's usually not a lot of pressure on the officials during the pregame warmup, it's not the time to mentally relax. Watch for player and team tendencies while they warmup. For example, if a target player is practicing a move to the net, take note of which way the player likes to spin with the ball. If the team is whacking a lot of balls during the pregame, remember that during the game. Look for the best corner kicker; determine if they will be inswingers or outswingers. Those clues and others will help you anticipate plays and get proper angles during the game.

Pregame procedure

There are additional pregame duties to perform for all officials. They include checking with the scorer, determining who will keep official time and conducting a captains' meeting. The order of those duties varies from referee to referee.

Checking with the scorer

The Federation manual states that the referee receives a lineup card at least five minutes before the game. The NCAA manual says 15 minutes. Typically in USSF matches, the referee gets the lineup roster and player passes about five minutes before kickoff. If you have an official scorer on hand, go over and make friendly introductions. If player introductions will be made, perhaps the announcers wish to have the referees' names. Many state associations mandate that coaches rate officials, so the officials must sign the scorebook. Follow local procedures.

Introduce yourself to the table crew. You might want to start up a conversation to find out how much experience they have. If they don't have much, prep them on their duties. Even if they do have many years of experience, it's a good idea to go over things with them.

If you arrive at the table and one (or both) of the teams doesn't have a roster turned in, let the coach know immediately.

An example of good common sense: If a coach is attempting to turn in his lineup, the scorer is not at the table, and the five-minute or 15-minute mark elapses, do not penalize the team. Sometimes the scorer is out taking care of other pregame duties, using the restroom, etc. The team shouldn't be penalized because they were trying to comply.

Next, while at the table, secure a game ball and approve it. Sometimes the ball is already at the table. Other times you might have to use one that the home team is warming up with or pull one from a ballbag.

Use the bounce test. The referee should carry an

inflation needle. If there's too much air in the ball, let a little out, then test again. If there's not enough air, either have it blown up or pick another ball. An advanced tip: have the home team captain select a ball from the ones the home team is using to warm up. If it meets your approval, give the ball to the visiting team's captain for approval. Though their input is not "official," that's a great way to build a rapport with both team leaders before the game. Plus, they're the ones that have to play with it so they might as well be happy. The vast majority of the time, the captains will approve the ball and appreciate your asking their opinions. Before applying that little trick, check with the appropriate governing body to see if you can use it.

Meeting the captains

Another pregame responsibility is meeting with both teams' captains. *Referee* recommends that the captains stand on their side of the field parallel to the halfway line; the referee stands between the players on one side (parallel to a touchline) while the assistants stand opposite the referee.

During that huddle with captains, the referee gives instructions and answers questions. Keep the meeting very brief; it should never last more than one minute. Also, there's no need to explain common rules or obvious things. The players are more interested in warming up than listening to you talk. Use the time with the captains to clear up any confusion, but don't hold a clinic.

Ask the captains if they have any questions (most of the time they don't). Flip the coin. Let the captains shake hands and it's over.

The Federation manual says to hold the captains' meeting "at least five minutes before the scheduled starting time."

After the captains' meeting, return to normal observatory positions. The more information you have about both teams, the better off you'll be during the game.

Halftime procedures

Where to go at halftime is up to the individual referee. Many referees mistakenly leave their gear between the team benches.

Some of the time, coaches will wait for you to come to the team area to voice their displeasure with the officiating. If you have left your gear between the benches, wait for them to leave before going over to the table, even if it takes an inordinate amount of time. Eventually, they'll give up, go to their team and resume coaching.

Do not leave the game ball at the center mark. Bring it

with you. Ensure that management will notify both teams when halftime is about to end. In most games, teams are notified three minutes before the end of the half.

During halftime, relax. Then, review the first half and discuss necessary adjustments. Hydrate. You've just lost a lot of fluid and need to replenish that to keep your concentration levels high. Return to the field with about two minutes remaining in the intermission.

On-field injuries

When an injury occurs and the coach or medical personnel are beckoned onto the field, move away from the area immediately. For liability reasons, you don't want to get involved in injury situations. You must avoid the urge to help.

Plus, if you're nearby, it's easier for someone to fire an emotional cheap shot at you. For example, if you're nearby, the angry coach on the way out to attend to the injured player may say, "This is your fault! The game's too rough!" There's even more of a chance for an emotional response if a parent is summoned from the stands onto the field. Avoid it all by moving well away from the injured player.

Under National Federation rules, neither coach may give coaching instructions to any player during an injury stoppage.

Postgame exit

There's an easy way to sum up postgame exits: When the final horn or whistle sounds, get out of there! There are no more duties that require you to be in the center circle. Assistants should jog to where the referee is standing and avoid confrontations. A game management representative should meet you near the exit from the field to ensure you get to your lockerroom safely. Stay well away from the players and coaches if you are going to observe the postgame handshakes. Too often, a postgame emotional comment leads to trouble, bad feelings and occasionally, referee assaults. Get well away.

Stay away from the scorer's table; it's too easy to be a target of emotional coaches, players or fans. If you've not stored your gear right there, there's no need to be over there.

If there's a need to sign the book, the official scorer can come to you, well away from the crowd.

Dead-ball officiating

There are many things to be done during dead-ball time. It's not the time to mentally relax. Handling dead-ball situations professionally and with common sense separates the great officials from the average ones.

Duties

- Do all your stretching exercises before entering the field.

- All referees observe the teams warmup.

- Keep the captains' meeting brief.

- Move away from injured players.

- You must stay alive when the ball is dead.

Quiz

Without referring back, you should be able to answer the following true-false questions.

1. Before the game, start with a walk around the field, looking for unsafe field conditions and verify important distances.

2. Under Federation rules, you have an obligation to ask the coach if the players are properly equipped.

3. When an injury occurs and the coach or medical personnel are beckoned onto the field, you should stand nearby to supervise.

1 – True, 2 – True, 3 – False

Chapter 6

Referee Signals

Referees communicate by using signals. Can you imagine trying to yell loud enough to be heard by all 120,000 spectators in the Stadia da Luz in downtown Lisbon, Portugal, during their big crosstown rivalry? Impossible. Bringing the scene closer to home, can you imagine trying to out-shout 100 excited parents of eight-year-olds? Nearly impossible.

Hand signals are the primary way you will be able to effectively communicate during the game. Spectators, coaches and players need to know what you want to happen next — who gets the free kick you just awarded, which team gets the throw-in now that the ball has gone into touch.

Whistle

After a season or two, referees learn to use the whistle more effectively. During most rookie seasons, it's hard for spectators and others to differentiate the whistle for a penalty kick from the whistle allowing a substitute to enter the field. Veteran referees should take the time needed to explain to less experienced referees why "talking with the whistle" adds to game control.

Body language

Your field presence has a lot to do with the respect you will gain on the soccer field. Preparation, timely arrival and a sharp appearance are a part of the equation. Are you standing on one foot? Do you check your watch at every stoppage? Are your arms folded across your chest? Do you yawn every few seconds? All of those imply you are bored with the game and can't wait for it to end.

90, 45 or straight up

With the arm straight at a 90-degree angle, with all the fingers fully extended, point in the direction of the restart. Some signals should be given with the arm at a 45-degree angle. In every case, make sure your arm is fully extended, with the fingers extended. Not rigid, not cartoonish but crisp. You want to achieve clarity. Do coaches and players ask you to repeat signals? That may be a sign that your signals are not clear.

Hold them for a second or two

Again, you want to fully communicate with those at the game. Coaches and spectators are watching play and watching the ball. It's going to take them a split second to react to the whistle, find you and observe your signal. If you've already given the signal and lowered your arm before they look, it is as if you had given no signal at all. Do coaches and players ask you to repeat

signals? That may be a sign that your signals are too quick.

Use signals to manage your game

Suppose a team winning by a single goal late in the match starts to use every substitution opportunity to switch out one player. Repeatedly. You can gesture in an exaggerated fashion to your watch to show everyone you are aware of the coach's tactics. You might also head off the complaint by the losing coach by giving the timeout signal after a few occurrences. Even if you don't physically stop your own watch, you let everyone know you're aware of the timewasting and are going to manage it.

Move to the spot, if needed

Move to the spot of the foul if necessary to prevent retaliation. Your presence is a signal. If you've taken the pains to run 15-20 yards to stand directly over the ball and maneuver between angry opponents, that is a clear signal that they had better focus their attention on the game and not each other.

Verbalization

Sometimes your signals are verbal. Not too often, for you want your whistle, arms and posture to convey the important messages. When you do verbalize, there are several people you want to hear you verbalize: the fouled player and the player who committed the foul; the player who winds up with the ball and who must decide to keep playing or wait for the whistle; the other players in the area; the coach of the player who was fouled so dissent is lessened by some small amount; the parents of the fouled player, for the same reason; and perhaps most important, the overly aggressive teammate of the fouled player, the protector. If the protector gets the message that you saw the action, that you recognized it as a foul, that you have some awareness of the fouling player's number and you have the situation in hand, then the protector does not feel the need to retaliate. Simply by loudly verbalizing a properly made decision, you've improved your match control and prevented problems.

Wait, don't restart

There are two closely related instances where you do not want play to restart immediately after a stoppage. Some referees make eye contact with the player with the ball and show a "stop sign" with the raised palm facing the player, for example, at a substitution. Play can then restart with a hand gesture or verbal signal. There are times when it is appropriate to tell a player,

"Wait for my whistle." You should then restart play with a whistle to avoid any confusion. Be certain you make eye contact with the players near the ball, show them your raised whistle, point at it for all to see and then say a few words, such as, "Wait for my whistle before kicking the ball." Don't let there be any confusion on anyone's part. Too many things can go wrong if you don't take positive action to control those restarts. Emotions boil over and everyone offers advice.

Quiet word

Sometimes your verbalization might be intended for a single player. You may not not want anyone else to know you "had a chat" with a player who needs a sportsmanship reminder. As the player runs up the field to get positioned for the next restart, run within a yard or two, say the necessary couple of words and move away.

Public word

Sometimes a stronger verbalization is needed. You may not need to raise your voice to get your point across. You can signal to everyone in attendance that you are making a point by asking a restart to be delayed, moving toward the player or players you need to address, saying your piece, moving into a good position for the restart and signaling for play to start up again.

Third party

One signal that referees fail to use often enough is the intervention of a third party. Use a coach. Use a team captain. Use a level-headed midfielder who can relay a message to a hot-headed goalkeeper. The players have been teammates for years, they practice together regularly — they know what buttons to push. You may come off too tough toward a player that needs kid gloves. You may be too lenient toward a player who only understands a hard, disciplined approach. Teammates and coaches know which approach will work best given the circumstances. Let them pass the message — the signal that something needs to change.

Television

You will watch many referees in televised matches and see signals that differ greatly from what is said in these pages. Know the culture of the match you are viewing. For six years that I worked in the German semiprofessional divisions, I had to un-learn the USSF signals that I had been taught. When I blew the whistle and walked north, the red team took the kick. When I walked south, the blue team took the kick. There was

only one signal — a raised arm for an indirect free kick. You will see South American referees display yellow cards with a dramatic flair. That's entirely out of place on your next U-14 game. It doesn't suit you, it doesn't suit your style of refereeing.

Film or video

Ask someone to videotape one of your games so you can analyze your signals. Are they up to par? Are you satisfied with the duration and crispness? Perhaps you don't have the expensive equipment needed to video the game. With a disposable camera and a roll of film, someone can catch you at 24 distinct moments during a game. Are you satisfied with each of those 24 moments?

Assessors and mentors

Ask an assessor, veteran referee or mentor to watch you. Get feedback about your signals. Are they appropriate? Are you only using authorized signals? Are they crisp? Does everyone clearly understand what you are trying to convey?

Practice

As with any endeavor that you want to do well, you must practice. Ten minutes in front of a mirror will do wonders. Teach your muscles what a perfect signal feels like through repetition. Learn what it feels like to hold your arm directly overhead, arm and fingers fully extended.

Pride

Take pride in your signals. Certainly when you submit a written product to your boss or to your teacher, you want it to reflect well upon you. The same can be said with your signals.

Standard diagonal

Most of the PlayPics and MechaniGrams will show referees on the standard diagonal, e.g., to the left of the goalkeeper. There are specific play situations later in the book where that assumption is critical. Having said that, *Referee* advises you to work the opposite diagonal on occasion, so that you and your assistants have some familiarity with how that feels during a game.

Play on! Advantage!

Direct free kick

The only two-handed signal used by the referee is also the only signal given both verbally and physically. Swing both hands forward from your hips at waist level while distinctly declaring, "Play on!" or "Advantage!"

There are several people you want to hear you verbalize: the fouled player and the player who committed the foul; the player who winds up with the ball and who must decide to keep playing or wait for the whistle; the other players in the area; the coach of the player who was fouled so dissent is lessened by some small amount; the parents of the fouled player, for the same reason; and perhaps most important, the overly aggressive teammate of the fouled player, the protector. If the protector gets the message that you saw the action, that you recognized it as a foul, that you have some awareness of the fouling player's number and you have the situation in hand, then the protector does not feel the need to retaliate. Simply by loudly verbalizing a properly made decision, you've improved your match control and prevented problems.

After you decide a penal (major) foul has been committed, blow your whistle with the appropriate tone, length and force and then signal for the direction of the restart. With the arm straight at a 90-degree angle, with all the fingers fully extended, point in the direction of the restart.

Move to the spot of the foul if necessary to prevent retaliation. Once you are satisfied the ball is properly placed in the approximate area of the restart, do not interfere with a team's opportunity to an immediate free kick. If one of the players on the kicking team near the ball requests help in dealing with opponents infringing on the minimum distance, step in to manage the wall. Ignore all pleas by spectators, coaches, goalkeepers and teammates that are 40 yards from the restart. While the ball is being retrieved and readied for play, glance at both assistants.

If you must make a comment or give instructions to a player, do it after you have signaled the direction.

While the players ready the ball for play, read the players and anticipate where the next significant action will take place. Take a position where you may see that play on a good angle. Avoid being straightlined. If you anticipate a long, clearing kick, you want to position yourself near the dropping zone, where you expect the ball will land. You can sense that area by watching players jostle for position.

Signals Approved By All Three Ruling Bodies

Indirect free kick

Goalkick

That is a two-part signal. The first part is to indicate the direction of the free kick. If the foul is not one of the major fouls but rather a technical foul or a violation, then the restart will be an indirect free kick. To signify that differentiation, raise your arm clearly overhead until a second player has touched the ball, play stops for another reason or the ball goes directly out of play.

While the ball is being retrieved and readied for play, glance at both assistant referees. Then look at the attackers to see if they are ready to restart. If not, drop your arm. The indirect free kick signal should not be held for an unnecessarily long time.

If the ball goes directly into the goal while you still have your arm raised (and thus it has not been played by a second player) you lessen the dissent by blowing your whistle loudly and pointing to your raised arm. Then signal for a goalkick and get the game restarted quickly.

Failure on your part to raise your arm, due to either your error or the quickness with which the game restarts, does not negate the indirect free kick. Even with your arm lowered, if the ball goes directly into the goal without touching a second player after you award an indirect free kick, no goal is scored. The restart is a goalkick if the attackers take the indirect free kick.

Point with a crisp motion toward the goal area, with emphasis on the downward extension of the arm. Stand erect and turn your head to look at a majority of the players. While the ball is being retrieved and readied for play, glance at both assistant referees.

You should not routinely whistle to stop play once the ball has left the field for a goalkick. Should the players have some doubt as to whether the ball left the field, a short, sharp blast of your whistle, followed by a clear signal avoids confusion.

While the players ready the ball for play, read the players and anticipate where the next significant action will take place. Take a position where you may see that play on a good angle. Avoid being straightlined. If you anticipate a long, clearing goalkick, you want to position yourself near the dropping zone, where you expect the ball will land. You can sense that area by watching players jostle for position.

Corner kick

Misconduct

Point with a crisp motion toward the corner flagpost on the side of the field where the kick is to be taken, using the hand closest to that corner. Emphasize the 45-degree upward extension of the arm. Stand erect and swivel your head to look at a majority of the players. While the ball is being retrieved and readied for play, glance at both assistant referees.

You should not routinely whistle to stop play once the ball has left the field for a corner kick. Should the players have some doubt as to whether the ball left the field, a short, sharp blast of your whistle, followed by a clear signal avoids confusion.

Observe top FIFA and MLS referees: a slight fool-the-eye used by top referees has them continue running until they cross into the penalty area. Only when they are inside the area, do they stop, stand tall and deliver a crisp signal. They may have been 14 yards outside the penalty area when the ball crossed the goalline but the appearance to the players and spectators is that they were perfectly positioned to make the call. Try it.

While the players ready the ball for play, read the players and anticipate where the next significant action will take place. Take a position where you may see that play on a good angle. Avoid being straightlined. If you anticipate a long, centering corner kick, you want to position yourself near the dropping zone, where you expect the ball will land. You can sense that area by watching players jostle for position.

Identify the player by number and begin moving toward the player. Ask the player to move toward you, drawing the player away from teammates and opponents. Position yourself so you can see beyond the player's shoulders and watch a majority of the other players on the field. Stop the clock if playing under Federation or NCAA rules. Stop about four feet from the player and record the time of the incident, the player's team and jersey number and a note to yourself to help you remember the incident ("USB – tug jersey" or "PI – kick"). Display the card directly over your own head. If you caution players, tell them, "If you persist in misconduct, you will be sent from the field."

If you send off a player (disqualify under National Federation rules or eject under NCAA rules), delay the restart of play until the player has left the field entirely. (Note: Under National Federation rules and some state association youth adaptations, a yellow-carded player also must leave the field, but may be replaced.)

The standard mechanics described above work well in the vast majority of cases. There will be instances in volatile situations, such as when you expect retaliation or other players becoming involved, when it is appropriate for you to display the card prior to recording any information or speaking with the player. Sprint to the location of the foul, display the card and loudly say something like, "Stay away. Leave him alone. I've got him already." After tempers settle and opponents move away from one another, draw the player aside, record the information and inform the player of your decision about the misconduct.

Penalty kick

An emphatic penalty kick signal helps "sell" the call. A long strident whistle usually delivered while running toward the penalty mark, and a strong arm signal fends off some of the expected pleas of innocence.

Continue moving to the intersection of the goalline and the penalty area line to avoid confrontation and dissent, unless needed near the spot of the foul to prevent retaliation. Deal with players who protest the decision by reminding them to set up for the restart, using body language to show them a stop sign or show a yellow card for their dissent by word or action. Stop the clock if playing under Federation or NCAA rules. While the ball is being retrieved and readied for play, glance at both assistant referees.

Throughout this book and in the *Guide to Procedures for Referees, Assistant Referees and Fourth Officials*, the recommendation is not to use a whistle unless necessary. The *Guide to Procedures* and the *Advice to Referees on the Laws of the Game* allow either a whistle of voice command to restart from a penalty kick, stating the referee must "signal for the kick to be taken." The penalty kick is such an emotional event and the probable outcome may lead to one of the few goals in the game, if not the only goal. We heartily recommend you verbally tell the kicker to wait for your whistle. Show everyone the whistle and tap it with your other hand as you instruct the kicker (see p. 54), check the other players' positioning, move to a position about six yards from the goalline and about 12 yards from the penalty mark toward the touchline, check your assistant referee, inform the goalkeeper who will take the kick and confirm the readiness of the goalkeeper and then blow a strident whistle to allow the penalty kick to proceed.

Timeout

The Federation and NCAA rulebooks specifically call for use of a timeout or "stop time" signal. The United Soccer League (professional divisions) *Referee Handbook 1999* section on clock management details limited occasions when the referee should stop the clock.

In matches played under FIFA, USYSA and USASA laws, the accepted method is to allow for time lost by adding time on at the end of the half. The amount of time added is at your discretion. Therefore, that signal would not normally be used in your matches.

Offside

The National Federation rulebook dictates that referees calling National Federation (high school) contests use the signal shown in the PlayPic to denote offside. Typically used for American football games, spectators may understand the reason for the whistle more readily if you use that signal.

Do not use the signal during NCAA or USSF contests.

Valid goal scored

The referee traditionally signals by pointing to the location of the next restart. That holds true after a team scores a valid goal. Point crisply to the center mark. Contrived signals such as the gridiron signal for a touchdown are not to be used. Before the signal is given, the referee should check visually with both assistant referees. Stop the clock if playing under Federation or NCAA rules.

The time immediately after a goal is often a turbulent time for referees. Emotions run high and you must manage the dead-ball period carefully. If opponents confront one another, referees must be ready to run to the hot spot to quell tensions. Each neutral official must listen for taunting comments. The goalscorer and teammates may attempt to prolong their celebration and some of that celebration may ridicule the opponents. Defenders may challenge the assistant referee, requesting an offside decision or pleading for an alleged foul. Each goal is unique and you must handle it according to the circumstances. The best mechanic is for the referee to backpedal away from the area, either toward the halfway line or toward the touchline, keeping constant vigil for trouble. There, record the goal in your game data wallet.

You should not routinely whistle to stop play once the ball has left the field for a goal. Should the players have some doubt as to whether the ball left the field, a short, sharp blast of your whistle, followed by a clear signal avoids confusion.

The *NISOA DSC Instructional Manual* calls for collegiate referees to blow the whistle after a valid goal. Whistle, make eye contact with the assistant, watch the assistant make a short run verifying the goal, give the timeout signal, point to the center circle to confirm the kickoff (optional) and run to the center circle for the restart.

Improper signal — indirect free kick

Improper signal — direct free kick

A common mistake is to give sloppy signals. That motion appears weak and indecisive. You invite dissent from a knowledgeable soccer audience when you give signals in that manner.

Give all referee hand signals with the arm straight at the indicated angle or direction, with the fingers fully extended.

Many newer referees officiate very young players and they are still in the role of teacher and official. Many newer referees are also still currently active players and know the game well. In those formative years, a word of caution, advice or encouragement from the referee helps those very young players learn more about the game. At the youngest ages, those helpful words might be appropriate, but do not neglect your primary duties. All too often youth referees discuss something with a young player before they communicate a direction and everyone stands around confused, defenses are not set up and coaches become frustrated at the lack of information or irritated if they believe you are taking their role.

Improper signal — misconduct

Improper signal — throw-in or free kick

Referees often mistakenly display the card too near the player. That action is confrontational and often leads to an already aggravated player swatting at the referee's arm or taking the card from the referee's hand and throwing it on the ground. Do not put yourself in the position of having to give a second card because of your improper mechanics.

A common mistake is to have both hands in the air while signaling. Referees try to show both the direction and the location at the same time. There is only one referee signal given with two hands — play on!

Give a proper signal to indicate the direction of the throw-in or free kick. Then drop your arm. If the players are confused about the proper location of the throw-in restart, use your voice or hand to guide them to the approximate location. Some referees advocate getting in line with where you want the player to take the throw-in, perpendicular to the restart location. That thought has some merit, but do not sacrifice your ability to judge fouls and contact where you expect the most likely next significant action will take place.

Whistle

Other than your voice, the whistle is the primary means of communicating with those people at the event — players, coaches, spectators and your referee partners. You will learn to talk with the whistle: a short chirp for a ball passing just over a boundary line; a longer blast for a pushing foul six yards outside the penalty area; and a deafening thunderbolt when you see an instance of serious foul play and want everyone to quickly know you will send the player off the field of play.

Do not routinely whistle for all stoppages in play or restarts. After a ball clearly passes over a boundary line, players know the proper restart and do not require your whistle to alert them to the restart. In those cases, use a hand signal or your voice, or allow the players to respond to the assistant referee's flag.

Learn to blow the whistle from your diaphragm, from your gut. Many referees are far too timid with a whistle and use what air is in their cheeks. That sound lacks authority. Another common mistake is to tweet your whistle. Top referees do not tweet their whistle, making three, four or even five short blasts. Whistling in that manner points to your inexperience with the whistle — players pick up on that and figure they can intimidate you because of your lack of experience.

A suggestion is to use a whistle with a lower tone or pitch (like a pea whistle). It allows the variations in tone, pitch and length that help you talk with the whistle.

Telling player to wait for a restart

During most phases of play, you do not want to delay the restart. There are some exceptions — penalty kicks and ceremonial free kicks.

Throughout this book and in the *Guide to Procedures for Referees, Assistant Referees and Fourth Officials*, the recommendation is not to use a whistle unless necessary. The *Guide to Procedures* and the *Advice to Referees on the Laws of the Game* allow either a whistle or voice command to restart from a penalty kick, stating the referee must "signal for the kick to be taken." *Referee* recommends you verbally tell the kicker to wait for your whistle. Show everyone the whistle and tap it with your other hand as you instruct the kicker to wait for your signal, check the other players' positioning, move to a comfortable position, check your assistant referee and then blow a strident whistle to allow the kick to proceed. In addition, inform the goalkeeper who will take the kick and confirm the readiness of the goalkeeper during penalty kick situations.

Many referees mistakenly believe they must verbally ask if the goalkeeper is ready. Is the keeper on the goalline between the goalposts and facing the field? Then the goalkeeper is ready.

Wave-down

Second yellow card leading to send off

When the referee does not wish to act on the raised flag of an assistant referee, common courtesy dictates some indication noting the raised flag. Some referees prefer a discrete signal at waist level. Some referees only give a verbal indication to lower the flag.

Giving a clearly visible signal and a thunderous, "Thank you," to the assistant does a couple of things to aid game control. It lets the assistant know to lower the flag and regain a position in line with the second-to-last defender or the ball. It lets players, coaches and spectators know the trio is functioning as a team. It reminds everyone that you are watching your assistant for input in controlling the game. If the assistant flagged for an offside decision, both the attacker and defender are aware of the signal. If the assistant flagged for a potential foul, it lets the fouled player feel protected and sends a sign to the miscreant that the deed was observed.

Though not an approved signal, the signal is common among officials. Check with the appropriate governing bodies to see if you can use it.

If a player persists in misconduct after having already received a yellow card, you should send that player from the field of play.

You need to let everyone know whether the sending off was for a second cautionable offense or for one of the other six offenses that leads directly to a red card (usually more serious infringements involving violence or preventing a goal). Although it is not your immediate concern, the tournament or league levies different punishment based on your decision.

If you decide the offense merits a caution, and it is that player's second caution of the game, the 1993 IFAB minutes detail the correct procedure: "The referee is required to show first the yellow card and immediately afterwards the red card (thus making it obvious that the player is being sent off because of a second cautionable offense and not because of an offense requiring immediate expulsion)."

For matches played under the National Federation code of rules, there is a different mechanic and a different punishment. For coaches or players who persist in misconduct and earn a second yellow card, you signal their disqualification by holding both the yellow and red card aloft together. That is commonly referred to as the "soft red." If the offender is a player, that team may replace the player. Coaches must leave the vicinity of the playing area immediately.

In a 1999 rule change, the NCAA states that the only card shown to a collegiate player after the first yellow card of a game is a red card.

End of game

Direction of throw-in

Referee recommends that you signal with three whistle blasts (as opposed to two at halftime) and point to the center of the field. Get the ball if you are near it and move to an area where it is convenient for both assistant referees to join you. Supervise the teams' departure from the field and clear the playing area after the teams depart.

If players, coaches or spectators wish to speak with you, make certain all three referees are together. While the best advice is not to engage them in conversation, a simple question about the laws or rules of competition can be easily answered as you replenish fluids and begin your own postgame analysis of your performance. Sometimes an individual will approach you in the most civil manner and kindly ask the first question. All too often, a second question has more emotion behind it and the situation soon escalates to raised voices, shouting, accusations and potential referee abuse or referee assault. Read the situation carefully and respond cautiously, if at all.

Point 45-degrees upward in the direction of the throw-in, using the hand on that side of your body. Do not cross your body to indicate direction. While the ball is being retrieved and readied for play, glance at both assistant referees. If the players are confused about the proper location of the throw-in restart, use your voice or hand to guide them to the approximate location.

The referee is primarily responsible for direction on the end away from the assistant referee. The referee will only point the direction of a throw-in in the assistant referee's end of the field to overrule an assistant referee's flag or to confirm a signal given by an assistant that meets with some dissenting comments.

You should not routinely whistle to stop play once the ball has left the field for a throw-in. Should the players have some doubt as to whether the ball left the field, a short, sharp blast of your whistle, followed by a clear signal, avoids confusion.

Wave to reposition

Kickoff

When the referee wants the assistant referee to cover the goalline at a ceremonial free kick, a signal starts the process. Some referees prefer a discrete signal at waist level or a nod of the head. Some referees give a large overhead sweeping motion to indicate the assistant should cover the goalline.

Giving a clearly visible signal to the assistant does a couple of things to aid game control. It lets the assistant know to reposition to the corner flagpost. It lets players, coaches and spectators know the trio is functioning as a team. It reminds everyone that you are watching your assistant for input in controlling the game. Lastly, a trained official who is already in place and not running to be properly positioned covers the goal/no-goal decision.

Though not an approved signal, the signal is common among officials. Check with the appropriate governing bodies to see if you can use it. If you are the referee, inform your assistants which signal you will use.

Referees must signal to start the match but the whistle is not mandatory. Just before whistling, the referee should make eye contact with both assistant referees and check to see their unfurled flags. You should position yourself where you are ready for the next phase of play, without being in the way of players or in a passing lane. Start your watch, then while whistling, raising an arm in the direction of attack to indicate the start seems a nice enough way for you to introduce your personality with your first crisp signal.

The referee should not obviously count players on each side of the field. If you feel compelled to count, or are working without neutral assistant referees, count the players in your mind's eye, grouping them by pairs and threes until you arrive at the proper number. Do not point to players as you count them. Also, above the most basic youth competition, do not shout to both ends of the field asking the keepers if they are ready. They are aware enough of the protocol to begin the game and if they are on the field, within the penalty area, properly attired and generally facing toward the center of the field, they are ready. With your sharp whistle blast, they will face whatever comes their way.

Referee signals

• The only two-handed signal used by the referee is also the only signal given both verbally and physically — "Play on! Advantage!"

• With the arm straight at a 90-degree angle, with all the fingers fully extended, point in the direction of the restart. Some signals should be given with the arm at a 45-degree angle.

• While the players ready the ball for play, read the players and anticipate where the next significant action will take place. Take a position where you may see that play on a good angle.

• You should not routinely whistle to stop play once the ball has left the field. Should the players have some doubt as to whether the ball left the field, a short, sharp blast of your whistle, followed by a clear signal avoids confusion.

• An emphatic signal helps "sell" the call.

Quiz

Without referring back, you should be able to answer the following true-false questions.

1. You can teach your muscles what a perfect signal feels like through repetition. Ten minutes in front of a mirror will do wonders.

2. You must move to the spot of the foul each time to prevent retaliation.

3. While the ball is being retrieved and readied for play, you should glance at both assistant referees.

4. When displaying a misconduct card to players, you should stand within two feet of the players so they can hear you clearly.

5. A referee must give the timeout signal under all three codes.

1 - True, 2 - False, 3 - True, 4 - False, 5 - False

Chapter 7

Assistant Referee Signals

Assistant referees communicate by using signals. Flag signals are the primary way you will be able to effectively communicate during the game. Referees count on you to provide valuable input into game management.

Listen to the pregame
Each referee has minor variations in their game management style. Perhaps they learned to referee in a foreign land or in a different state. Perhaps their mentor was a former international referee. Those differences in background account for minor variations in signals that the referee wants from you. It's your job to communicate with the referee, not the referee's job to understand the signal you are giving. At a comical extreme, if the referee wants you to signal goalkicks by standing on your head, start practicing that difficult skill right away. Listen to the pregame. Ask questions if a point is unclear. Do what the referee wants during that game, even if it differs from the standard mechanics in the *Guide to Procedures.*

Bury the flag
While running up and down the line, especially while sprinting, take pride in keeping the flag pointed directly at the ground. That skill takes practice to master. Once mastered, there is no confusion about partial signals — the flag is either all the way up or all the way down.

Phantom flags
Assistant referees create problems by raising a flag part way, or all the way for a second or two, and then lowering it before the referee sees it. Spectators and coaches who view that phantom flag yell at the referee, who had no idea the flag was raised. That creates game control problems and the teams will attempt to divide the referee trio at every turn.

Lowering an offside flag
The most common occurrence for phantom flags is during offside situations. Perhaps the flag goes up a split second early or as you are raising the flag you spot another defender and realize the signal is in error. There are only five times you should lower a flag raised for an offside violation: the referee blows the whistle to signal the infraction, the referee waves your flag down, the ball goes out for a goalkick, the ball goes out for a defensive throw-in or the defensive team gains clear, un-pressured control of the ball.

Be careful where you hold discussions
There are instances during a game where the referee and the assistant need to hold a discussion. It may only happen a few times during a season but it is almost always at a critical juncture in the game — how a player received an injury, which player committed misconduct behind a referee's back, why the ball that went into the net should not count as a valid goal, etc. Be extremely careful not to let those private conversations be overheard by spectators, coaches or opposing players. Once the referee has the proper information, the referee will signal the trio's decision. No one needs to overhear the preliminary reports.

When asked
Throughout this book and in many pregame discussions, you'll note the term "when asked." The NISOA pamphlet *Assistant Referee Duties & Responsibilities* has a clear definition: "When the referee looks to the assistant referees for information. There is no verbal exchange. It is done entirely through eye contact."

Flag
After a season or two, referees learn to use the flag more effectively. Veteran referees should take the time needed to explain to less experienced referees why "talking with the flag" and giving proper flag signals aids game control.

Film or video
Ask someone to videotape one of your games so you can analyze your signals. Are they up to par? Are you satisfied with the duration and crispness? Perhaps you don't have the expensive equipment needed to video the game. With a disposable camera and a roll of film, someone can catch you at 24 distinct moments during a game. Are you satisfied with each of those 24 moments?

Pride
Take pride in your signals. Certainly when you submit a written product to your boss or to your teacher, you want it to reflect well upon you. The same can be said with your signals.

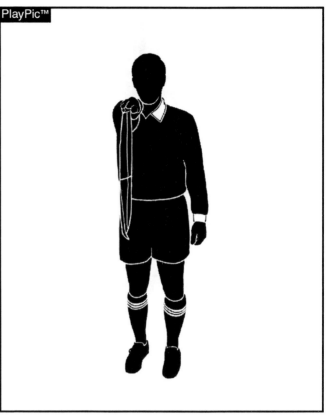

Goalkick

Goalkick

For balls that wholly cross the goalline in your half of the field, come to a complete stop, square to the field and using the hand closest to the goalline, point horizontally toward the goal area. Drop the flag when the restart and direction are clearly established. Make eye contact with the referee while signaling and if the referee overrules you, drop the flag immediately. While the ball is being retrieved and readied for play, glance at the referee.

This is the players' and referee's view of the goalkick signal for a ball that has gone out on the assistant referee's side of the field.

If the ball departs the field over the crossbar or on the referee's side of the field, then the assistant only flags when requested.

If the ball has momentarily left the field by inches and there is confusion among the players as to whether the ball is out of play, you may give the request for stoppage in play signal (see p. 64) first and when the referee whistles to stop play, move the flag into the position as shown.

Corner kick

Substitution

Point with a crisp motion at a 45-degree angle downward toward the corner flagpost on the side of the field closest to you. Stand erect and turn your head to look at a majority of the players. While the ball is being retrieved and readied for play, glance at the referee.

If the ball clearly crosses the goalline for a corner kick on the far side of the field, make no signal unless the referee makes eye contact to request assistance. If the ball wholly crosses the goalline for a corner kick and quickly returns to play, raise the flag vertically until acknowledged by the referee and then point at a 45-degree angle downward toward the corner flagpost.

Observe top assistant referees: a slight fool-the-eye used by top assistants has them continue running until they get within one yard of the corner flagpost. Only when they are near the flag, do they stop, stand tall and deliver a crisp signal. They may have been seven yards from the goalline when the ball crossed the goalline but the appearance to the players and spectators is that they were perfectly positioned to make the call. Try it on routine corner kicks when it is obvious and the referee does not need your immediate assistance. In cases where the ball touches several players on the way out of play and the referee is waiting for you to make the distinction between a goalkick and a corner kick, you must relay that information with a quick, emphatic signal regardless of your position.

Regardless of which side the kick comes from, position yourself in line with the goalline, behind the corner flagpost, out of the player's way. If the kick comes from your side, ensure proper placement of the ball around the corner arc. (Note: The National Federation directs assistant referees to move to the junction of the goalline and the penalty area line if the corner kick is taken from the far corner.)

Raise the flag horizontally, well above your head, between both hands. Lower the flag as soon as the referee acknowledges your signal. If you are working without a fourth official, jog to the halfway line to supervise the player coming off the field and then allow the properly equipped substitute to step onto the field to become a player, or otherwise as instructed in the pregame discussion with the referee. Collect the player pass if appropriate.

The *NISOA Assistant Referee Duties & Responsibilities* says, "When a substitution is about to be made, both assistant referees shall indicate to the referee by raising their flags over their heads as shown. The flags shall be lowered simultaneously when the referee signals the substitutes to enter the field of play. Again, this indicates *teamwork* and gives the referee the freedom to observe the field as desired."

Direction of throw-in

For balls that wholly cross the touchline in your end of the field, signal with the flag 45-degrees upward in the direction of the throw-in, using the hand on that side of your body. Do not cross your body to indicate direction. If you have been running up the line or down the line, come to a stop, square up to the field and give a crisp signal. Drop the flag when the restart and direction are clearly established. Make eye contact with the referee while signaling and if the referee overrules you, perform the flag signal requested by the referee. Some referees prefer you drop the flag immediately, while some prefer you switch the flag to the other hand to confirm the direction.

While the ball is being retrieved and readied for play, glance at the referee.

The referee is primarily responsible for direction on the end away from you. If the ball passes wholly out of play and immediately returns to the field and players continue to play the ball, give the request for stoppage in play signal (see p. 64) in the appropriate hand (the hand on the side of your body that the throw-in will go when play restarts) and make eye contact with the referee. When the referee whistles to stop play, lower the flag to a position which is 45-degrees upward in the direction of the throw-in if the ball departed the field in your end of the touchline. The hand indicates the direction of the throw-in on the referee's end of the field in which you hold the flag.

Follow any special pregame instructions regarding which elements of the throw-in the referee expects you to watch.

Request for stoppage in play

Offside — near side of field

That is the basic signal for assistants wishing a stoppage in play. That is the first part in many multi-part signals: offside, ball narrowly passing wholly over a boundary line, foul or misconduct.

Come to a complete stop and raise the flag as an extension of your straight arm. Establish eye contact with the referee. If the referee waves your signal down, quickly lower the flag and regain your position with the ball or second-to-last defender to judge offside.

If the referee misses the flag, stay at attention with the flag raised until it is no longer appropriate, given the circumstances. You should discuss those situations with the referee during the pregame conference.

In those rare cases when it is a flag that should not be waved down, such as a ball that passed wholly over the goalline, under the crossbar and between the goalposts but came back into the field, continue to hold the flag vertically.

The *NISOA Assistant Referee Duties & Responsibilities* dictates a few mechanics differences:

• stop moving at the point of the offside.

• hold the signal for a slow three count (1000, 2000, 3000) or as directed by the referee in the pregame conference.

• once play stops for the offside infraction and you indicate one of the three positions, hold the flag in that position until the ball is placed.

That is the second part of a two-part signal. Once the referee acknowledges your signal by stopping play, drop the flag to a 45-degree angle downward, directly in front of your body. That indicates the offside infraction was on the near side of the field, closest to your position.

Offside — middle of field

Offside — far side of field

That is the second signal of a two-part signal. Once the referee acknowledges your signal by stopping play, drop the flag to a 90-degree angle, directly in front of your body. That indicates the offside infraction was in the middle of the field. While that signal looks exactly like the goalkick signal, there can be no confusion because of the preliminary signal and the circumstances of play.

That is the second signal of a two-part signal. Once the referee acknowledges your signal by stopping play, drop the flag to a 45-degree angle upward, directly in front of your body. That indicates the offside infraction was on the opposite side of the field, furthest from your position.

Not ready for the start of play

Ready for the start of play

Assistant referees are to carry their flags from the moment they enter the field together with the referee. A furled flag indicates the assistant is not ready for the start of play, for whatever reason. Before the flag is unfurled, the assistant must make a final check of the net at that end of the field, visually check to make sure the goalkeeper is ready to play, silently count 11 players on that end of the field, move to the touchline in line with the second-to-last defender, set the stopwatch to 0:00 and make sure that no outside agents are on the field of play. While making eye contact with the referee, each assistant unfurls the flag and prepares for the kickoff.

At the start of each half of play and any period of extra time, the referee checks each assistant referee to see if they are prepared to start. An assistant who is ready will unfurl the flag, hold the flag straight down in view of the referee and make eye contact with the referee after doing several things: make a final check of the net at that end of the field, visually check to make sure the goalkeeper is ready to play, silently count 11 players on that end of the field (less in a short-sided game), move to the touchline in line with the second-to-last defender, set the stopwatch to 0:00 and make sure that no outside agents are on the field of play.

The referee simply checks to see if both assistants are ready with unfurled flags and then whistles to start the match.

The *NISOA Assistant Referee Duties & Responsibilities* offers a slight mechanics addition: "Should anything go wrong at the start of play, the assistant referee raises the flag straight up (do not wave the flag) to indicate to the referee."

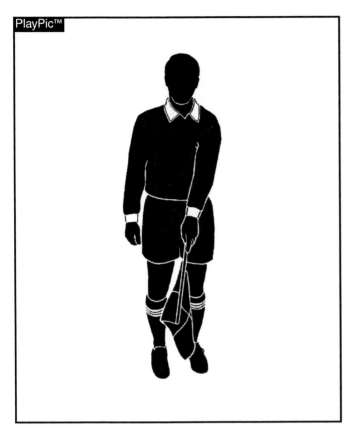

Assistant helps with location — inside the area

Assistant helps with location — outside the area

If the referee is well behind play on a counterattack and sees a foul near the penalty area, the referee may need some assistance with the exact location of the infraction. As the assistant in that case, establish eye contact with the referee. If the referee requires assistance (as indicated by a questioning eye contact), and the defense committed the foul inside the penalty area, hold the flag straight downward in front of your body (between your legs).

After the referee sees your covert signal and indicates a penalty kick, move quickly to the goalline and then move to the junction of the goalline and the penalty area line to prepare for duties assigned by the referee in the pregame conference.

The *NISOA Assistant Referee Duties & Responsibilities* indicates a slight mechanics difference: "The assistant referee, facing the referee, moves the flag from along side the leg to a position in front of the body, centered and extended downwards towards the ground, *then the assistant referee moves quickly to the corner flag after the referee blows the whistle and stands in position.*"

If the referee is well behind play on a counterattack and sees a foul near the penalty area, the referee may need some assistance with the exact location of the infraction. As the assistant in that case, establish eye contact with the referee. If the referee requires assistance, and the defense committed the foul outside the penalty area, make no discernible signal.

After the referee sees your covert signal and indicates a direct free kick, move quickly to get even with the second-to-last defender or other duties assigned by the referee in the pregame conference.

Not a valid goal

Assistant concurs valid goal scored

If you observe the ball wholly cross the goalline under the crossbar and between the goalposts and believe the goal was scored in accordance with law 10, make eye contact with the referee and start a short jog 10-15 yards up the touchline. If defenders challenge you, go further up the touchline.

Observe player behavior as opponents pass one another and listen for taunting comments. The goalscorer and teammates may attempt to prolong their celebration and some of that celebration may ridicule the opponents. Defenders may challenge you, requesting an offside decision or pleading for an alleged foul. Each goal is unique and you must handle it according to the circumstances.

Take up a position even with the second-to-last defender and record the goal on your game data wallet.

If you observe the ball wholly cross the goalline under the crossbar and between the goalposts but believe the ball was not scored in accordance with law 10, stand in place. It is clearer to the referee if you even stiffen slightly, similar to a military person at the position of attention.

If a player other than the goalscorer was in an offside position, and in your opinion, interfered with play or with an opponent, stand at attention with no flag signal. If there was a foul by a member of the attacking team that contributed to the goal, stand at attention with no flag signal.

If the goalscorer was offside, give the request for stoppage in play signal (see p. 64), standing with the flag raised.

Experienced partners may be able to piece together what occurred without consulting. Most likely, the referee will come to your location, turn so that both of you are watching the majority of players on the field and ask what you saw. Based on the information you give, the referee will decide on a restart and communicate it via hand signal. You should then assume your proper position based on the restart.

If the referee disallows a goal based on your information, expect some disagreement with your decision. Players may voice comments about your positioning, your eyesight and your ability. Strong referees will temper those comments by using their personality and body language. If the comments reach the point of misconduct, referees will use cards to deal with the offenders.

If you find comments directed at you offensive, insulting or abusive, give the request a discussion signal (see p. 80), call the referee to you and describe the circumstances.

According to correspondence from NISOA on this point, "The NISOA mechanic also directs the referee to have the assistant referee in view at all times in the event a violation or infraction is called by the assistant. If a signal is given by the assistant referee to the referee that there was a possible infraction or violation, the referee withholds blowing the whistle until after conferring with the assistant, if the referee so chooses. That mechanic is covered in the pregame conference."

To indicate a foul

Foul/misconduct indicated by trail assistant referee

Law 6 dictates assistants indicate "when misconduct or any other incident has occurred out of the view of the referee."

That is a three-part signal. The movement starts after the flag raises vertically, is in the wrist only and the wig-wag should only be repeated once or twice. The assistant is looking directly at the referee while signaling. Should the referee wave the flag down, it should come down immediately. Once the referee honors the request by blowing the whistle to stop play, the assistant should immediately give the third part of the signal, pointing 45-degrees upward in the direction of the restart.

Advanced assistant referees quickly develop the habit of raising the flag in the hand the restart will be going. An experienced referee working with a veteran assistant referee will know the signal pictured here is against a defensive player because the flag is in the right hand. Soon you will master the technique of switching the flag to your left hand before raising the flag and performing the wig-wag with the left hand, then lowering the flag to a 45-degree upward angle to indicate a foul against the offensive player.

Your pregame discussion with the referee should include whether you may request a penalty kick. If so, once the wig-wag signal in your right hand is noted by the referee, lower your arm and move directly to the goalline and stand in front of the corner flagpost to indicate a penalty kick. Once the referee gives a signal to verify a penalty kick decision, move to the junction of the goalline and penalty area line.

If the referee does not see a flag offered by the trail assistant referee, the lead assistant referee mirrors the request for stoppage in play signal and, after making eye contact with the referee, points across the field to the trail assistant referee while waving the flag slightly.

The trail assistant referee will continue to hold the flag vertically. Once the referee looks at the trail assistant referee, the assistant does a single wig-wag to show that a foul/misconduct has been committed. The referee will whistle to stop the game and, as needed, confer with the trail assistant referee. The referee will deal with the incident as appropriate.

Do not use that simply to indicate a foul was committed. As the trail assistant referee, you should determine the foul was at least reckless or involved the use of excessive force. At a minimum, the referee should give a yellow card. More likely, you will not request a stop in the action unless a send off offense occurs or some action brings the game into disrepute or the referee's game control in dispute. You may go an entire 10-year career and never use that signal, but it is critical that you understand the signal because of the consequences involved.

Time remaining

Time has expired

As each half ends, indicate the last five minutes with the appropriate number of fingers pointing downward against the background of the shorts. Make sure you have eye contact with the referee before initiating the signal.

That is particularly important in tournament settings where the halves may be of a different duration than referees are accustomed to. It is also particularly helpful to referees who work a variety of age groups throughout the season.

If you are the referee observing the signal, do not simply nod your head or give a thumbs up. To assure the assistant that the exact message was accurately passed, signal the minutes remaining on your shorts. The numbers may not correspond exactly as you may be giving back time including an allowance for time lost.

One of two possible alternatives, the closed fist across the patch while making eye contact with the referee tells the referee that, according to your watch, time has expired. The other alternative is a closed fist over your thigh.

Assistant referee moving up the line

Assistant referee moving down the line

As the attack retreats and the assistant referee runs to stay with the second-to-last defender, the flag stays "buried" to the ground and stays "field side."

The flag is in the right hand as the assistant moves away from the corner flagpost on a standard diagonal, which we will refer to as moving up the line. Also, the assistant's head turns toward the referee. That allows eye contact with the referee and allows the assistant to watch for off the ball incidents, as well as monitor the second-to-last defender.

As the attack develops and the assistant referee runs to stay with the ball or second-to-last defender, the flag stays "buried" to the ground and stays "field side." Some assistants tend to allow the flag to come above their waist while sprinting. That motion is very distracting to many experienced referees, who often act on the first flicker of a raised flag.

The flag is in the left hand as the assistant moves toward the corner flagpost on a standard diagonal, which we will refer to as moving down the line. Also, the assistant's head turns toward the referee. That allows eye contact with the referee and allows the assistant to determine if attackers are in the offside position.

Square to the field

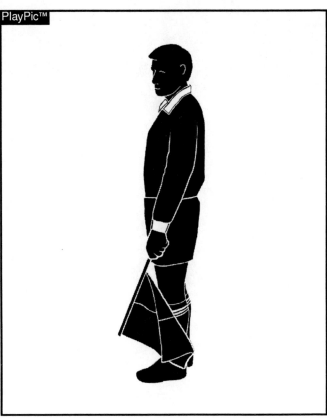

Square to the field

Stand as shown before making any signal: come to a stop, stand erect, make eye contact with the referee and turn your body square to the field.

If you are making positioning adjustments of only a few yards, make side-to-side movements, remaining square to the field. If you must move 10-15 yards to follow the ball or second-to-last defender, then switch the flag to the proper hand and move up the line or move down the line. Once you gain the proper position, turn so you are again square to the field.

That is another view of an assistant referee standing square to the field. Get in that position when you wish to give a signal to the referee.

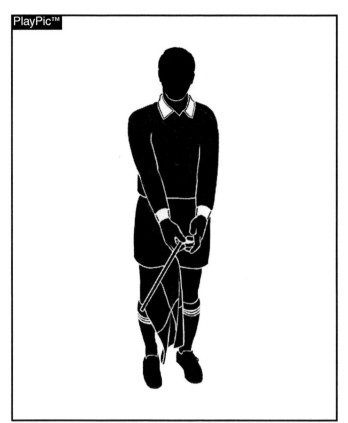

Switching hands

Scanning

Many of the signals shown involve switching hands to get the flag on the proper side of your body. You need to keep the flag field side as you move up the line or down the line, and the only way to do that is to switch the hand carrying the flag. That motion should be done low, near waist level.

You've seen examples of assistant referees raising the flag, having the referee blow the whistle and then the assistant lowers the flag, switches hands and then raises the flag in the opposite direction. Or even worse, you've witnessed assistant referees reach up with their second hand to switch the flag from hand to hand overhead. Both those are improper mechanics.

Practice moving the flag from hand to hand until it becomes a comfortable motion for you. You must grow accustomed to doing that without looking at the flag, for you should be concentrating on the second-to-last defender, opponents in close physical proximity and scanning eye contact with the referee. It is not easy, but it is essential.

When the ball moves to the other half of the field, all the defenders have moved beyond the halfway line and you are properly positioned near the halfway line, take up a comfortable position and scan the field. The best rule of thumb is to concentrate 80 percent of the time on the ball in play and 20 percent of the time on your offside position when you are the trail assistant. Every few seconds you should switch your view, rotating your chin across the full spectrum of the field, viewing the goalkeeper, benches, opposite side assistant referee and referee. Once you are satisfied there are no problems, then watch play with awareness of the areas behind the referee's back for potential misconduct.

Have your feet in a comfortable position. You may be stationary for 45 seconds and suddenly have to sprint with teenagers on a quick counterattack. Hold the flag where the referee can quickly see it with a glance. If the referee turns in your direction, make eye contact and be ready to respond to any directions given. If the referee is doing a good job, smile and give a barely perceptible thumbs up.

Side steps

Improper — crossover steps

When making small adjustments up or down the line, the preferred mechanic is to side step your way along the touchline. If you have to make a 10-15 yard adjustment, place the flag in the proper hand and sprint or run along the touchline. When you are back in line with the second-to-last defender, square up to the touchline (see both PlayPics on p. 72) and place the flag in the hand facing the referee.

As the second-to-last defender makes minor adjustments in field positioning, say a yard or two, you should side step to regain a level position with the defender.

If play is at the other end of the field, every few seconds, swing your head to look for the second-to-last defender. If you need to make a minor position adjustment, side step into place.

If you get in the habit of making crossover steps, you increase the likelihood of tripping. With play quickly moving downfield and you lying on the ground, you are of no help to the referee.

If you have a small adjustment to make, side step into place. If you have a major adjustment to make, turn and run into the correct position.

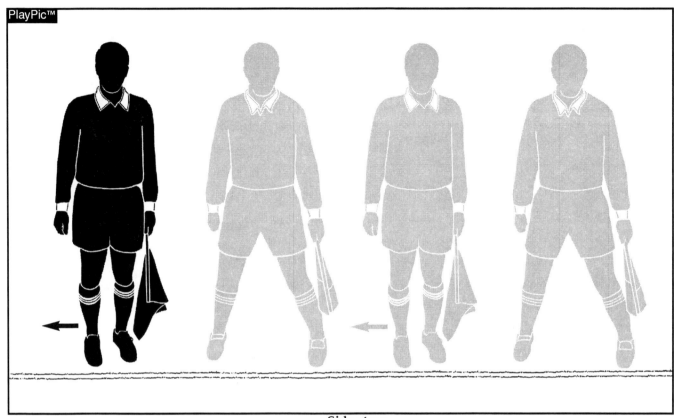

Side steps

Crossover step

Improper signal — throw-in

Improper signal — direction of throw-in

Give the throw-in signal from the touchline. Some assistant referees run five or six feet onto the field or run well behind the touchline. You cannot effectively do your job unless you are along the touchline.

If coaches, strollers, umbrellas or water coolers are in your way, ask for their removal. You need one to two yards along the touchline to safely patrol your area. Get it.

Some tournaments add an additional chalk line three yards beyond the touchline. Field marshals keep spectators and reserve players behind that line so assistants can concentrate on the task at hand. Ask your local league if they will do that.

A common mistake is to signal across the body. The flag should never point across your body. Switch hands before raising the flag. That mistake occurs because you are focusing heavily on the playing action.

Improper signal — flag in wrong hand

Improper signal — throw-in

To give the referee the greatest chance to see the flag, you should hold the flag in the hand toward the referee. Many assistant referees get comfortable with the flag in their dominant hand and improperly leave it there throughout the game. Be attentive to the referee's position and adjust the flag as needed.

A common mistake is to look at the flag while signaling. Allow the referee, the players and the crowd to admire your perfect, straight-armed signal — you have work to do: look at the referee to see if you are overruled on throw-in direction, watch the players for misconduct, check the far-side assistant to see if the flag is raised indicating a problem behind the referee's back, check your watch to see if it is still functioning or a reminder needs to be given to the referee that the game is near the end of the half.

Improper signal — switching hands

Improper signal — substitution

A common mistake is to switch the flag overhead. Signaling well is a learned art. In their first few games, many assistant referees feel a rush to get the signal up in the air. That haste leads to sloppy signals, not well thought-out and not well executed.

Do not switch signals from side to side while the flag is overhead. First, the appearance is unprofessional. Second, the perception is that you were going to give the signal favoring team A and then a player or coach from team B said something, so you changed your mind to favor that team.

When you observe an action, think about what information you want to convey. Think about how the mechanic should look in its final form. Think about where the flag is now. If need be, switch the flag into the proper hand and then make a professional appearing signal. Less than two percent of all flags must be given instantly to help sell a call. By the time you are seasoned enough to know which two percent need your quick action, you'll be practiced enough to switch hands quickly and properly at waist level.

A common mistake is to hold the flag while signaling for substitution. Some rulemaking bodies used that substitution signal for several years, so you may still see some assistant referees using it. No code uses that signal at present.

PlayPic™

Player came from an offside position to an apparent onside position

Often used when an attacker is in the opponent's half of the field, in an offside position, at the moment the ball is passed, the signal helps sell the call to the referee. The referee may look quizzically at you when you've called a player offside and the referee notices that the player is 10 yards or more from being in an offside position. The minor rotation of the wrist over an imaginary line conveys the message quickly.

Some referees use the same signal to quickly convey the same message to a coach who is yelling from the touchline.

Though not an approved signal, the signal is common among officials. Check with the appropriate governing bodies to see if you can use it.

Assistant requests a discussion with referee

A few occasions arise when an assistant must communicate directly with the referee in a manner for which no signal has been adopted: two squabbling players teetering near misconduct, a coach or spectator behind the assistant that must be dealt with by the referee, a bleeding player that has gone unnoticed by the referee, a dangerous weather condition the referee is unaware of or an urgent message from the tournament staff that cannot wait until halftime.

Discretely hold the unfurled flag across the center of the chest for a brief moment, after you establish eye contact with the referee. Ideally, the coaches, substitutes and spectators behind you will not even see that signal.

Though not an approved signal, the signal is common among officials. Check with the appropriate governing bodies to see if you can use it. Discuss it during your pregame. Some referees prefer you cover your badge with your free hand.

Substitution placard by fourth official

If asked to serve as a fourth official in a competition, one of your responsibilities will be to monitor a substitute's entry into the contest. After checking the player's equipment, check the player's pass (or substitution ticket), alert the nearest assistant referee and, with both of you well back from the touchline, watch for the next stoppage in play. (Under the *Laws of the Game*, substitutes may enter at any stoppage. The competition rules may have special provisions, so know what those provisions are and follow them.) If the referee makes eye contact with the assistant referee first, the assistant gives the substitution signal and the referee will make eye contact with you. After you have eye contact, raise the placard showing the number of the departing player high above your head so it is clearly visible for all to see. Angle it so the referee has a clear view of it first, and then angle the placard so it is most visible to the departing player. Once the player is aware, slowly turn the placard so everyone can see it. As soon as the player being substituted departs the field, allow the substitute to enter. Record the entering and departing players' numbers and the game time on the fourth official's log.

Hint: To freeze the entering substitute along the touchline, and to prevent the substitute from entering the field before the player being substituted departs, do not take the player pass or substitution ticket until after the departing player steps across the touchline.

Assistant referee signals

• Make eye contact with the referee while signaling and if the referee overrules you, drop the flag immediately or change your signal to confirm the referee's ruling, as directed in the pregame discussion.

• While the ball is being retrieved and readied for play, glance at the referee.

• If the ball has momentarily left the field by inches and there is confusion among the players as to whether the ball is out of play, you may give the request for stoppage in play signal first and, when the referee whistles to stop play, move the flag into the position for a throw-in, goalkick, corner kick or kickoff.

• One of two possible alternatives, the closed fist across the patch while making eye contact with the referee tells the referee that, according to your watch, time has expired. The other alternative is a closed fist over one of your thighs.

• As the attack develops and the assistant referee runs to stay with the ball or second-to-last defender, the flag stays "buried" to the ground and stays "field side."

Quiz

Without referring back, you should be able to answer the following true-false questions.

1. Lower the substitution signal as soon as the referee acknowledges your signal.

2. When signaling, you should come to a complete stop and raise the flag as an extension of your straight arm.

3. A furled flag indicates the assistant is ready for the start of play.

4. If you believe the goal was scored in accordance with law 10, make eye contact with the referee and jog 45 yards up the touchline.

5. If you are making positioning adjustments of only a few yards, make side-to-side movements, remaining square to the field.

1 - True, 2 - True, 3 - False, 4 - False, 5 - True

Chapter 8

Sequenced Signals

Some of the signals shown in the previous two chapters do not make sense in isolation. Many of the signals shown are the second part of a multi-part signal.

Observe
Watch the top referees working MLS matches and professional division matches in your area. They have sufficient training and experience to know which signal to use — and when. Their signals flow. If you will focus on their signals, you will often see a dialog. You may see the assistant try to get the referee's attention, convey a short message, look to the referee for a response, send a clarifying signal and then watch as the referee gives a thumbs up to express appreciation.

Practice
Clear and distinct signals help the communication process. When you give crisp signals and gestures that leave no room for doubt, your partners will receive and understand the intended message. In each of the prior two chapters, we've tried to point out common mistakes that detract from clear communication and are unprofessional. Work with a partner or practice in the mirror but get your signals clear and distinct.

Flow
You want to establish a nice flow to your signals, especially when the signal has several parts. Figure out what you want to do with the signal and keep giving that signal until the message is passed. If you want to stop play for an offside infringement, do not lower the request for stoppage in play signal until the referee notices your flag. After that, give a clear signal for where the incident took place.

Rush
Many referees are in a rush to convey information, so they instantly give a signal. Then once they've had a chance to think about that signal, they have to reverse themselves or switch the flag to the other hand. Be patient. Do your thinking before you offer the signal.

Eye contact
Each signal offered as a part of a sequence must have eye contact between the refereeing partners. The three signals offered up on the chapter title page tell a story. If the referee isn't looking at the assistant when the first signal is given and the assistant starts to run up the line to signal a valid goal, the referee is likely to think the assistant is pulling out to stay level with the second-to-last defender. That would be like walking in halfway through a movie. If the referee notices the flag straight

up but neglects to keep eye contact until the assistant starts the jog toward the halfway line, the referee might think an offside decision was given and award the wrong restart. That would be like leaving the movies halfway through the picture. Eye contact is the key. Establish it and keep it while the message is being passed.

Demeanor
Be pleasant. Smile. It's a game, you are outdoors in the sunshine, you're getting some exercise and you should be having fun. Let that show on your face. If you're hoping for more eye contact with your partners, smile at them when they look at you. The players will think you are enjoying their game, your partner is more likely to look at you to receive your message and it may encourage your partner who is having a tough game.

Change in demeanor
The nice thing about having a smile on your face most of the time is that it allows a dramatic change when a player does something to upset you. If you are the referee and have had a pleasant game with a few fouls to this point, you're smiling. Here comes a defender with a hard tackle a split second late — your changed expression is as much a signal to him as a yellow card or a public word. If you're the assistant referee hustling to keep up with play on every kick of the ball and some silly attacker parrots, "It's when the ball is kicked, linesman," your sudden change from a smile to a blank look may be just the warning that player needs to stop the dissent at an early stage.

One-part signals
Some signals are intended to be given in one fluid motion. Examples of those are routine throw-in signals by either the referee or assistant, the referee offering a direct free kick signal or the assistant giving a routine corner kick decision. Some referees mistakenly complicate those simple signals — an assistant raises the flag straight up in the right hand to indicate the ball is out, then lowers it to a 45-degree angle in the right hand to show direction. That's great if the ball was inches off the field and came back into play. Routine one-part signals should be given in one part.

Two-part signals
The referee offering an indirect free kick is an example of a two-part signal. The direction for the restart must be the first part of the signal and then the raised arm denotes what type of kick it is. An assistant referee offering an offside indication needs a two-part signal to

convey the complete message. Likewise, an assistant who offers help with a foul indication needs to point the restart direction as the third part of the signal.

Options

Sometimes, when an assistant offers one signal, the referee has several options. This chapter will point out several of those times and lay out the full range of options for the referee.

Courtesy

All assistant referee signals which are seen should be acknowledged by either doing what the assistant requests or waving down the signal. Waving down the signal is "acting on" the assistant's signal — it simply means that for whatever reason the referee has decided not to do what the assistant requested.

As a simple courtesy to your partners, there should never be a signal given that doesn't have some sort of response. It may be as simple as a nod, thumbs up or a verbal, "Thank you." For example, if the assistant signals you on her shorts that she shows three minutes left in the half, give that same signal back. Don't just nod. Show three fingers to indicate clearly you got exactly the same message she passed to you. If you wish to add a minute of referee's discretionary time, display four fingers on your shorts. But give her the courtesy of a reply, the same as you would do in conversation.

Request for stoppage in play

That is the basic signal for assistants wishing a stoppage in play. That is the first part in many multi-part signals: offside, fouls or misconduct not seen by the referee or a ball narrowly passing wholly over a boundary line but continuing to be actively played.

Come to a complete stop and raise the flag as an extension of your straight arm. Establish eye contact with the referee. If the referee waves your signal down, lower the flag and regain your position with the ball or second-to-last defender to judge offside.

If the referee misses the flag, stay at attention with the flag raised until it is no longer appropriate, given the circumstances. You should discuss those situations with the referee during the pregame conference. If you raised the flag for an offside, lower the flag when the referee awards a goalkick or throw-in to the defense.

In those rare cases when it is a flag that should not be waved down, such as a ball that passed wholly over the goalline, under the crossbar and between the goalposts but came back into the field of play, continue to hold the flag vertically.

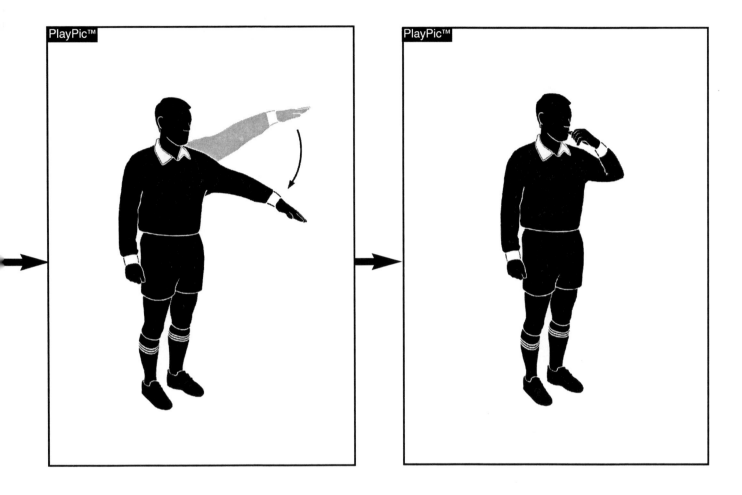

Wave-down

All assistant referee signals which are seen should be acknowledged by either doing what the assistant requests or waving down the signal. Waving down the signal is "acting on" the assistant's signal — it simply means that for whatever reason the referee has decided not to do what the assistant requested. Some referees prefer a discrete signal at waist level. Some referees only give a verbal indication to lower the flag.

Whistle

Other than your voice, the whistle is the primary means of communicating with those people at the event — players, coaches, spectators and your referee partners.

A strong whistle and a motion that says thank you to your partners does a lot for their self-esteem, foul recognition skills, teamwork and motivation. Your using their input to control the game pays huge dividends later in that game and in future games when you work with those same partners.

Wig-wag to request a foul

Law 6 dictates assistant referees indicate "when misconduct or any other incident has occurred out of the view of the referee."

That is the first part of a two-part signal. The movement starts after the flag raises vertically, is in the wrist only and the wig-wag should only be repeated once or twice. The assistant is looking directly at the referee while signaling.

The referee has three basic options, as shown on the next page. Should the referee wave the flag down, it should come down immediately. If the referee honors the request by blowing the whistle to stop play, the assistant referee should immediately give the second part of the signal, pointing 45-degrees upward in the direction of the restart.

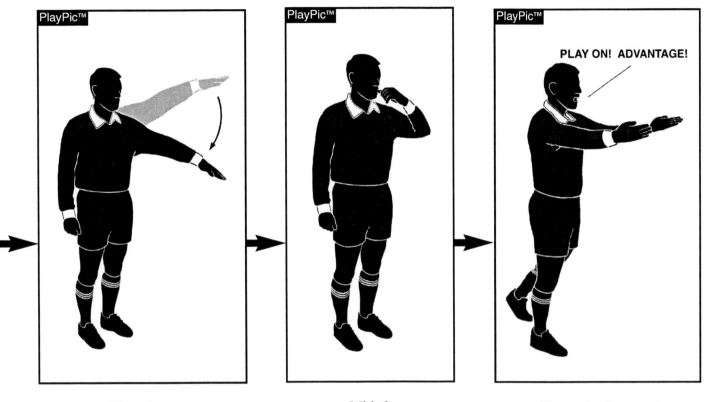

Wave-down	Whistle	Play on! Advantage!

All assistant referee signals which are seen should be acknowledged by either doing what the assistant requests or waving down the signal. Waving down the signal is "acting on" the assistant's signal. Some referees prefer a discrete signal at waist level. Some referees only give a verbal indication to lower the flag.

Giving a clearly visible signal and a thunderous, "Thank you," to the assistant does a couple of things to aid game control. It lets the assistant know to lower the flag and regain a position in line with the second-to-last defender or the ball. It lets players, coaches and spectators know the trio is functioning as a team. It reminds everyone that you are watching your assistant for input in controlling the game. If the assistant flagged for a potential foul, it lets the fouled player feel protected and sends a sign to the miscreant that the deed was observed.

Other than your voice, the whistle is the primary means of communicating with those people at the event — players, coaches, spectators and your referee partners.

A strong whistle and a motion that says thank you to your partners does a lot for their self-esteem, foul recognition skills, teamwork and motivation. Your using their input to control the game pays huge dividends later in that game and in future games when you work with those same partners.

The only two-handed signal used by the referee is also the only signal given both verbally and physically. Swing both hands forward from your hips at waist level while distinctly declaring, "Play on!" or "Advantage."

The signal is an indication to the assistant that you saw the signal. However, based on your position, experience, feel for the game and understanding of the players involved, you are choosing not to stop play.

Take care in exercising this option — a qualified, certified assistant has brought to your attention a foul or misconduct which occurred outside your view, which is not doubtful or trifling infraction and which the assistant believes warrants stopping play, or else the assistant would not have given the signal in the first place.

Proper mechanics by the assistant — offside by player who scored

That is the basic signal for assistants wishing a stoppage in play. That is the first part in many two-part signals, such as offside.

Come to a complete stop and raise the flag as an extension of your straight arm. Establish eye contact with the referee.

If the referee misses the flag, stay at attention with the flag raised until it is no longer appropriate, given the circumstances. You should discuss those situations with the referee during the pregame conference.

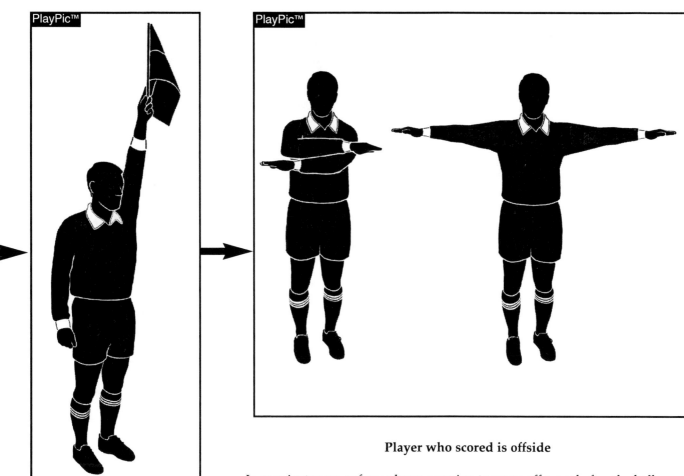

Continue to hold

Player who scored is offside

Standard mechanics as stated in the *Guide to Procedures for Referees, Assistant Referees and Fourth Officials* dictate that if the player who put the ball into the net was the player guilty of the offside infraction, continue to hold the flag straight up, even after the ball is in the net.

In rare instances, referees have occasion to wave off a goal after the ball winds up in the net. There might have been an offside indication just as the ball was kicked and the ball was in the net before the whistle could sound.

Referees may also have to consult with assistant referees to get information about action that occurred just prior to a goal being scored. When the assistant referee stands stiffly near the corner flagpost with the flag raised, as opposed to making a 15-yard sprint toward the halfway line, the referee must find out why. Based on information provided by the assistant, the referee may have to deny the unfairly scored goal. Signal to all concerned by waving off the goal as shown above.

Most soccer referees use the same signal adopted by basketball and football officials. Though not an approved signal, the signal is common among officials. Check with the appropriate governing bodies to see if you can use it.

Standard mechanics as stated in the *Guide to Procedures for Referees, Assistant Referees and Fourth Officials* dictate that if the player who put the ball into the net was the player guilty of the offside infraction, the assistant continues to hold the flag straight up, even after the ball is in the net. That should eliminate any need for a consultation with the assistant. But, if there is uncertainty, consult and get the call right.

Request for a stoppage in play

That is the basic signal for assistants wishing a stoppage in play. That is the first part in many multi-part signals: offside, foul or misconduct.

Come to a complete stop and raise the flag as an extension of your straight arm. Establish eye contact with the referee.

You may have taken this position and displayed this signal during a phase of play immediately prior to a ball entering the goal. The *Guide to Procedures* 3K dictates two instances when you would lower the flag and stand in place: if there was a foul by an attacker or if a player other than the scorer was in an offside position and, in your opinion, interfered with play or with an opponent. In either of those cases, as soon as the ball enters the net, lower the flag, continue to make eye contact with the referee and stand in place.

Sequenced Signals

Proper mechanics by the assistant — attacking team fouled leading to a goal
(The same mechanics are to be used when a player who did not score
was in an offside position)

Not a valid goal. If you observe the ball wholly cross the goalline under the crossbar and between the goalposts but believe the ball was not scored in accordance with law 10, stand in place. It is clearer to the referee if you even stiffen slightly, similar to a military person at the position of attention.

If a player other than the goalscorer was in an offside position, and in your opinion, interfered with play or with an opponent, stand at attention with no flag signal. If there was a foul by a member of the attacking team that contributed to the goal, stand at attention with no flag signal.

If the referee disallows a goal based on your information, expect some disagreement with your decision. Players may voice comments about your positioning, your eyesight and your ability.

No goal. In rare instances, referees have occasion to wave off a goal after the ball winds up in the net.

Referees may also have to consult with assistant referees to get information about action that occurred just prior to a goal being scored. When the assistant referee stands stiffly near the corner flagpost with the flag at his side, as opposed to making a 15-yard sprint toward the halfway line, the referee must find out why. Based on information provided by the assistant, the referee may have to deny the unfairly scored goal. Signal to all concerned by waving off the goal as shown above.

Most soccer referees use the same signal adopted by basketball and football officials. Though not an approved signal, the signal is common among officials. Check with the appropriate governing bodies to see if you can use it.

Proper mechanics by the assistants — foul/misconduct behind the referee's back

Foul/misconduct indicated by trail assistant referee. If the referee does not see a flag offered by the trail assistant referee, the lead assistant referee mirrors the request for stoppage in play signal and, after making eye contact with the referee, points across the field to the trail assistant referee.

Request for stoppage in play. That is the basic signal for assistants wishing a stoppage in play. That is the first part in many two-part signals, such as behind-the-back misconduct.

Come to a complete stop and raise the flag as an extension of your straight arm. Establish eye contact with the referee. If the referee misses the flag, stay at attention with the flag raised until it is no longer appropriate, given the circumstances. You should discuss those situations with the referee during the pregame conference. In the case of misconduct (yellow or red card), you want to get the referee's attention to improve game control.

Wig-wag to request a foul. Law 6 dictates assistant referees indicate "when misconduct or any other incident has occurred out of the view of the referee."

The assistant is looking directly at the referee while signaling. Since there may have been a long delay between the time you saw the incident until the other assistant noticed your flag and got the referee's attention, you have a lot to remember. Go over those incidents once again in your mind.

Proper mechanics by the assistants — misconduct behind the referee's back

Whistle. Talk with the whistle: use a deafening thunderbolt when you know that you had an instance of serious foul play or violent conduct behind your back and want everyone to quickly know you will send the player off the field of play.

Go to the assistant. Since you do not yet know what happened, you must confer with your trail assistant referee. Sprint or jog to the assistant and turn so that you are side-by-side — both of you facing the field of play and the players. Get the needed information. Ask questions until you have a clear picture of what you are going to do. Know who was involved by jersey number and jersey color.

Display the misconduct card. During this emotional period, tempers are liable to be high. You want to get the game restarted and get the fans, coaches and players focused on playing action. With a minimum of conversation, say what needs to be said, display the appropriate misconduct card and get ready for the restart. If players need to leave the field, urge them off quickly and restart.

Sequenced signals

• Be pleasant. Smile. It's a game, you are outdoors in the sunshine, you're getting some exercise and you should be having fun.

• If the referee misses the flag, stay at attention with the flag raised until it is no longer appropriate, given the circumstances. You should discuss those situations with the referee during the pregame conference.

• Clear and distinct signals help the communication process. When you give crisp signals and gestures that leave no room for doubt, your partners will receive and understand the intended message.

Quiz

Without referring back, you should be able to answer the following true-false questions.

1. While the referee and fourth official monitor the substitution, the assistant referee should observe the field and watch for incidents that may occur behind the referee's back.

2. When an assistant referee offers a signal, the referee has no option other than to act on that signal.

3. Standard mechanics as stated in the *Guide to Procedures for Referees, Assistant Referees and Fourth Officials* dictate that if the player who put the ball into the net was the player guilty of the offside infraction, continue to hold the flag straight up, even after the ball is in the net.

1 - True, 2 - False, 3 - True

Chapter 9

Kickoff And Goals

The kickoff is one of eight ways to start or restart a soccer match. To start the game, start the second half, start any period of extra time or restart play after a goal, the attacking team gets a kickoff.

Since 1863

The kickoff has survived the test of time. The original *Laws of the Game*, codified in a London pub in December, 1863, said, "The game shall be commenced by a place kick from the center of the ground by the side winning the toss, the other side shall not approach within 10 yards of the ball until it is kicked off. After a goal is won the losing side shall be entitled to a kickoff." So the provisions of the kickoff are virtually unchanged after 136 years. About the only change was the removal of the provision that "the two sides shall change goals after each goal is won."

Simplicity

All players in their own half of the field. No opponents within 10 yards of the ball. Make sure everyone is ready. Start your watch and make sure it is running before you signal. Give the signal for the start. That is not a difficult restart to manage.

Referee's role

For the start of play, it is usual for the referee to cover the ball, the kicker, the taking of the kick and encroachment. The assistants usually cover encroachment violations by players not immediately involved in the kickoff. Whatever position the referee takes should allow the referee to move quickly to the diagonal pattern as soon as the play begins. Some referees like being ahead of the ball, others behind it. Some referees like to be to the left of the kickers, others to the right. Those are matters of personal choice.

Other aspects to manage

Your game management must not fall by the wayside during that facet of the game. You need eye contact with your assistants, you need to scan the field to look for hot spots and displeased players. Since the ball is not in play, it serves as a perfect time for you to have a quiet word with a player regarding improper behavior. Maybe that player just had a go at your assistant regarding an offside decision. Stand near the player and quietly and privately explain you will protect your teammate just as strongly as the player will act to protect his teammates. Order the kickoff taken from your spot near the player and offer some encouraging words as the ball is put into play.

Some try to gain an advantage

In a cyclical pattern, teams in one area reinvent the wheel and bring back an illegal technique that has been going on for decades. Most often it's the youthful players who figure it out for themselves or viewed someone else try it and get away with it — one of the wingers will get a 10-15 yard head start before the ball is kicked off, the two players in the center circle legally place the ball into play and the second player to touch the ball whacks it 40 yards to open space behind the defenders. If you see it, whistle it and order the retake. If you sense it happening, watch the entire length of the halfway line immediately before signalling for the restart. If your assistant flags the action that you missed, whistle to stop play and order the restart. Catch the teams a few times, tell your fellow referees at the next association meeting and within a month the cycle is broken until the next time.

Goals scored

That is a good time for the entire referee team to have their heads up. Look for those unwanted actions and listen for the unkind words. Prevent what you can by being close to hot spots. The easiest way to see the hot spots is to begin backpedaling toward the center circle, keeping as many players in view as possible.

Celebration

Perhaps taken to a new level during the 1999 Women's World Cup final, players spontaneously react to show their joy at scoring. Some inventive players create and rehearse their "moves" to express themselves, such as MLS star Digital Takawara with his "crawl" or the aged Cameroon World Cup star Roger Milla dancing near the corner flag. One Brazilian inflamed his opponents, nicknamed "The Rabbits," by taking a carrot out of his shorts after a goal and biting into it during his midfield celebration. At some point, those celebrations become taunts or excessively eat into valuable playing time. While you have the power to display a caution card for delaying the restart of play, make an attempt to use your voice and your personality to encourage the celebration to end, a jog to the other half of the field and a speedy restart.

Advice to Referees 12.29.4 lists excessive celebration of a goal as a reason to display a discretionary caution. It is recommended that referees give a prior explicit warning to the team before cautioning a team member.

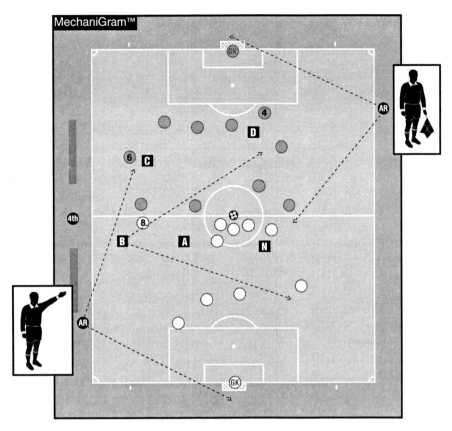

Referee positioning

Action on the field:

To start the game, start the second half, start any period of extra time or restart play after a goal, the attacking team gets a kickoff.

Referee Responsibilities

Move to a position where you can observe the most important aspects of play. Typically, position A works well for most referees. If you get a sense that ⑧ is moving into the opponent's half well before the kick is taken, move toward the touchline to observe ⑧ (position B). For the initial kickoff to start each period, start the clock under all codes of rules.

Nothing requires you to move into the half of the field behind the ball. If either ④ or ⑥ dispute some aspect of the goal or are chastising the assistant, you may wish to remain near them (positions D or C) and use your personality to lessen the dissent or clear up some point of the law. Start the clock if playing under Federation or NCAA rules.

From the *NISOA DSC Instructional Manual*, "For the start of play, it is usual for the referee to cover the ball, the kicker, the taking of the kick and encroachment. The assistants usually cover encroachment violations by players not immediately involved in the kickoff." Position N is detailed in their manual, but it says, "Some referees prefer other positions. Whatever position is taken should allow the referee to move quickly to the diagonal pattern as soon as the play begins."

Assistant Referee Responsibilities

Return to your position level with the second-to-last defender. If immediately after a goal, record the time, team and scorer. Unless directed otherwise by the referee during the pregame discussion, the assistant on the far end records first and then watches players as the assistant on the near end records the vital information. Work quickly so you do not hold up the game. Establish eye contact with the referee when you are ready.

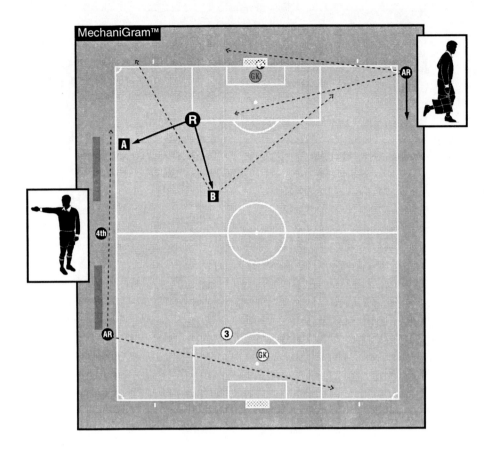

Valid goal — no onfield difficulties

Action on the field:
The ball enters the goal, under the crossbar, between the goalposts for a valid score by the attacking team.

Referee Responsibilities
Check visually with your lead assistant to see if there is any reason to believe it is not a valid goal. Most top referees also check visually with the trail assistant referee before awarding the goal. Perhaps something was clear from that perspective that was not able to be picked up from the standard diagonal. Point to the center circle to confirm the goal. Backpedal away from the playing action to gain a broader perspective on the greatest number of players, such as to position A or B. Stop the clock if playing under Federation or NCAA rules. Move to the jubilant players to curb the celebration if it begins to consume too much time. Record the goal in your game data wallet.

Assistant Referee Responsibilities
Make eye contact with the referee. If you are at the end where the goal was scored, run a short distance up the touchline. Wait for the other assistant to record the goal, then record the goal in your game data wallet. Observe the players. Move laterally to stay even with the second-to-last defender.

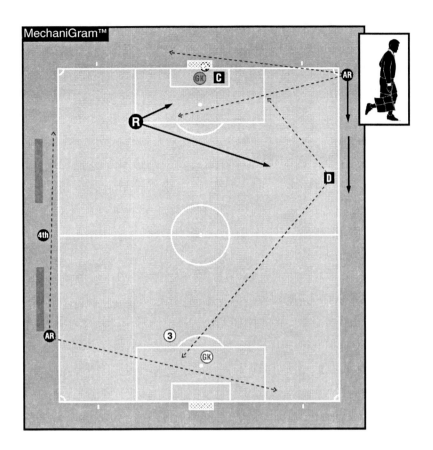

Valid goal — problems with players

Action on the field:
The ball enters the goal, under the crossbar, between the goalposts for a valid score by the attacking team.

Referee Responsibilities
Check visually with your assistants to see if they have any reason to believe it is not a valid goal. Point to the center circle to confirm the goal. Stop the clock if playing under Federation or NCAA rules. Often a member of the scoring team goes into the goalmouth to retrieve the ball for a quick restart and the goalkeeper or defender physically tries to deny access to the ball. Sometimes a defender runs to dissent with the assistant referee. In any case, move to the trouble spot (such as position C or D) and use your personality or tools to fix the problem. Move between angry opponents. Funnel joyous scorers to one side of you while soothing defenders on the other side. Record the goal in your game data wallet.

Assistant Referee Responsibilities
Make eye contact with the referee. If you are at the end where the goal was scored, run a short distance up the touchline. If players run to confront you, move further up the touchline. Wait for the other assistant to record the goal, then record the goal in your game data wallet. Observe the players. Move laterally to stay even with the second-to-last defender.

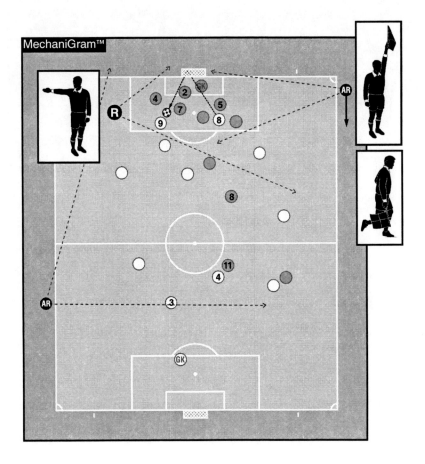

Valid goal — ball rebounds into play

Action on the field:

⑧ shoots and scores a valid goal but the ball quickly rebounded off some hard surface into the field toward ⑨ and ⑦. There is confusion on the part of some players; defenders quickly making a long clearance and attackers initiating celebrations.

Referee Responsibilities

If you suspect that a goal was scored, observe the lead assistant referee. If the assistant signals to request a stoppage in play, whistle to stop play and watch to see what the assistant does next. If the assistant runs 10-15 yards up the touchline, point to the center circle and follow procedures for a goal scored. Stop the clock if playing under Federation or NCAA rules.

Assistant Referee Responsibilities

Raise the flag vertically to indicate the whole of the ball passed completely over the goalline. Establish eye contact with the referee and, as soon as the referee whistles, lower the flag and run 10-15 yards up the touchline. Follow procedures for a goal scored.

Valid goal — ball rebounds into play

When the ball crosses wholly over the goalline, under the crossbar and between the goalposts, the ball is out of play and a valid goal is scored. In most cases, the ball causes the back of the net to flutter and the goal is obvious to everyone.

Some cases are not so obvious. One notable example is the 1966 World Cup final match between England and West Germany. With the scored tied, 2-2, after regulation time, in extra time Swiss referee Gottfried Dienst was forced to rule on a ball that hit the crossbar, drove quickly into the ground near the goalline and rebounded into play. Without the benefit of a common language, Dienst and his Russian assistant spoke and gesticulated. The final result — a goal was awarded and England went on to win their first World Cup trophy.

Using standard mechanics, you can convey the same message in four simple steps. Even if the referee crew shares a common language, there is no need to speak.

PlayPic A shows an assistant requesting a stoppage in play because the ball passed wholly over the goalline. The referee honors that request by blowing the whistle, as shown in PlayPic B.

The referee must continue to watch the assistant for the next action conveys the vital information. PlayPic C shows the assistant running 10-15 yards up the touchline, the same signal used when a valid goal is scored. The referee concurs with the valid goal by pointing to the center mark, shown in PlayPic D.

Defenders will yell, "But ref, you've got to go talk to your assistant." You already have. You've had a concise, clear communication with each other that can have only one meaning — the ball was out of play and a valid goal was scored.

Restart the game with a kickoff. Keep tuned to defenders who might continue to make rude comments to your hard-working assistant.

Watching players at a goal scored

The emotional lift of a goal scored, as well as the despondent faces of those scored upon, lead to a variety of actions on the field. Defenders will claim an attacker held or impeded them, some run to the assistant to protest for a possible offside and some have the awareness that a more skillful player bested them. Keepers hate to be scored upon and project the blame on anyone but themselves; yelling at referees, assistants, teammates, etc. Those words are often unkind, occasionally abusive.

Attackers who have just halved the goal differential from two to one will want to go into the net and pick up the ball to get it into play as quickly as possible. Keepers and defenders with a lead want to delay that as long as possible and might push or fight with jubilant attackers to waste precious seconds. If the ball hit the net and bounced a yard or two back onto the field, a second attacker may rekick the ball into the net several seconds later to taunt the opponents.

That is a good time for the entire referee team to have their heads up. Look for those unwanted actions and listen for the unkind words. Prevent what you can by being close to hot spots. The easiest way to see the hot spots is to begin back pedaling toward the center circle, keeping as many players in view as possible. Make eye contact with the assistant referee to confirm a valid goal. Also, note if defenders claiming offside besiege the assistant. If they do, control that action via your personality or cards, as needed.

Here the players have gotten in front of a referee who hustled to the goalline. The referee is checking with the assistant and sees that no attackers are going into the goal to carry the ball back to the center mark. ⑩ and ⑪ are focused on their teammate and not turning to taunt any opponents. If other teammates drag ❸ to the ground and pile on him, give it a few seconds, lean down and say something like, "Nice goal, 3. OK fellas, let's get to the other side and get it going." If the celebration becomes prolonged, or use field equipment such as the corner flags, display a caution for unsporting behavior.

Misconduct — unsporting behavior

There are dozens of offenses that fit under the umbrella of unsporting behavior: late challenges, reckless tackles or deliberately handling the ball to thwart a counterattack. ❾ may not even be saying anything but his actions to incite the emotions of the opposing crowd are at least unsporting.

Goalscorers are happy. They worked hard to create a significant chance and made the most of that chance. They beat their opponents. That is reason to celebrate and join with the other teammates who made it possible. Those emotions elevate when it is in the closing moments of a tight game or toward the end of a championship match.

In the Fair Play campaign, there is no move to inhibit celebrating goals. Players may raise their voices, dance and hug to recognize the effort. When those actions become a prolonged celebration, referees must step in. A valuable commodity — time — is being wasted as one team celebrates and the other team waits to score the tying goal. Referees should also step in when the celebrations turn outward, away from the joy of the team scoring the goal, and begin to taunt and demean the opponents. In the PlayPic above, if you see ❾'s actions as inflammatory behavior or an action that brings the game into disrepute, caution ❾ for unsporting behavior. Modern-day morality and the influence of cultural icons aside, those are decisions you have to make on the field.

If you think the gesture is offensive, insulting or abusive, send off the offender.

Federation rules deal differently with a high school player that taunts an opponent or the opposing fans. The player is shown both the yellow and red card together, that player is disqualified for the remainder of the game and the offender's team may replace the player. Some referees call that the "soft red." The Federation definition of taunting (12-8-2 Note) is "intended or designed to embarrass, ridicule or demean others under any circumstances including on the basis of race, religion, gender or national origin."

Kickoff and goals

• For the start of play, it is usual for the referee to cover the ball, the kicker, the taking of the kick and encroachment.

• The assistants usually cover encroachment violations by players not immediately involved in the kickoff.

• Establish eye contact with the referee when you are ready.

• Whatever position is taken should allow the referee to move quickly to the diagonal pattern as soon as the play begins.

Quiz

Without referring back, you should be able to answer the following true-false questions.

1. You are required to move into the half of the field behind the ball.

2. To start the game, start the second half, start any period of extra time or restart play after a goal, the attacking team gets a kickoff.

3. At a kickoff, both assistants should be level with the second-to-last defender.

1 - False, 2 - True, 3 - True

Chapter 10

Throw-in

The throw-in is probably the most common restart you will administer during a game. With a narrow field, you may have 50 to 60 throw-ins during a 90 minute game. As the field gains width and the players gain ballhandling skills, the number of throw-ins decreases.

In the beginning

The original *Laws of the Game* stated that when a ball went into touch (out-of-bounds over the touchline), "the first player who touches it shall kick or throw it from the point on the boundary line where it left the ground." While some elements have changed (the referee now designates which team is entitled to the throw-in and it must be thrown), some aspects of the throw-in remain constant, such as the location.

The Inner Game of Soccer

When I was first learning how to referee this great game, I was guided by a few early soccer refereeing books. One thought about throw-ins stayed with me over two decades. Eric Sellin wrote in *The Inner Game of Soccer* (World Publications, Mountain View, Calif., © 1976) that, "In all of these instances, however, it is possible for the throw-in to be quite legal, even if it is not necessarily elegant. The referee must decide whether the throw is foul or not and whether it is incorrect in so trifling a manner that he should allow play to continue. That most players and coaches are basically unaware of what constitutes a lawful throw-in is attested to by the fact that they often claim that an opponent's throw is foul but seldom argue in their own behalf when the referee has charged them with a foul throw." Confirming Sellin's observation that referees should not interrupt play just because a throw-in might be only slightly incorrect, *Advice to Referees* 15.5 directs referees to ignore doubtful or trifling errors in performing a throw-in if, in fact, the ball was otherwise put into play quickly and with no unfair advantage to the thrower.

Sellin continues on page 191 with, "Let me insert a mildly relevant story. I once heard tell of a coach of younger players who noticed that 75 percent of both teams' throw-ins went to the opponent. He therefore instructed his players to deliberately make foul throws and, if boxed in on the sideline, not to kick the ball out off the shins of the opponent as one is wont to do but rather to kick the ball straight out of touch. These tactics were adopted in order to exploit the percentage factor when the ball was put back into play. Not very good soccer training, no doubt, but this coach's strategy bears out the notion that — with a few notable exceptions — the throw-in is seldom the major contributing game

factor that players would make it out to be as they wring their hands in despair over a referee's directional signal in favor of the opponent."

Tactics

There are several tactical variations during the throw-in that you must sense. Does a team want to take a long throw-in for a scoring opportunity? Do they want a short throw-in to maintain team possession? Will they bleed as much time off the clock as possible with a one-goal margin of victory in the latter stages of a match? Be aware of those changing tactics and read play to gain the best position possible. Talk with a team captain to speed the ball into play before it becomes a problem. Caution as needed if the team continues its stalling tactics.

Dynamics change

Just as the tactics change given the score, time remaining and players involved, the dynamics of the throw-in change as play moves up and down the line. Do you expect the ball to be thrown down the line, with the likely possibility of another throw-in direction decision? Will the ball be thrown to the goalkeeper? If so, remind yourself of what to do if the keeper handles the ball. Will the throw-in be thrown to a midfielder who may whack the ball long? Your awareness of that may allow you to clear the passing lane so you are not struck by the ball.

The short throw

Because it is a difficult skill for players to master, judging short throw-ins tends to be more difficult than judging longer throw-in. Most often, players violate the provision stated in *Advice to Referees* 15.3, "The throwing movement must be continued to the point of release." When making a short throw-in, a high percentage of players deliver the ball from over and behind their head, move the ball in front of their body, stop all motion and then drop the ball to their teammate. If you have trouble judging that motion at game speed, work with a senior mentor or role-play several proper and improper short throw-ins at your next training session.

Don't make up your own rules

There are referees who love to spot and call illegal throw-ins. Some referees boast at association meetings they caught 12 or 15 illegal throws in their last game. Don't be one of those referees. As Sellin says, "quite legal, even if it is not necessarily elegant." Other referees contend that flip throw-ins present a danger to the thrower and whistle them as an infraction.

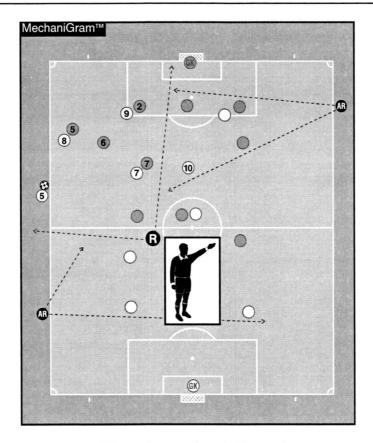

Throw-in on referee's diagonal

Action on the field:

A player attacking the goal on that end of the field takes a throw-in from the referee's side of the field and from the referee's end of the field.

Referee Responsibilities

During the game, you face positioning decisions on throw-ins dozens of times. When the throw-in is along your diagonal, you face several options. You can take an extreme position (see the MechaniGrams on the next two pages), you can move off your diagonal toward the center of the field or you can remain behind play. With ⑤ taking the throw-in, if you choose to get into the middle of the field along your normal diagonal, you get into the passing lanes between ⑦ and ⑩ or ⑧ and ⑩. Here is one case where you should remain behind the play, observe who receives the throw-in, wait until the first pass is made and then react to player movement. Most likely, you want to move toward ⑧'s present position if white continues its attack. If the defense intercepts one of the first few touches, you'll cross to the other side of the center circle and let play get in front of you.

Assistant Referee Responsibilities

Be aware that a player who receives the ball directly from a throw-in, even though in an offside position, cannot be offside. Move laterally to stay even with the second-to-last defender.

From the *NISOA DSC Instructional Manual*, "The referee normally observes to assure correct position at the line for the throw, and observes for hand faults by the thrower. The assistant observes for foot faults by the thrower, and can usually best see that the ball enters the field directly into play. The division of responsibilities at the throw-in should be addressed by the referee in the pregame briefing." That mechanic is also stated in the *NISOA Assistant Referee Duties & Responsibilities*.

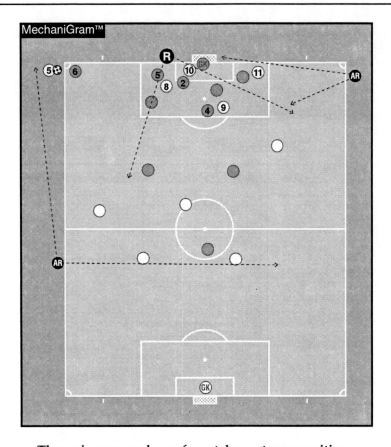

Throw-in near goal — referee takes extreme position

Action on the field:

A team uses a throw-in as an attacking weapon. A skilled player with a long throw in can be as effective as a corner kick. Look for two types of long throw-ins: a high looping throw that a tall attacker tries to drive directly into the goal; and a line drive that an attacker at the near post tries to flick on to a teammate on the far post.

Referee Responsibilities

You might read that a long throw-in is about to take place when a particular player moves out of normal position to take the restart. Listen for a coach to call a certain player to throw. Look for the cluster of offensive players (or the target person on a line drive throw) and position yourself so you have a good angle on the next significant action.

From position R, you have an excellent view of a line drive throw to ⑧, who has three choices to flick the ball: ⑨, ⑩ or ⑪. An airborne ⑧ may fling arms and elbows into the defenders or may be pushed or pulled as the ball draws close. You have a superb, close view to see if ⑩ impedes the goalkeeper and your goal/no-goal decision will not be disputed if the ball hits the woodwork and rides the goalline. Perhaps most important, by being across the goalline you are not in the way of a shot on goal or a clearance.

The one drawback is the same as any time you take an extreme position — in case of a counterattack, you may be an extra 10-15 yards behind play and must sprint in a straight line to catch up. That straight sprint causes you to follow play and you get straightlined or flat, not being able to see diagonally through the players.

Assistant Referee Responsibilities

Be aware that a player who receives the ball directly from a throw-in, even though in an offside position, cannot be offside. Move laterally to stay even with the second-to-last defender.

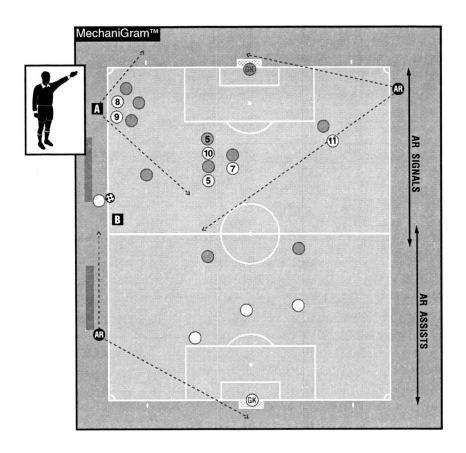

Throw-in — referee takes extreme position

Action on the field:

The referee anticipates that the white team will take a long throw-in and the most likely place for the ball to land will be near the touchline along the referee's diagonal.

Referee Responsibilities

Read that a throw-in down the line is about to take place. Listen for a coach to call a certain player to throw. Look for the cluster of offensive players and position yourself so you have a good angle on the next significant action.

From position A, you have an excellent view of a line drive throw to ⑨, who has three choices: flick the ball to ⑧ or ⑩ or chest trap the ball and make a centering cross. An airborne ⑨ may fling arms and elbows into the defenders or may be pushed or pulled as the ball draws close. Perhaps most important, by being across the touchline you are not in the way of a shot on goal or a clearance. Remaining near the thrower, at position B, leaves you too far from the next significant action.

The one drawback is the same as any time you take an extreme position — in case of a counterattack, you may be an extra 10-15 yards behind play.

Assistant Referee Responsibilities

Remain level with the second-to-last defender. Offside decisions are yours. Note the words in the MechaniGram's right margin. The *Guide to Procedures* 3C and 3D spells out that on balls that depart on the assistant's end of the field, the assistant gives a primary signal with the flag raised 45-degrees upward. For balls that depart in the referee's end of the touchline, the assistant referee assists with a vertical flag in the appropriate hand, if necessary.

Throw-in — the flip throw

Most spectators attend a soccer match to see exciting play. In a 1982 collegiate match between the University of Virginia and the University of San Francisco, about 500 spectators were 20 yards onto the far end of the field as a UVA player took a flip throw-in near the corner flagpost. It was exciting — they wanted to see that play.

Some referees contend they will not allow a flip throw-in because of the possible dangers to the thrower: the thrower may slip off the ball and land awkwardly, the thrower may wrench her back or the thrower's feet may slip. Nonsense. You have no authority to rule a throw-in as dangerous.

Advice to Referees 15.3 allows the acrobatic throw-in, if the throw-in meets all the other legal requirements mentioned in law 15.

Throw-in — unfair distraction

The throw-in originated as a simple means to get the ball back into play once it crossed over a touchline. The rulemakers wanted to make it an awkward motion so the throwing team did not gain a huge advantage but simple enough so that almost everyone could do it properly after minimal training.

The beauty of soccer is when the ball is at the feet of the 20 field players. That's the most exciting portion of the game. Your job is to keep the ball in play for a majority of the time. Do not allow an opponent to delay a throw-in by unfairly distracting or impeding the thrower. If you or an assistant referee can stand close enough to do some preventive officiating before the distraction takes place, do it. If ㉓ is already waving his arms, yelling or gesticulating, caution ㉓ for unsporting behavior and show the yellow card. That is one of the mandatory cautions, as pointed out in *Advice to Referees* 15.7.

There is much misunderstanding on that simple point. An opponent may stand anywhere on the field, even directly on the touchline in front of the thrower. But ㉓ needs to be there before the ball is thrown in. If ➐ moves two feet to create the space to throw the ball into play, ㉓ may not move two feet in the same direction to block the throw. Some referees ask a defender to move 10 yards away during a throw-in. You have no such authority. Be very wary of a defender who yells just as a thrower releases the ball, even if he is yelling directions to a teammate. That may happen once as a legitimate need to reposition a teammate but the second time it happens you should consider it a tactical move to distract.

Throw-in — legally turned at the hips

Some referees tend to call too many foul throw-ins. Think of the criteria called for in law 15. If the thrower violates none of those criteria, the throw-in is legal.

That PlayPic tests three of the criteria. Is ❻ facing the field of play? Yes, clearly the feet position show ❻ is facing into the field. He is not facing toward the stands or the corner flagpost or some other odd angle, so he is facing the field of play.

Will ❻ use both hands? Yes, the hand placement while holding the ball and the elbows indicate use of both hands.

Will ❻ deliver the ball from behind and over his head? Yes, the ball is in that position now, so any continuous forward motion with his arms leads to a proper throw-in.

So against the criteria listed in the *Laws of the Game*, ❻ will execute a proper throw-in. The fact that it looks unusual does not make it a violation. The fact that his hips are twisted is not a violation. The fact that he initially was going to throw to his right but saw that teammate covered and instead twisted to his left to find an unmarked teammate is not a violation.

Judge throw-ins against the criteria found in the laws. Do not evaluate throw-ins on hearsay or the cries of parents and coaches. Some referees take great pride in being able to spot a foul throw-in from six fields away. At monthly meetings, some referees have commented they called 18 foul throw-ins in a single game. They were bragging about how well they had done — most of the other members thought they ruined the game.

Advice to Referees 15.5 discusses trifling infringements of the throw-in law. "Apparent technical infringements of law 15 should often be deemed trifling or doubtful so long as an advantage is not obtained by the team performing the throw-in and the restart occurs with little or no delay."

Throw-in — ball not delivered from over the head

There is a point where a throw-in is illegal. Often, it is at the younger, untrained age groups that are learning the skill for the first time. Perhaps in a player's haste to get the ball back into play to take advantage of a momentary defensive lapse, a player makes an illegal throw-in.

As the assistant referee looking at that throw-in, you can clearly see the throw is not delivered from over and behind the head. Since that is one of the criteria for a valid throw-in, you recognize it as illegal. But do you raise your flag to indicate the improper throw-in?

That depends on which elements of the throw-in your were told to supervise during the pregame instructions from the referee. The referee is counting on you to watch your area of responsibility. If that's the feet, that's where your focus must be. If the referee told you to watch the players contesting for the ball on the field before the throw-in, you should not even be aware of the thrower's motion. That direction changes from referee to referee, so listen to the pregame instruction and follow the guidance given that game.

Short throw-ins — squatting

There is often a tactical advantage to a team taking a short throw-in, that is, a throw that doesn't travel more than six to 15 yards before a teammate controls the throw-in. For example, team A has a striker controlling the ball down the left flank and a teammate comes over with an overlapping run. A defender slide tackles the ball away which just crosses the touchline. With the defender still on the ground, tactically it makes sense for the overlapping runner to make a short throw-in to his teammate who stands alone. A cross or a chip would almost certainly lead to an exciting scoring opportunity.

There is nothing in the laws about short throw-ins, so here are some do's and don'ts for referees. The thrower may use the body of a teammate or opponent in hopes of collecting the rebound. Say a lone defender were standing near the touchline, with his head turned, shouting directions to a teammate. The thrower could legally bounce the ball off the defender's back, collect the rebound and continue playing.

Of course, if he tried that same trick by hitting the referee, it would be illegal for the laws clearly state the ball must touch another player before the thrower may play the ball a second time.

Be on the watch for a thrower, angry about the last challenge or frustrated by an opponent with superior skill, trying to get even with the opponent by throwing the ball very rapidly and striking the defending player. That would be violent conduct and grounds for sending off the player.

Clever players will quickly figure out that if the ball is thrown from a lower height, the ball will not travel as far. Some players will choose to squat down, as shown in the PlayPic above. That is legal, if all other aspects of the throw-in are legal.

Short throw-ins —Kneeling

The PlayPic above shows a player who is kneeling on the ground. Some will argue that the player's feet are on the ground, but USSF's *Fair Play*, Fall 1996 issue's question and answer section dealt with that specifically. "**Q**. Is a player allowed to take a throw-in kneeling or sitting down. **A.** No. As the throw-in has not been taken correctly, it shall be retaken by a player of the opposing team." See *Advice to Referees* 15.4

At the other end of the spectrum is the player trying to achieve maximum distance on the throw-in by doing the flip or somersault throw (see PlayPic p. 112). That is legal, as long as all other aspects of the throw-in are legal.

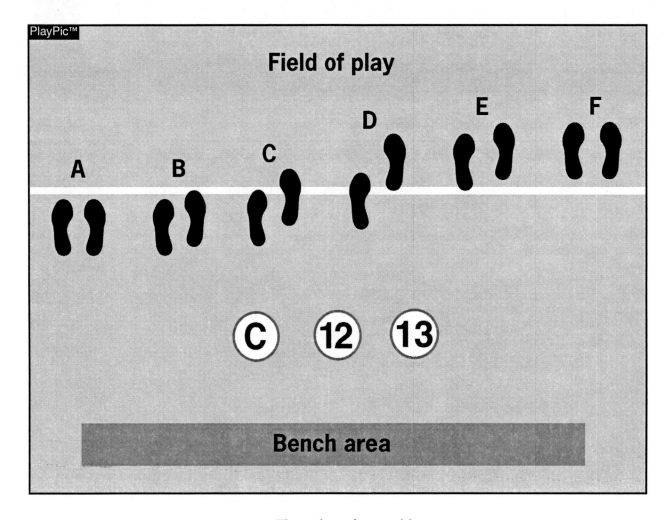

Throw-in — foot positions

There continues to be much confusion about the proper foot placement for throw-ins. It stems from the time when each of the three codes had different variations on what was legal and illegal. Now the three codes agree. For sporting people who follow American football and basketball, there is room for confusion.

The diagram above shows six different alternatives for foot placement during a throw-in. Judging each of those against the criteria in the *Laws of the Game*, A, B, C and D are all legal. Only in E and F does the player not have "part of each foot either on the touchline or on the ground outside the touchline." In E, the left foot is legal but the right foot is not, so judge it as an illegal throw-in. In F, both feet are on the field, leading to a violation and a throw-in for the other team from that same location.

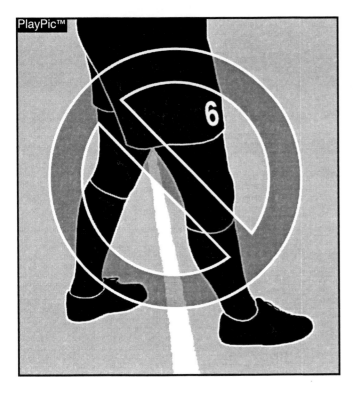

Improper — throw-in foot placement

Throw-in — proper foot placement

One requirement for a proper throw-in is that part of each foot remains on the touchline or on the ground outside the touchline. Since **❻**'s right foot is entirely within the field of play, it is improper. Penalize that infringement by awarding a throw-in to the opposing team.

The NISOA *Assistant Referee Duties & Responsibilities* directs that "during the taking of the throw-in, the assistant referee looks for foot faults." The mechanics for the other codes are not that specific, so do as instructed during the pregame conference.

Although players, coaches and spectators loudly proclaim that action to be illegal (usually when the other team is doing it), **❼**'s right foot placement is legal. It seems unusual to the coaches and spectators, for during a majority of throw-ins, the player's feet remain completely behind the touchline.

Historically, under some codes, the foot placement pictured above was illegal. Now all three codes agree — legal foot placement. Don't let players talk you out of the correct ruling.

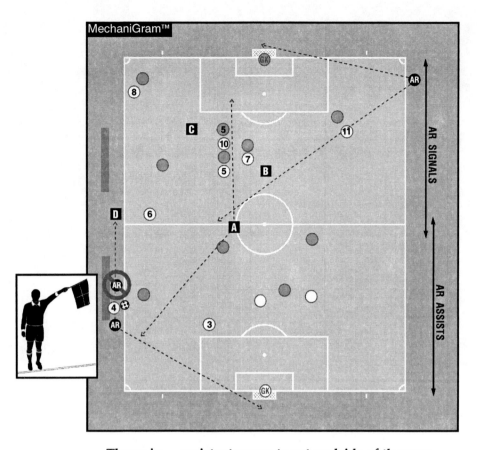

Throw-in — assistant moves to get goalside of thrower

Action on the field:

The attacking team has a throw-in from its own half of the field. The ball angled out of play from midfield and ④ had to run back 20 yards to get the ball from a reserve player on the bench.

Referee Responsibilities

Position yourself so you may view the next significant action. Anticipate the direction of play by reading who the key players are and remember what the attacking team did in similar circumstances earlier in the game. Judge the approximate length of the throw to position yourself at an angle where you can view the action.

Assistant Referee Responsibilities

Do not allow ④ to get goalside of you. Sprint if you must but be certain to position yourself between any player taking a throw-in and the goalline.

If you do not, and ④ decides to throw the ball to the goalkeeper, you are not in position to judge if the whole ball completely crosses the goalline or clearly see if the goalkeeper touches the ball with the hands or arms in violation of law 12. As you try to move toward the goalline and ④ tries to move onto the field of play, you may collide or tangle. That delay may cause you to make an inaccurate decision, simply because of poor positioning at a restart.

Throw-in — hand placement

Improper — throw-in hand placement

Not everyone will have the same hand placement around the ball. Players with small hands tend to get a wider grip, as shown in the PlayPic. Some players will draw the ball behind their head in one hand, then when both hands come together behind their head will deliver a legal throw-in with both hands. Do not penalize that legal play.

Many players, coaches and spectators will yell because the ball spins coming off the thrower's hands. Some referees firmly believe that indicates a foul throw. Incorrect. *Advice to Referees* 15.3 says, "There is no requirement in law 15 prohibiting spin or rotational movement." *Advice to Referees* 15.5 also allows you to ignore a minor illegality on a throw-in if it is doubtful or trifling.

One requirement for a proper throw-in is that the thrower must use both hands. In the PlayPic, **7** is clearly only throwing the ball with the right arm while the left arm merely guides the ball. Clearly, **7** falls short of the criteria for a legal throw-in and the infringement may be penalized by awarding a throw-in to the opposing team.

In a rule difference, NCAA rule 15 mandates the "thrower shall use both hands equally," while the Federation says the thrower "shall use both hands with equal force."

Throw-in

• The referee normally watches to assure correct position at the line for the throw, and watches for hand faults by the thrower.

• The assistant normally watches for foot faults by the thrower, and can usually best see that the ball enters the field directly into play.

• The division of responsibilities at the throw-in should be addressed by the referee in the pregame briefing.

• Look for two types of long throw-ins: a high looping throw that a tall attacker tries to drive directly into the goal; and a line drive that an attacker at the near post tries to flick on to a teammate on the far post.

Quiz

Without referring back, you should be able to answer the following true-false questions.

1. You can read that a throw-in down the line is about to take place by listening for a coach to call a certain player to throw.

2. A flip throw-in is not allowed because of the possible dangers to the thrower: the thrower may slip off the ball and land awkwardly, the thrower may wrench her back or the thrower's feet may slip.

3. Referees should ask a defender to move 10 yards away during a throw-in.

4. There is no requirement in law 15 prohibiting spin or rotational movement.

1 - True, 2 - False, 3 - False, 4 - True

Chapter 11

Goalkick

Goalkick

Goalkicks are one of the more common restarts. Since the objective of the game is to put the ball into the goal more often than your opponent, it makes sense that the offensive team would put the ball across the goalline frequently.

Dropping zone

Referees must position themselves to see the next significant action. One concept that helps most referees understand that principle is to learn about the dropping zone, or where the referee expects a long kick will return to a playable height. Goalkeeper punts, corner kicks and goalkicks are the three most common incidents where referees see that concept in action. You can start reading the best position to assume during the pregame. Watch who warms up by taking a series of long kicks, such as corner kicks to warmup the goalkeeper. While the goalkeeper wants a variety of placements to test agility and coverage, you can take a hint regarding the kicker's leg strength. Watch the goalkeeper take some pregame punts. Do most of them cross the halfway line? If so, that is a clue to you for your coverage during the game.

Assistant referee positioning

The assistant is to move to the top of the goal area "to check for proper placement" of the ball. If the goalkeeper is taking the goalkick, the assistant "moves to a position to judge offside." During those times when one or more attackers are near the top of the penalty area, the assistant should move to the top of the penalty area to verify the ball is properly put into play, i.e., passes wholly outside the penalty area before it is touched by a player on either team. If the ball is touched by a player on either team, it must be a retake of the goalkick. The ball never entered play.

Because a series of questions were raised to Alfred Kleinaitis, USSF manager of referee development and education, he issued a clarification to the *Guide to Procedures*, paragraph 3E. "What actions should the assistant referee take if a defender other than the goalkeeper takes the goalkick? First, if as above, there are one or more attackers at the top of the penalty area, the assistant referee's position should be even with them in order to judge the ball being properly put into play with no failure to respect the required distance by an attacker. Second, if a defender other than the goalkeeper is taking the goalkick and a teammate is positioned closer than 18 yards to the goalline (i.e., closer than the top of the penalty area), usually to receive the goalkick, the correct position for the assistant referee is to be even with that teammate. The

purpose of that position is to judge that the ball was permitted to leave the penalty area before being played by the teammate. Once that is determined, of course, the assistant referee is expected to quickly take the normal position with the second-to-last defender or the ball for judging offside."

Wasting time

Once a goalkick is awarded and the team winning by a slim margin places the ball on the ground in preparation for the restart, they should kick the ball from that location. If the ball "then is moved unnecessarily to another location," the referee should warn the team to stop indulging in delaying tactics. Top referees use their personality to prevent problems. A kind word with the team captain or team leader in the midfield might work. Making eye contact with the goalkeeper and gesturing as if to say, "You and I both know you're doing that to waste time and if you do it again, what other options do I have?" may be enough to get the message across. If the team persists after the warning, you may caution and show the yellow card. Think before you do that. Make sure you don't show the yellow card to a person on the losing team. Is a caution the best way to handle the problem in a game with the score 8-0?

Untouched ball crosses the kicking team's goalline

From a goalkick, if either due to wind or a mis-kick on the ball, the ball crosses the kicking team's goalline untouched, there are two possible courses of action.

If the ball crosses wholly over the goalline before it leaves the penalty area, the restart must be a retake of the goalkick. The ball never entered play — it never departed the penalty area.

If the ball crosses wholly over the goalline after leaving the penalty area, award a corner kick. The ball legally entered play as soon as it passed outside the penalty area and into the field. Thus, a live ball played over the goalline last touched by a member of the defending team equals a corner kick.

Goalkick

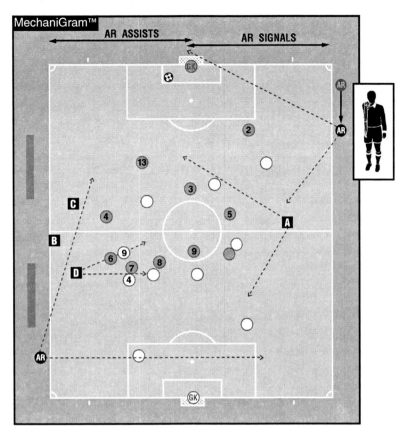

Goalkick

Action on the field:

The goalkeeper is taking a goalkick. The game is being played by older age players who are able to kick the ball farther.

Referee Responsibilities

Read the play and find the dropping zone. Anticipate where the ball will land and get a proper angle to look through the players rather than looking at player's shoulders or backs. Positions A, B, C and D are good candidates but adjustments might be needed based on the flight of the ball. If the ball goes to ⑤, ⑦, ⑧ or ⑨, position D works effectively. If the ball goes to ⑥, you are looking directly into ⑥'s back as ⑥ and ⑨ jostle for position; in addition, you are too close to the play. Moving a few steps to the center of the field opens that angle and you have a clear view between the players.

A suggestion to assist in positioning: Stand on the side of the center circle away from the side where the goalkick is to be taken. If the goalkeeper moves the ball to the far right corner of the goal area, position A is a good starting point for most goalkicks. Increasingly, position A is being recommended for all goalkicks, especially if you believe the team taking the goalkick will continue the attack. That places you on your diagonal.

Assistant Referee Responsibilities

Move to the top of the goal area to check proper ball placement. If players are near the top of the penalty area, observe the ball wholly cross outside the penalty area before it is touched. Move laterally to stay even with the second-to-last defender. If the referee has not read play well and you determine that an infringement was not or could not be seen by the referee, signal an infraction.

For games played under Federation rules, the assistant referee moves in line with the penalty area line after checking placement of the ball. Remain there to see that the ball leaves the penalty area before it is played a second time.

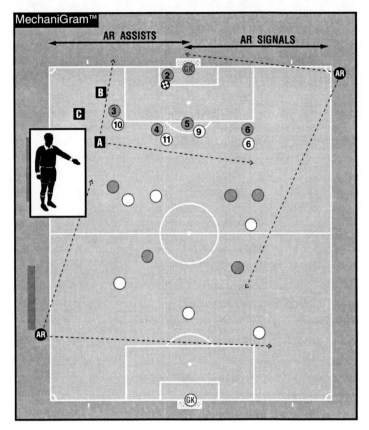

Younger-age goalkick — referee positioned properly

Action on the field:

A younger age player, someone whose leg strength limits the distance of a kick to about 12-15 yards, is taking a goalkick.

Referee Responsibilities

The proper alignment for a referee in the diagonal system of control allows you to look across the field at your assistant. You want the ball between you and the assistant most of the time. That positioning covers gaps in field coverage. If ③ and ⑩ begin a pushing match or taunt one another verbally, you are nearby. If ⑥ and ⑥ create some havoc, the assistant is nearby to solve the problem.

If the ball does not wholly depart the penalty area, order the kick retaken. If ② kicks the ball a second time before it departs the penalty area, order the kick retaken.

Assistant Referee Responsibilities

Move laterally to stay even with the second-to-last defender. Assist as needed if the ball does not wholly cross outside the penalty area before another player touches it. Notice the words in the MechaniGram's top margin. If the ball passes over the goalline on your side of the field, you have primary responsibility for signaling the goalkick. If the ball passes over the goalline on the other side of the field, the referee may look to you for assistance.

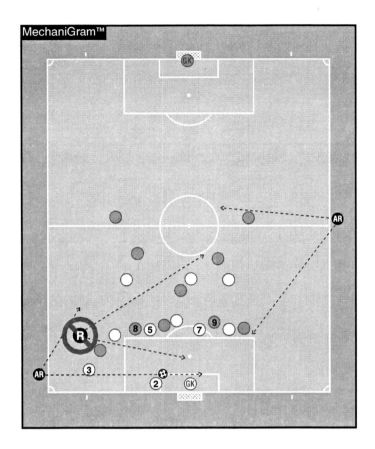

Improper position — referee on a younger-age goalkick

Action on the field:

A younger age player, someone whose leg strength limits the distance of a kick to about 12-15 yards, is taking a goalkick.

Referee Responsibilities

The opposite page shows the proper alignment for a referee in the diagonal system of control. You want to look across the field at your assistant. You want the ball between you and the assistant most of the time. Some referees tend to get their backs turned toward the lead assistant referee so both officials have the same view of the play. That is ineffective. In addition, that positioning leaves gaps in field coverage. If ⑦ and ❾ begin a pushing match or taunt one another verbally, no referee is within 40 yards of that action.

Referees contend they need to be out of the player's way and need to be along the top of the penalty area to view if the ball enters into play. Both of those statements are true. However, crossing to the other side of the field while the ball is being readied for play is much more effective for the DSC.

Assistant Referee Responsibilities

Move laterally to stay even with the second-to-last defender.

Goalkick

• A suggestion: Stand on the side of the center circle away from the side where the goalkick is to be taken.

• If the ball does not wholly leave the penalty area, order the kick retaken. If a player kicks the ball a second time before it leaves the penalty area, order the kick retaken.

• Anticipate where the ball will land and get a proper angle to look through the players rather than looking at player's shoulders or backs. Read the play and find the dropping zone.

Quiz

Without referring back, you should be able to answer the following true-false questions.

1. The assistant referee should assist as needed if the ball does not wholly cross outside the penalty area before another player touches it.

2. For games played under Federation rules, the assistant referee moves in line with the penalty area line after checking placement of the ball and remains there to see that the ball leaves the penalty area before it is played a second time.

3. If the ball goes wholly and directly over the goalline after leaving the penalty area from a goalkick, award a corner kick.

1 - True, 2 - True, 3 - True

Chapter 12

Corner Kick

When the ball goes over the goalline last touched by a member of the defending team, the restart should benefit the attacking team in some small way. The game offers them a free kick from within the corner arc.

It is a free kick

Referees must remember that a corner kick, like a penalty kick, is a very specialized free kick. It has its own law in the *Laws of the Game* but many of the characteristics are the same: the ball must be stationary, the kicker may not play the ball twice in succession, the opponents must be at least 10 yards from the ball, etc. Do not allow the opponents within 10 yards of a corner kick, any more than you would allow them to get within 10 yards of a direct free kick. If the fields you regularly work on do not have the optional mark 11 yards from each corner flagpost along the goalline, ask them to chalk those lines for you.

Referee positioning

Teams are developing new tactical approaches to taking corner kicks and referees need to stay up-to-date about how to deal effectively with them. The "short corner" is a good example. Appearing in World Cup play for the first time in 1994, referees and assistant referees were at first unsure about the best position each should take and what each should be watching for (an offside violation can more easily occur unobserved in a short corner situation).

On some occasions, position yourself among the combatants between the penalty mark and the six-yard goal area line, on the near or far goalpost, on top of the goal area or near the corner of the penalty area. On some occasions, make your initial location known to players, then a split-second before the kick, quickly shift to another observation location. When the kick is airborne and you blow your whistle for a foul, players look at your earlier location (thinking you were where they initially saw you) to see the direction for the restart. That should confirm to you that your sudden shifting of location spotted a predetermined action on the player's part.

Read play

Look at what teams have been doing earlier in the game to get clues about what they might do. Factor in the score and the time remaining. Realize that substitution patterns may alter what teams attempt to do during corner kicks. Because MLS teams are starting to bring goalkeepers the length of the field during corner kicks, look for teams in your area to start mimicking those tactics.

Goalkeepers

Goalkeepers present a wonderful challenge for referees during corner kicks. The *Laws of the Game* offer them no special protection. Yet their fans and teammates will cry, protest and demand they be protected. Many referees interpret the spirit of the game to infer that goalkeepers should be given that little edge in a 50-50 contest. Are you one of those? If you are, it deserves some additional thought. It should not be done automatically.

Your stock as a referee and game manager can soar in the eyes of the defenders when you appropriately handle an attacker roughing up a goalkeeper. Watch for someone fronting the keeper and moving their heels continuously. They are trying to "accidently" step on the keeper's toes with one of two thoughts in mind: get the keeper's mind focused on the painful toes instead of the ball heading goalward, or get the keeper to retaliate with a push in full view of the referee.

Goalkeepers also become very aggressive in their endeavor to keep a clean slate. They will go over and through people to punch or collect the ball. Sometimes their aggressiveness is careless or reckless.

You must try to bring a balance to those actions. Your positioning to see all those subtle dramas is a great start. A well-spoken word of warning as soon as the actions start places you in firm control. An authoritative whistle as soon as the actions become careless lets everyone know where the limits are during the later stages of your game. For those few who do not heed your earlier messages, a card may turn out to be your moment of truth when you demonstrate you will act as needed for player's safety.

Assessors

Assessors may share information about how they used to handle corner kicks. Although I may be going out on a limb here, most assessors are quality soccer people, trying to share their accumulated knowledge from a long career. Many discussions you have with assessors will increase your knowledge of the game and your awareness of positioning. But there are tales of woe out there as well. There are rumors that assessors are telling referees *that* is where you must stand at corner kicks. There is no one right location. If an assessor dictates you take a certain location during a postgame debrief, listen to the comment, say "Thank you very much" after the debrief and the use common sense positioning based on your reading of the play.

Common sense

Let's walk through a typical scenario and see where

common sense takes us: A ball last touched by a defensive player (goalkeeper) passes wholly over the goalline directly over the center of the crossbar. In this example, the late afternoon game is tied with six minutes to play.

The referee must decide where the next restart occurs. When faced with that choice, all things being equal, it might not matter which corner is used. However, faced with the setting sun in a tie game, the referee should use law 18 to decide to have the kick taken from the east corner. That way the goalkeeper does not have to defend while looking into the rays of the sun. That decision is not based on law, but one instance of common sense that makes up much of officiating.

To go along with that play, here's a tip for the assistant referee: Rather than look straight into the setting sun, look a few degrees away and use your peripheral vision to view playing action.

Law 18

Too many people think the *Laws of the Game* stop at law 17. As detailed in *Advice to Referees on the Laws of the Game,* that is not so. While corner kicks are detailed in law 17, you need to flip the page to get the essence of refereeing. Former FIFA referee and World Cup veteran Michel Vautrot was quoted in 6/97 *FIFA magazine* as saying, "Law 18, still unwritten but frequently quoted as the ultimate goal of refereeing: 'Intelligence in the perception of the game, the attitude of the players, the place and the moment of the offense.'"

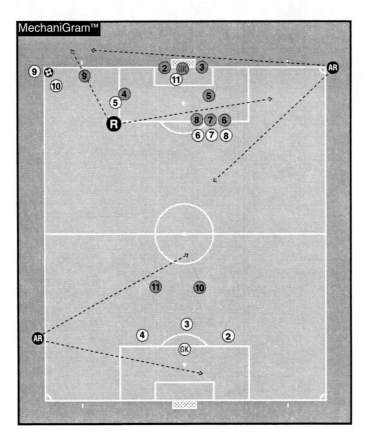

Corner kick — complexities that can arise

Action on the field:

A player takes a corner kick from the referee's side of the field. ⑩ has come over to assist, opening the possibility of a "short corner." ⑨ is defending against that and will attempt to move within 10 yards of the ball before the kick is taken. ⑤ and ④ are bumping one another as the attacking team opens the possibility of a flick-on. ⑪ is fronting the goalkeeper, often with an amount of body contact as both jostle for position. ⑥, ⑦ and ⑧ are lined up to make crossing runs to the near post, far post and penalty mark to confuse the defenders and possibly create contact situations that will leave a player unguarded.

Referee Responsibilities

This variation of the normally simple corner kick can place you in task overload due to the attacking team's strategy to complicate the defense. There is simply too much activity for you to see all in one glance, so you must prioritize your focus and react to the most probable plays. Good referees read what the players offer them — use those clues to help you successfully position yourself for the optimum view of the next significant action.

Become unpredictable in your positioning while maintaining oversight over all the essential elements: your assistant referee, the ball, the goalkeeper and those players who participate in action around the ball.

Assistant Referee Responsibilities

Attackers cannot be offside if they receive the ball directly from a corner kick. The trail assistant referee must be ready to observe a counterattack. Although not the USSF guidance, Federation assistant referees should move down the goalline to a position approximately where it intersects with the penalty area line. Move laterally to stay even with the second-to-last defender.

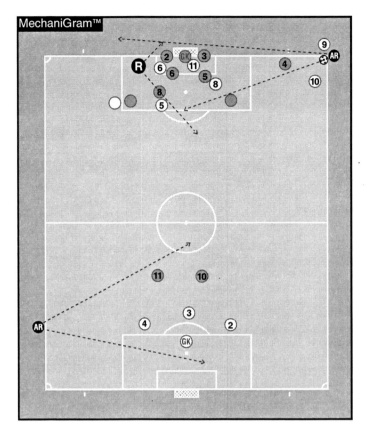

Corner kick — assistant referee's near corner

Action on the field:

A player takes a corner kick from the assistant's side of the field. **10** has come over to assist, opening the possibility of a short corner. **4** is defending against that and will attempt to move within 10 yards of the ball before the kick is taken. **5** and **8** are bumping one another as the attacking team opens the possibility of a flick-on. **11** is fronting the goalkeeper, often with an amount of body contact as both jostle for position. Attackers have packed the mixer to confuse the defenders and possibly create contact situations that will leave a player unguarded.

Referee Responsibilities

Good referees read what the players offer them — use those clues to help you successfully position yourself for the optimum view of the next significant action.

9 is getting ready to make a left-footed kick, which means it will be an inswinger. Defender **5**, the tallest player on the white team, has pushed forward for a probable header. White has packed the goal area to limit the goalkeeper's movement. The ball will be crossed toward the penalty mark and as many as 11 bodies are going to hurl themselves toward it. Focus, concentrate, observe, decide and then communicate your decision.

Assistant Referee Responsibilities

Start three to five feet behind the corner flagpost. Stay in line with the goalline until at least the next play of the ball. Recognize that attackers cannot be offside if they are the first to touch the ball directly from a corner kick. The trail assistant referee must be ready to observe a counterattack.

The *NISOA DSC Instructional Manual* says "an alternate position for the assistant, if the control of possible encroachment is involved, is outside the field along the goalline." Federation assistant referees may also move down the goalline to control encroachment.

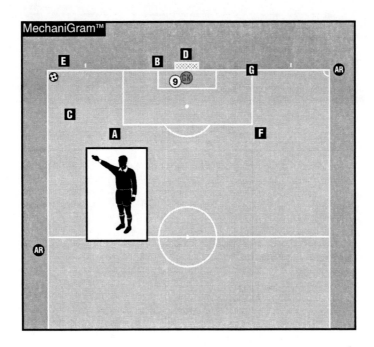

Corner kick — referee's near corner

Action on the field:
A player takes a corner kick from the referee's side of the field.

Referee Responsibilities
Become unpredictable in your positioning while maintaining oversight over all the essential elements: your assistant referee, the ball, the goalkeeper and those players who participate in action around the ball.

Standard position A places you outside the penalty area, about 18 yards from the goalline and looking into the mixer. That position is comfortable because it allows a diagonal line of vision and offers a 20-yard head start in case of a counterattack. Before assuming that position, check to see that the ball is properly placed within the corner arc (see MechaniGram p. 135) and deal with any failure to respect the required distance.

While position A is perhaps the best position considering all the variables, if you assume that position on every corner kick, opponents take advantage of your predictable positioning. They pull jerseys, step on insteps and set picks (similar to basketball) to successfully defend or score. You cannot disallow a valid goal due to your lack of mobility.

Good referees read what the players offer them — the players' positioning tells you if the kick will be near post or far post. The kicker lets you know if it will be an inswinger or an outswinger. (From the set-up pictured, a left-footed kicker approaching the ball from the touchline will kick an outswinger.) Use those clues.

Positions B, C and E are unconventional but based on circumstances, player behavior and your reading of the next significant action, might be useful. Positions D, F and G are not recommended under most circumstances. There are drawbacks to each and you should quickly work to balance the field after taking any of those positions at a restart.

Assistant Referee Responsibilities
For games played under Federation rules, the assistant referee moves down the goalline to a position approximately where it intersects with the penalty area line. Move laterally to stay even with the second-to-last defender.

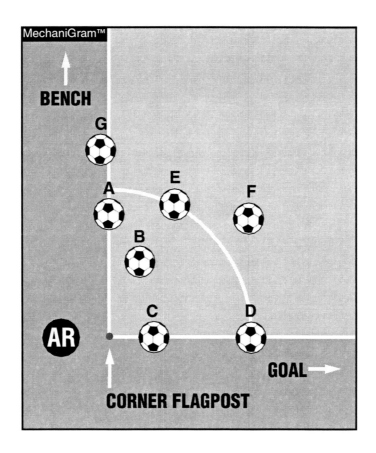

Ball placement on a corner kick

Action on the field:
Here are several possible ball placements. Locations F and G are illegal. Locations A, C, D and E are legal, although only a portion of the ball is within the corner arc.

Referee Responsibilities
When a corner kick is awarded on your side of the field, move to a location where you can determine if the ball is properly placed. Deal with any failure on the part of the kicker to place the ball properly, then move into position to manage the corner kick — typically nearer the goal area.

Assistant Referee Responsibilities
If the corner kick is taken from your side of the field, your position three to five feet behind the corner flagpost allows you to see proper ball placement. If the ball placement is improper, ask the player to reposition the ball. If the player does not respond to your request, call the referee over to deal with the offender.

Corner kick

• Become unpredictable in your positioning while maintaining oversight over all the essential elements: your assistant referee, the ball, the goalkeeper and those players who participate in action around the ball.

• Focus, concentrate, observe, decide and then communicate your decision.

• Good referees read what the players offer them — use those clues to help you successfully position yourself.

• The trailing assistant referee must be ready to observe a counterattack.

Quiz

Without referring back, you should be able to answer the following true-false questions.

1. Although only a portion of the ball is within the corner arc, that is acceptable ball placement for a corner kick.

2. NISOA allows an alternate position for the assistant, if the control of possible encroachment is involved, as outside the field along the goalline.

3. Federation assistant referees should not move down the goalline to a position approximately opposite the penalty area line.

4. Attackers cannot be offside if they receive the ball directly from a corner kick.

1 - True, 2 - True, 3 - False, 4 - True

Chapter 13

Direct Free Kick

If one of the 10 penal (major) fouls is committed by one team, the other team is entitled to take a direct free kick.

Restores the balance

Listening to USSF national instructor and national assessor Pat Smith during a 1999 USL clinic in Chicago, the group of senior referees was reminded that when a referee awards a direct free kick, it restores the balance that was lost due to the illegal actions of the team that committed the act. You are making the playing field level again.

Balance the skills

Quoting from Eric Sellin's *The Inner Game of Soccer*, "As with the other laws, law 12 is designed to permit the player to demonstrate his soccer skills for his own pleasure and that of his teammates and his fans. It is especially law 12 which, if correctly enforced, prevents brute strength from prevailing over ability, might from becoming right."

Sellin continues by saying, "Inevitably a player who substitutes strength for ability will commit fouls and run the risk of disqualification. That is a good thing, and referees must see to it that the player with ability is not made the subject of pre-emptive physical action on the part of less-skilled players. If law 12 had been more strictly enforced in the 1962 and 1966 World Cup games, Pele would not have been brutalized as he was and forced to sit out some games to the regret of the many fans who loved to see him play. The laws are so constructed that a 5'2" player can compete with a six-footer on equal terms, that is on the basis of his skills."

World Cup level

In The Eye Of The Whistle, II: The Refereeing at the 1990 World Cup (edited by David J. Ross © 1991 Onereal, Ontario, Canada) addresses how strict interpretation of law 12 benefits the game. Les Jones, a freelance writer accredited during the games, writes, "On the positive side, French manager Platini stated that, 'If referees had officiated like that (before) I would have been kicking a ball about for two years longer.' And, as FIFA rightly point out, not one player had to leave the field through an injury caused by a foul." Platini joins Dutch star Marco Van Basten and others who had their careers tragically shortened by repeated hard fouls.

Your level

You may never have the opportunity to referee at a World Cup. But the players in your games deserve the same level of protection and they deserve a restoration of the balance after an opponent commits a foul. When those fouls are not called, frustrations build. You notice it first via verbal comments, as players try to express that frustration in hopes that you will whistle more fouls (on their behalf but far fewer that benefit the opponents). Once they realize their words are not getting the desired reaction, some tend toward vigilante justice — taking their frustrations out on opponents' legs. Occasionally, you will hear frustration from players because you are calling the game too tight. They do not have their typical level of play, there are too many stoppages and there is no flow to the game. Most often, referees hear that in the first few games after advancing a level or age group. Work with a mentor or experienced partner before those first few contests and discuss what to expect in terms of which actions deserve a direct free kick at that new level.

Signals the restart

The current version of the *Laws of the Game* says that referees have a duty to "restart the match after it has been stopped." Veteran referees remember the provision in the laws before the general rewrite that said referees shall "signal for recommencement of the game after all stoppages." You may consider that requirement met when you announce or signal what the restart is, which team is entitled to the restart and if necessary, from where. Unless it is a ceremonial restart, a separate signal allowing the team to take the restart is unnecessary.

A ceremonial restart is when the referee informs all the players that the ball may not be put back into play without a specific signal from the referee. The best example is a penalty kick. The most common example is a direct free kick near the opponent's penalty area and the attacking team asks the referee for the proper distance between the ball and the defending wall.

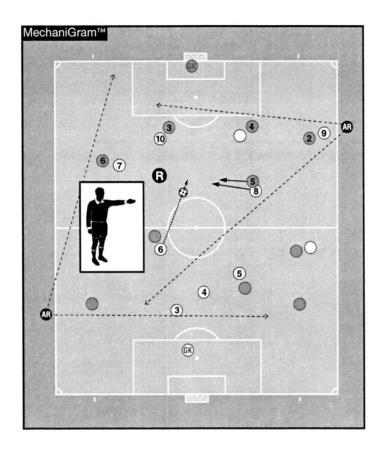

Direct free kick — referee observes foul

Action on the field:
⑥ plays the ball forward into space. ⑧ begins a run toward the ball and ⑤, sensing ⑧ will win the ball, holds ⑧.

Referee Responsibilities
Stop the game with a whistle. If you sense it is needed, move to the spot of the foul to prevent retaliation. Ensure the ball is properly placed. Allow the quick free kick unless the defensive team prevents it by failing to respect the required distance of 10 yards. Deal with the interference.

Assistant Referee Responsibilities
Move laterally to stay even with the second-to-last defender. Do not flag that foul since you determine that the infringement was or could be seen by the referee.

KEY
R Referee   AR Assistant Referee   4th Fourth Referee   CL Club Linesman   A Optional Position   ●----→ Coverage Area   ○ Offense   ● Defense

→ Movement   Initial Position AR ——→ AR Current Position   ⊗ Ball   ------⊗→ Ball Movement   ▨ Goal

Soccer Officials Guidebook **139**

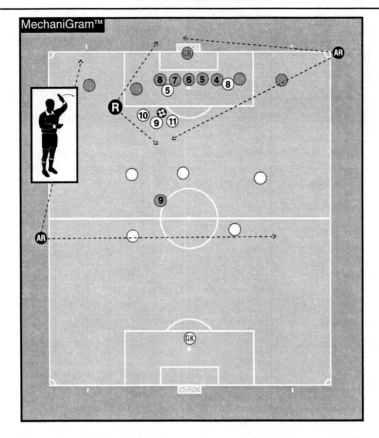

Direct free kick near goal — assistant referee sent to goalline

Action on the field:

The attacking team is awarded a direct free kick within 25-30 yards of goal. They request your help to set up a ceremonial free kick and want the defense moved at least 10 yards from the ball. It is a serious threat on goal and the referee and lead assistant have a number of duties to attend to: offside, goal/no-goal decision and physical play as opponents line up near each other. The trail assistant referee remains with the second-to-last defender to officiate a counterattack and observe misconduct behind the referee.

Referee Responsibilities

The referee waves the assistant referee to the corner flagpost with a clear signal (see PlayPic A). The referee makes offside decisions and spots any foul play in the wall. Some referees tend to station themselves exactly in line with the wall (several players are equidistant as the second-to-last defender) so they are straightlined or flat. By taking that position, they overlook the shirt pulling, pushing and stepping on insteps that often goes on in the wall. You must sacrifice some precision on the offside decision to maintain control over those physical actions. If not, your game control may suffer while you pride yourself on making perfect offside choices.

Assistant Referee Responsibilities

Some referees prefer to send the assistant referee to the corner flagpost to serve as goal judge. That is particularly helpful if the referee expects a counterattack, the referee's fitness is not the best or the referee wants to view the physical play in the wall at close quarters. The referee should give a definitive, predetermined signal to you and allow time for you to get ready before allowing the kick to proceed. Serve as primary goal judge and assist with fouls you determine go unobserved by the referee or as instructed in the pregame discussion.

The *NISOA DSC Instructional Manual* says that is "the preferred position of the assistant for the restart." Further, "that mechanic should be covered by the referee in the pregame briefing."

The I-formation

Some referees refer to what you see in PlayPic B as flat or straightlined, so if your view of half a dozen players consists of a side view of one shoulder, you are not in the proper position.

There could be untold mayhem going on in the wall. Literally, everyone in the stands and the technical area will see elbows into ribs, tugging shorts and shirts and larger players trying strong-arm tactics on smaller opponents. Everyone but you — the most important person to view those offenses.

Most often, when referees send their assistants to the goalline, they feel compelled to stand *directly* in line with the second-to-last defender. The offside decision is important, critical even, but you cannot allow game control to suffer at the expense of that offside decision. Of course, if there are no opponents in the wall, then potential misconduct is not an issue and you may line up directly in line with the wall.

Move just far enough off that direct line to open an angle — to be able to see through the players, to see their hands. While some referees like to go behind the players, there are benefits to remaining in front of them. When a hard shot goes directly into the wall, you want to see the defenders' hands. If the ball strikes a stationary arm, you'll allow play to continue. However, if a defender deliberately handles the ball or purposefully redirects that shot by overt arm movement, the player committed an offense — one you will only see if you are in front of the wall. Give yourself an edge — note any prior patterns of wall behavior and move to a location that allows you an angled look at the behavior.

Increasingly, attackers are committing misconduct in wall situations. A USSF memorandum, dated Jan. 26, 1999, notes that referees must become more aware of such misconduct and position themselves to prevent such actions. The full text of the memorandum is in the appendix to this book.

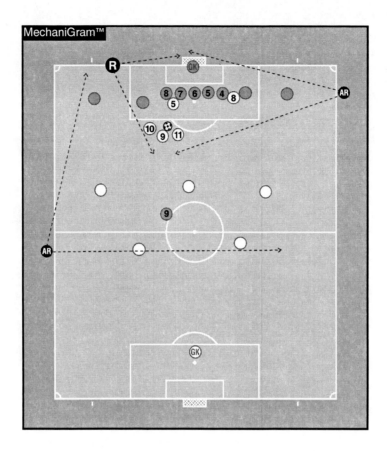

Direct free kick near goal — referee goes to the goalline

Action on the field:

The attacking team is awarded a direct free kick within 25-30 yards of goal. They request your help to set up a ceremonial free kick and want the defense moved at least 10 yards from the ball. It is a serious threat on goal and two officials have a number of duties to attend to: offside, goal/no-goal decision and physical play as opponents line up near each other. The lead assistant referee remains level with the second-to-last defender to officiate a counterattack.

Referee Responsibilities

Some referees prefer to go to the goalline to serve as goal judge. That is particularly helpful if the referee expects a dangerous shot on goal, the referee's fitness is unquestioned and the referee wants to dispel any doubt as to who makes offside decisions throughout the game. You should inform the kicker to delay the kick, allowing time for you to take up the desired position. Some referees find it helpful to wait three yards off the goalline, toward the wall, until the ball clears the defensive wall and then step toward the goalline to make the goal/no-goal decision. Some referees close in very tight to the goalpost, remaining just off the field of play. That is helpful if you expect some contact between the goalkeeper and an attacking player.

By taking that extreme position, you have a diagonal look at the shirt-pulling, pushing and stepping on insteps that may go on in the wall. That method retains precision on the offside decisions and allows more control over those physical actions. The one drawback is the same as any time you take an extreme position — in case of a counterattack, you may be an extra 10-15 yards behind play.

Assistant Referee Responsibilities

The assistant referee retains offside decisions and helps with any foul play in the wall or as instructed in the pregame.

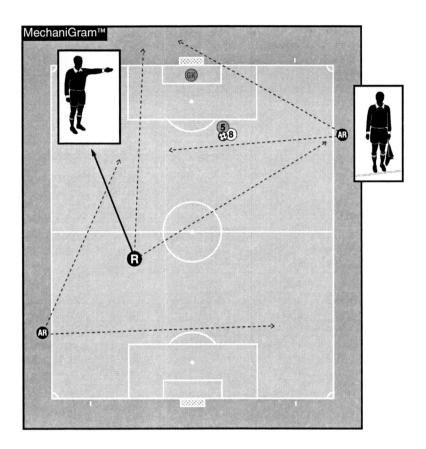

Direct free kick — referee caught on counterattack

Action on the field:
One of the 10 penal fouls takes place near the penalty area line and the referee whistles to stop play. The referee was caught in a counterattack and needs help to determine if the foul occurred outside the penalty area.

Referee Responsibilities
Blow a hard whistle and continue to sprint to the spot of the foul so it gives the appearance you were closer to the play than you were. While running, make affirmative eye contact with your assistant referee who gives no discernible signal, to indicate the foul occurred outside the penalty area. Once you see no signal, move to the spot of the infraction and signal the direct free kick. Quickly move out of the way to allow the team to take the free kick. Set the wall for the ceremonial free kick, if requested by the attacking team. Conduct the direct free kick in the standard fashion.

Assistant Referee Responsibilities
Move to stay with the second-to-last defender. Once you hear the referee's whistle and know the foul occurred outside the penalty area, come to a stop. If the referee looks to you for help, face the field of play and make no discernible signal. Once the referee announces the direct free kick, move quickly to become level with the second-to-last defender. Perform those duties as assigned by the referee in the pregame discussion, including watching for a signal moving you to cover the goalline for goal/no-goal decisions.

Respecting the required distance

As you progress into higher levels of competitive play, teams want the opportunity to take the quick free kick. If you are in the initial stages of upgrading to higher levels, be more patient than you have been in the past. Wait for the kicking team to invite you in to deal with the defenders.

While referees maintain discretionary powers to caution defenders in a wall situation, some are almost automatic. Caution the player who picks the ball up to prevent a play, the defender who runs 40 yards and squats down three yards in front of the ball to tie a shoe and the defender who stands a yard or two behind the ball (between the ball and attackers) to direct the wall placement. They politely asked you, via their actions, for a card, so do not let them down.

Here, Ⓧ and ⑪ see no obvious opening on goal, so they ask your help to restore the chance of scoring via a free kick. With one exception, defenders must be "at least 9.15 meters (10 yards) from the ball" in all directions. If defenders already meet that criteria, inform the attackers to put the ball in play. If defenders are within that distance, ask the attackers to withhold taking the kick, reposition the defenders to the proper distance and give the signal to proceed, usually a whistle. If a defender you have placed 10 yards from the ball moves within that distance before the ball comes into play, *Advice to Referees* 13.5 suggests you stop the restart to deal with the offender via a card. Retake the restart.

There are some very easy pleas to ignore: mom and dad in the stands; the coach along the touchline; and the goalkeeper stationed 83 yards away. When those people cry out for 10 yards, ignore them. Unbeknownst to all those well-intentioned folks, Ⓧ and ⑪, stationed within a few yards of the ball, may want the quick free kick.

A few hints to help you with walls: Once the ball is on the ground, do not lose sight of it. Attackers may feel free to move the ball forward two or three yards and then stand innocently by as a nearby teammates continues to ask for 10 yards. Use field markings to help you judge 10 yards. Use every tool at your disposal: penalty arc, goal area, center circle and penalty mark. Use markings from the American football field if they are available.

Do not pace off the 10 yards. Partially because it forces you to take your eye off the ball, it is not recommended. It also invites an attacker who feels the distance is short to pace off the steps behind you. One possibility to deter that player from following you is to not let the player get more than six steps before you display a yellow card.

If you regularly work with the same partners, in the pregame discussion, ask whichever assistant referee is lead to move to a location 10 yards from the spot of the ball on a wall situation. They'll need to factor in diagonal distances, etc., but as soon as they realize the attackers invite you to deal with a wall, they should move along the touchline parallel to the location of the wall. While watching the ball, you simply jog to a position in line with your assistant, invite the defenders to line up with you and signal the restart. It's quick and easy. More important, it gets the game restarted more quickly.

Unnatural arm motions

Players in a wall are there to defend against goals. Staring down the barrel of a direct free kick from 10 yards away brings fear to many. Both male and female players will station their arms to protect vulnerable body parts. That pre-positioning is unlikely to produce an infringement.

Using the definition of deliberate contact in *Advice to Referees* 12.9, it "means that the player could have avoided the touch but chose not to, that the player's arms were not in a normal playing position at the time or that the player deliberately continued an initially accidental contact for the purpose of gaining an unfair advantage."

If **❺** or **❾** is struck in the arms by that direct free kick, it should not be whistled. However, if **❻** were struck anywhere along the hands or arms, it would be the offense of deliberately handling the ball because the arms are not in a normal playing position. **❼** and **⓫** form the middle ground — parts of their arms are in a normal playing position, but their forearms are thrust out to the side to make their bodies wider.

Coaches are teaching that technique and referees need to be aware that players willfully try to take advantage. Here the dark-shirted team has made a wall that is six bodies wide with only five players. The defenders fill the gaps and creases with hands and forearms. That leaves one extra defender available to cover an attacker, giving a significant advantage.

Restarts — running to the spot of the foul

Preventive officiating. Take care of small problems when they are small so you do not have to deal with bigger problems. Use your voice. Use your personality. Use your whistle. Convey your unhappiness with a player's action but do it in a way that doesn't inflame the situation. The referee could easily be having a quiet word with any one of the five players pictured and it would lower the emotional temperature. The referee can do that because he put in the extra effort to run to the spot of the foul.

Do you ever wonder why all the football referee assaults take place in peewee football and Pop Warner football and not in the NFL? The NFL officials hustle to the spot of the infraction or confrontation, look that mean middle linebacker in the face and say, "That's enough. Just go on back and huddle with your team." The inexperienced referee throws a yellow rag 40 yards and screams out, "Hey kid, knock off the cheap shots." That loud comment sets off dad like New Year's fireworks and the coach has to stick up for his team, so he verbalizes at the referee.

Use your personality. Almost 20 years ago, now-FIFA referee Brian Hall was refereeing an ethnic game in San Francisco. After a hard physical challenge, the two opponents squared off to face one another with Hall running toward them. As they glowered at each other from six inches away, Hall calmly said four or five words to them and they both doubled up with laughter. If humor is in your repertoire, use it.

Be very attentive when opponents help a fallen player from the ground. While, in many cases, it is a gesture of good sportsmanship, there are hazards. Be certain that ⑩ is ready to get up. Some players truly need a second or two to collect their thoughts after a hard physical challenge and you do not want an opponent to drag them up, as if to say, "Come on. Get up. You're not hurt." Some cynical players have been known to offer a hand up and then just about the time ⑩ regains his balance, ❹ lets go and ⑩ tumbles to the ground again. That usually circles the wagons — which is not a good thing. If ❸ and ❹ genuinely assist ⑩ to his feet and offer a kind word, it's OK for you to verbally praise that act of sporting behavior.

Free kick — ball does not leave the penalty area

Action on the field:

The referee awards the dark-shirted team a direct free kick from within its own penalty area. **2** sees all teammates are covered, so decides to pass the ball directly to the goalkeeper for a punt well upfield. The ruling is the same for an indirect free kick.

Referee Responsibilities

As soon as the goalkeeper touches the ball, either with a hand, foot or other body part, blow your whistle and order a retake of the free kick. The ball must pass completely outside the penalty area into the field before any player on either team may touch it. Even **2** may not touch it again.

Coaches and players will yell at you for your supposed ignorance. They will yell, "But ref, it was a free kick, not a goalkick." Many people familiar with the game hold that misconception. It must be a retake. The ball is not in play until it departs the penalty area. If the ball does not properly go into play, it must be a retake.

That same principle holds true for all eight restarts, not just in that case. If a dropped ball does not touch the ground, it must be a retake. If a kickoff moves backward, it must be a retake.

Assistant Referee Responsibilities

Move laterally to stay even with the second-to-last defender. If the opportunity is there and the temperament seems right, offer a quiet explanation of the ruling to a coach who approaches you.

Direct free kick

• Stop the game with a whistle. If you sense it is needed, move to the spot of the foul to prevent retaliation.

• Allow the quick free kick unless the defensive team prevents it by failing to respect the required distance of 10 yards. Deal with the interference.

• The referee and lead assistant have a number of duties to attend to: offside, goal/no-goal decision and physical play as opponents line up near each other.

• The trail assistant referee remains with the second-to-last defender to officiate a counterattack and observe misconduct behind play.

Quiz

Without referring back, you should be able to answer the following true-false questions.

1. The assistant referees should not flag fouls if they determine that the infringement was or could be seen by the referee.

2. If your view of half a dozen players consists of a side view of one shoulder, you are in the proper position.

3. As the referee, you may not look to your assistant referee for help in determining the location of a foul near the penalty area.

1 - True, 2 - False, 3 - False

Chapter 14

Indirect Free Kick

If a minor or technical foul is committed by one team, the other team is entitled to take an indirect free kick. Just as with direct free kicks, your decision to penalize a team should be with the objective of restoring a balance that was lost due to the infraction.

Offside

Since offside is the most common reason for awarding an indirect free kick, a subsection of this chapter will be devoted to offside.

Wall management

The team that has been awarded the indirect free kick is entitled to an unimpeded chance to get the ball into play without undue interference by the offending team.

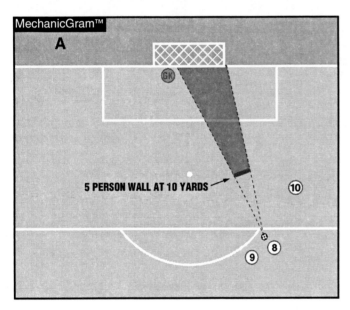

MechanicGram™ A

5 PERSON WALL AT 10 YARDS

The laws dictate that all opponents remain at least 9.15 meters, or 10 yards, from the ball until the ball is put into play. (There is an exception for an indirect free kick awarded to the attacking team within 10 yards of the goal.) While the *Laws of the Game* do not mention a wall at any point, referees know that is a big portion of the tactics within a game. Most defenders tend to take up a position five to seven yards from the ball and wait to be moved back. Some referees get the full allotment of 10 yards. Others do not. Sellin's *The Inner Game of Soccer* offers this advice for your thoughtful consideration. "However, if it is manifestly less than 10 yards, the offended team has a right to have the law enforced. Two yards less than the lawful distance on the part of the defensive wall can radically reduce the [proportion] of goal mouth open to the kicker. In an interesting article, Les Radunchev demonstrates the decreasing area to be protected on a straight shot by the goalkeeper.

"In taking a wall of five players to be about 2.10 meters wide (MechaniGram A), the available strikable area of the goal diminishes radically if a wall cheats by two meters (MechaniGram B) on the prescribed 9.15 meter distance. In the following metric chart, DG = distance from ball to goal, DW = distance from the ball to the wall, DA = area of goal defended by the wall and SA = the strikable area of the goal.

DG	DW	DA	SA
17	9.15	3.90	3.42
20	9.15	4.60	2.72
25	9.15	5.72	1.60
DG	**DW**	**DA**	**SA**
17	7	5.11	2.21
20	7	6.00	1.32
25	7	7.50	---

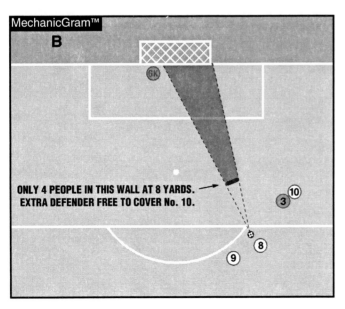

MechanicGram™ B

ONLY 4 PEOPLE IN THIS WALL AT 8 YARDS. EXTRA DEFENDER FREE TO COVER No. 10.

It would appear, from this calculation, that cheating yields better results for the defense on a kick from some distance out, but there are other factors to consider: a shot from 25 yards out will be more easily curved up, over and down into the goal than one close up, but the latter will require greater reactions on the part of the goalkeeper. Suffice it to say that each yard is statistically important down in the area of pay-dirt!" Whether a superior mathematician can verify those figures or not, the perception of the attacking team is what matters.

Indirect Free Kick

An exercise

There are some referees who don't give the full 10 yards because they are unaware of how far 10 yards really is. Are you getting feedback from players that your wall is too close or too far away? Are you willing to try an interesting experiment?

Materials needed are a soccer ball, a length of string cut to 30 feet and a dozen different-colored sticks with pointed ends. Take your group of referees outside (during the monthly meeting or before the first game some Saturday) where there is open space and soft ground. Hand each one a pointed, colored stick. Place the ball on the ground. Ask them to move until they think they are exactly 10 yards from the ball, and lightly drive their stick into the ground to mark their place. You will be amazed (and frightened) at the different distance each individual chooses.

Then ask someone to hold one end of the string directly over the ball while you extend the other end of the string and walk the entire 10-yard circumference of the circle. Let each person see how well they estimated the distance. Move the ball 40-45 yards and try it again and the variance will be far less. Again, give feedback with the string.

Stubborn walls

Most walls will move back upon your request. Some players may be a little slow in moving back or may grumble as they inch backward. That's almost to be expected. But some players refuse to cooperate. Perhaps they think your distance is too far. Some coaches like to test referee's resolve to see how much it takes before the first card is shown.

Whom do you caution when you have several players who jointly persist in moving the wall forward once you set the 10 yards? There is no right answer. Here are some questions to consider:
- Who's the instigator?
- Who's given you the most grief during the game?
- Who's the leader — the one you will receive the most effect by giving the card?
- Who's the closest to you?
- Who was involved in similar, unpenalized behavior previously?
- Who was the first brick on the wall and then told teammates to move forward?
- Who's the biggest?
- Is the team captain in the wall?
- Who already has a caution?

As you can see, there are many reasons to select the player that is shown the yellow card. You have to base your decision on what's gone on so far in that game.

Only in the last case, the player with one caution already, should you avoid that player, in most cases. If you need to send a particularly strong message, do so. But think about having the punishment fit the crime.

Communication

Do you ever ponder why you see so few indirect free kicks on televised matches? Watch an MLS game. Other than offside, you may watch an entire game and not see a single indirect free kick whistled. Those referees are communicating with the players to prevent technical infractions. They tell a midfielder to pass the word back to the goalkeeper to get rid of the ball more quickly. They run alongside a player who attempts to hinder a goalkeeper distribution. "No more of that," is enough of a warning to a professional player from a professional referee. You can easily adopt those same habits and reduce game stoppages. It takes a little more effort on your part. Occasionally a player may not heed your warning and you will have to whistle the infraction but you tried. Plus, the player who was warned and then had it whistled has learned a valuable lesson. The player now knows, "If that referee asks me to do something (or not do something), I better listen. The next time it gets called."

Study the laws horizontally

Most referees study the laws vertically. They open the book and read law 1, then law 2, then law 3. Read the laws horizontally and look for trends. To know which restarts require the ball to go forward, you must analyze laws 8 and 14. To know all the reasons a referee may award an indirect free kick, you must compile information from laws 3, 4, 8, 11, 12, 14, 15, 16 and 17.

Preventing the goalkeeper from releasing the ball

Goalkeepers are notorious for wasting time by holding the ball. All codes cracked down by imposing time limits on how long a keeper may control the ball. The objective is to get the ball to the feet of the 20 field players and let their skills determine the outcome of the game. Referees are encouraged to speed play, because that makes it more enjoyable and more entertaining.

Players who attempt to block goalkeeper distributions hinder that objective. Tempers flair as goalkeepers and defenders yell at those offenders. Time ticks by as defenders yell to you to protect their keeper. The keeper holds the ball until the attacker clears away. All that yelling and no playing.

Here is where smart referees think before they act. The law is clear and specific: "An indirect free kick is also awarded to the opposing team if a player … prevents the goalkeeper from releasing the ball from *his hands*" (PlayPics B and C). Yet, PlayPic A also suggests penalizing an attacker from trying to block a punt. Authority for doing that is in *Advice to Referees* 12.17. Does the defensive team want an indirect free kick from deep in its own penalty area? No. That kick puts them at a severe disadvantage. The goalkeeper loses the flexibility of rolling or throwing the ball and must kick the stationary ball from the ground instead of a punt or drop kick. That might cut 20-25 yards off the distance of a kick. Referees who automatically whistle the infraction and award the free kick, without at least warning the attackers, place undo hardship on the defense.

Communicate with the players. Without blowing your whistle, run to the players and say to the goalkeeper, "Keep, I'll give you an extra few seconds while I talk to ⑤. Don't put it in play yet." Then turn to the attacker and say, "OK, ⑤. My job is to keep the ball in play. You're preventing that. Let's see that nobody wearing a grey-colored shirt does that again today." Sprint toward midfield and call for the keeper to play the ball. With an effective warning, ⑤ will not go near the keeper and if a teammate wanders in that direction, you have an ally in helping you. ⑤ should speak up, "Sue, the ref said we can't do that. You better back off." Caution players who do not heed that advice.

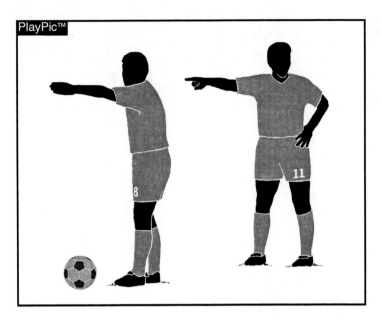

Respecting the required distance

As you progress into higher levels of competitive play, teams want the opportunity to take the quick free kick. If you are in the initial stages of upgrading to higher levels, be more patient than you have been in the past. Wait for the kicking team to invite you in to deal with the defenders.

Here, ⑧ and ⑪ see no obvious opening on goal, so they ask your help to restore the chance of scoring via a free kick. With a few exceptions, defenders must be "at least 9.15 meters (10 yards) from the ball" in all directions. If defenders already meet that criteria, inform the attackers to put the ball in play. If defenders are within that distance, ask the attackers to withhold taking the kick, reposition the defenders to the proper distance and give the signal to proceed, usually a whistle. If a defender you have placed 10 yards from the ball moves within that distance before the ball comes into play, *Advice to Referees* 13.5 suggests you stop the restart to deal with the offender via a yellow card. Retake the restart.

There are some very easy pleas to ignore: mom and dad in the stands; the coach along the touchline; and the goalkeeper stationed 83 yards away. When those people cry out for 10 yards, ignore them. Unbeknownst to all those well-intentioned folks, ⑧ and ⑪, stationed within a few yards of the ball, may want the quick free kick.

A few hints to help you with walls: Once the ball is on the ground, do not lose sight of it. Attackers may feel free to move the ball forward two or three yards and then stand innocently by as a nearby teammates continues to ask for 10 yards. Use field markings to help you judge 10 yards. Use every tool at your disposal: penalty arc, goal area, center circle and penalty mark. Use markings from the American football field if they are available. Do not pace off the 10 yards.

If you regularly work with the same partners, in the pregame discussion, ask whichever assistant referee is lead to move to a location 10 yards from the spot of the ball on a wall situation. They'll need to factor in diagonal distances, etc., but as soon as they realize the attackers invite you to deal with a wall, they should move along the touchline parallel to the location of the wall. While watching the ball, you simply jog to a position in line with your assistant, invite the defenders to line up with you and signal the restart. It's quick and easy. More important, it gets the game restarted more quickly.

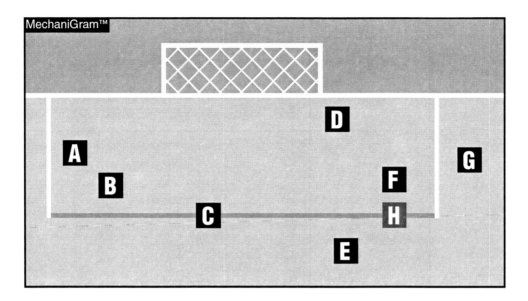

Ball location — attacking indirect free kicks

Action on the field:
The referee stops play for an infraction by the defending team in the goal area. The restart is an indirect free kick to the attacking team. The special circumstances in law 8 require a specific location for the restart.

Referee Responsibilities
The restart must take place along the goal area line that runs parallel with the goalline, six yards from the goalline (darkened in the MechaniGram above). You should move the ball perpendicular to the goalline from the location of the restart. An example: If the indirect free kick foul or misconduct was at location F when you stopped play, you should restart with the ball in location H. Similarly, restarts in locations A, B and D need to be moved. A restart at location C is already at the proper location. Restarts at locations E and G would not be moved.

In either case, the goal area will be tightly packed with players trying to score or defend. Be aware of increased emotional play.

Assistant Referee Responsibilities
Move laterally to stay even with the second-to-last defender. Assist the referee with game control. Be aware of players on the fringes taking unfair advantage of the referee's diverted attention.

Offside is the most common reason for awarding an indirect free kick.

Calls to do away with offside

Despite considerable misunderstanding about offside, it is a part of the game. Very young children tend not to play with offside as a part of their 4-v-4 games, for they are still trying to learn the elementary aspects of the game.

Changes in interpretation

The written law regarding offside has not changed much in the past 130 years. With the general rewrite of the *Laws of the Game* in 1997, law 11 became a little more precise, but most aspects of the written law are the same. However, there have been substantial changes in the interpretation. The lawmakers want a more open style, more attacking soccer, more goal-scoring chances. When you raise your flag on a questionable offside decision, you thwart that ambition.

Cultural differences

Having lived and refereed overseas for almost a decade, I've become aware that different cultures view offside in dramatically different ways. Playing in England and Spain, you better not have even a big toe in an offside position, even if you are 50 yards across the field from the play. But that is not the interpretation the IFAB is trying to instill in the game.

USSF interpretation

Even two decades ago, the USSF taught a style that reinforced two key points: it is not an offense to simply be in an offside position; and if the player was not involved in the play, do not flag for an offside infraction.

Assistant flags offside, referee waves it down

While the assistant is in a perfect position to judge offside position as far as the length of the field is concerned, referees must apply their particular perspective regarding the width of the field.

Consider an assistant looking across the width of the field. The assistant observes attacker A6 ahead of the ball and the second-to-last defender at the moment the ball is played by A8. The assistant also observes that the ball is going in the direction of A6 and that A6 is doing nothing affirmative to take himself out of the play. The assistant's flag should go up.

The problem comes when it happens on the referee's third of the field — some 70 yards away from the assistant. What about depth perception?

The referee (given where the referee probably is in that play) is the only one who can determine if that ball is indeed going in the direction of A6 to justify a call. The referee is the only one close enough to A6 to determine definitively if A6 is indeed not affirmatively taking himself out of the play. And the referee is the only one who can wait for a moment to see if A8 might be running forward to pick up his own play forward.

In those cases, the assistant properly raises the flag and the referee properly waves the flag down. It is not a case of the assistant flagging too early, while waiting would have produced a better call. The assistant flagged exactly when he should have and then the referee did exactly what he should have done — evaluate the information instead of reacting blindly to the flag. The referee can make a decision based on the additional facts at his disposal. The assistant is providing data from one direction and the referee is adding that to the data from an almost 90-degree different direction: the result is a better call than either would have made alone.

Hard work

To be an effective assistant referee and make correct offside decisions takes a great deal of effort and concentration. It is hard work. As the PlayPics and MechaniGrams in this section show, you must be in the right position. You must be patient and make judgements about the speed and direction of the ball and opponents.

Widen your scope

During an interview with then-FIFA assistant referee Steve Olson, he told how, even as an experienced international assistant he had difficulties with offside decisions because of the speed of the Brazilian attackers. They would start overlapping runs 20 and 25 yards behind the second-to-last defender. Split seconds before they would pass that defender, a teammate would play the ball into space. The very experienced Olson had not seen that tactic used so effectively before. He was able to compensate by broadening his field of view, focusing on a wider angle of the field. That might work for you, if you're getting some feedback that your offside decisions don't agree with the player's opinions.

Up-to-date

There is a new philosophy in the game. If there is any doubt, leave the flag down. Almost weekly, the MLS referees and assistant referees hear that phrase: If there is any doubt, leave the flag down. If you are trying to improve, adopt that new philosophy.

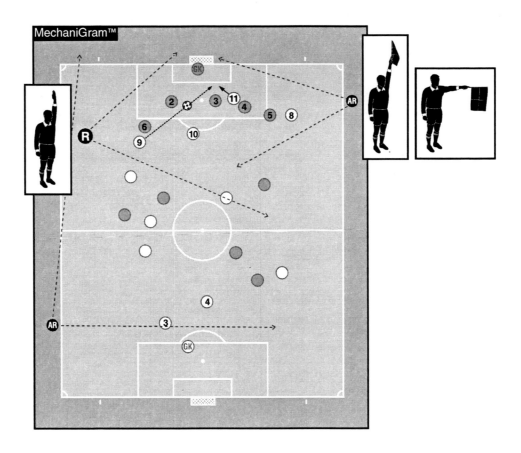

Offside

Action on the field:

At the moment ⑨ passes the ball to ⑪, ⑪ is nearer to the opponent's goalline than the second-to-last defender.

Referee Responsibilities

Acknowledge the lead assistant referee's flag by blowing the whistle to stop play. Hold the indirect free kick signal from when the ball is put into play until it touches another player or goes out of play.

Assistant Referee Responsibilities

As soon as you determine ⑪ becomes actively involved in the play, raise the flag vertically. Hold the flag until the referee acknowledges the flag by stopping play, waves your flag down, the ball is clearly controlled by the defense, goes out for a goalkick or a defensive throw-in. If the referee stops play, indicate the position of the offside player by holding the flag at a 45-degree upward angle (indicating the far third of the field), straight out from your shoulder (the middle third of the field) or at a 45-degree downward angle (the near third).

KEY

| **R** Referee | **AR** Assistant Referee | **4th** Fourth Referee | **CL** Club Linesman | **A** Optional Position | Coverage Area | ○ Offense | ● Defense |

Movement   Initial Position **AR** → **AR** Current Position   ● Ball   ● ► Ball Movement   Goal

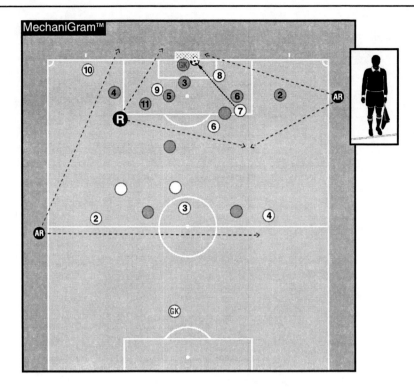

Goal to be disallowed — offside by player other than scorer

Action on the field:

At the moment ⑦ shoots the ball on goal, ⑧ is nearer to the opponent's goalline than the second-to-last defender. ⑧ moves to the left, impeding the progress of ③ to defend against the shot. The ball enters the goal. ⑩, although in an offside position, is not involved in active play and is not to be judged offside.

Referee Responsibilities

Acknowledge the lead assistant referee's signal (standing at attention rather than the expected action of running toward the halfway line) by blowing the whistle to stop play. If you must, jog to the lead assistant and find out why the assistant believes the goal should be disallowed. If you are aware of ⑧ being in an offside position and believe the goal should be disallowed for that infraction, give an indirect free kick signal. Hold the indirect free kick signal from when the ball is put into play until it touches another player or goes out of play.

If you choose to overrule the assistant because you believe ⑧'s actions did not interfere with play, interfere with ③ or gain an advantage, wave down the assistant's flag, point to the center circle and allow a goal. Stop the clock if playing under Federation or NCAA rules.

Assistant Referee Responsibilities

You might have momentarily raised the flag vertically at the time the shot was taken due to ⑧'s offside infraction. As soon as you realize the ball enters the goal, lower the flag. If, in your opinion, ⑧ interfered with play or with ③'s ability to defend against the shot, stand at attention with no flag signal and make eye contact with the referee.

The referee may jog over to consult with you, to ask questions about what you saw and what effect those actions had on the play and the goal. If the referee awards the goal, jog 10-15 yards up the touchline and follow the normal goal procedures. If the referee acts on your information to disallow the goal, move laterally to get even with the second-to-last defender. Expect some criticism from the attacking team.

The *NISOA DSC Instructional Manual* directs NISOA referees to "stand at the corner area immediately after the goal (where the running pattern should occur), obtain eye contact with the referee," and provided needed information.

Goal to be disallowed — offside by scorer

Action on the field:

At the moment ⑦ passes the ball to teammate ⑧, ⑧ is nearer to the opponent's goalline than the second-to-last defender. ⑧ traps the ball, shoots and the ball enters the goal. ⑩, although in an offside position, is not involved in active play and is not to be judged offside.

Referee Responsibilities

Acknowledge the lead assistant referee's signal by blowing the whistle to stop play. A longer, more strident whistle is appropriate for that unusual situation where you disallow what appears to be a goal. Hold the indirect free kick signal from when the ball is put into play until it touches another player or goes out of play.

The lead assistant may receive some criticism from the attacking team while the ball is being readied for play, so listen to protect your partner and encourage the dark-shirted team to put the ball into play quickly.

Assistant Referee Responsibilities

If, in your opinion, ⑧ interfered with play or gained an advantage, raise the flag vertically and make eye contact with the referee. If the scorer was the player you judged to be offside, continue to hold the flag vertically even after the ball entered the goal. Listen for the referee's whistle before making the second part of your two-part signal. If the referee does not notice your flag at first, continue to hold the flag vertically. The noise from the players, coaches and spectators will direct the referee's attention to your flag.

Indicate the position of the offside player by holding the flag at a 45-degree upward angle, straight out from your shoulder or at a 45-degree downward angle. Expect some criticism from the attacking team.

The *NISOA DSC Instructional Manual* directs NISOA referees to "stand at the corner area immediately after the goal (where the running pattern should occur), obtain eye contact with the referee," and provide needed information.

Torsos lined up — not offside

Law 11 states that "a player is in an offside position if he is nearer to his opponent's goalline than both the ball and the second-to-last opponent." Nearer is the key word in that phrase. Remember that "as near as" does not mean the same thing as nearer. If you are level with the ball or with the defender, you are not nearer the goal.

In the PlayPic above, the line shown is not the halfway line. It exists to help you align the torsos of the opposing players. ❹ and ⑧ are even. Sure, ⑧'s arm and head are in front of ❹, but those body parts are not judged for offside position. It is the torso — and their torsos are level. That is not an offside position.

The only way you are going to see that minor difference is to be in position.

Torsos are not even — offside position

In the PlayPic above, the line shown is not the halfway line. It exists to help you align the torsos of the opposing players. ⑩ is clearly nearer the goalline than ❹, by almost a full body width.

Advice to Referees 11.1 says, "It is not necessary to 'see daylight' between them for one to be considered nearer than the other." That common misconception of "even" spread soon after the law was changed making even onside. Allow more scoring opportunities, allow more attacking soccer and create more flow in your games. *Advice to Referees* 11.7 says, "If an assistant referee is in any doubt as to whether a player is actively involved or not, he should decide in favor of the attacker; in other words, he should refrain from signaling offside."

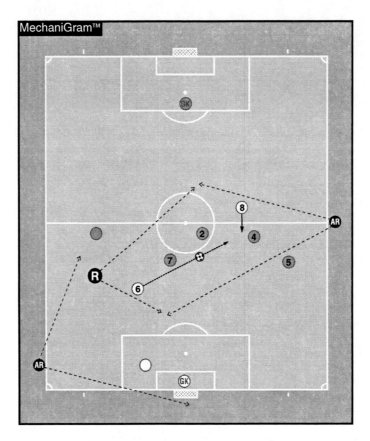

Offside position — player comes back to own half to receive ball

Action on the field:
At the time of the pass, ⑧ was in an offside position in the opponent's half of the field. Teammate ⑥ kicked the ball toward ⑧ so that ⑧ was forced to retreat into her own half of the field to control the ball.

Referee Responsibilities
With proper positioning, the referee in the MechaniGram had all the elements directly in front of her: ball, assistant referee, halfway line, second-to-last defender and the two light-shirted teammates. As soon as the flag rises to indicate the offside position and involvement in active play, the referee will understand the reason for the flag and be able to explain it to any player who questions the decision.

For a referee who is not positioned as well, or for someone focused on a contact situation away from the lead assistant referee, that flag might come as a surprise. Seeing an offside flag for a player who is five yards inside her own half of the field is unusual and may lead to a wave-down. Eye contact will help.

Assistant Referee Responsibilities
The assistant should patiently wait until she is certain that the pass is coming toward ⑧ and that ⑧ is running to the ball. Once certain, raise the flag directly overhead to request a stoppage in play. The referee may look quizzically due to ⑧'s positioning in her own half. Sell the call to the referee with eye contact. Once the referee stops play with a whistle, lower the flag 45-degrees downward to indicate the nearside offside position.

While non-standard signals are not normally used, the unusual circumstances and the doubtful look from the referee may call for the PlayPic signal on p. 163 to help sell the call to the referee. You are not making those signals to sell the call to the crowd or the players. That's the referee's job.

Assistant referee signal — player was on opposite half

Offside — National Federation only

With a limited-use signal, assistant referees can clarify to the referee why an offside decision was offered when the player who was flagged for offside is now clearly standing in her own half of the field of play or otherwise not apparently in an offside position.

After you signal for offside, the referee may look quizzically at you because the player appears to be 10 yards in her own half of the field. With the two-part signal shown in the PlayPic above, you can quickly convey the information that at the time of the kick, the player was in the opposite half of the field when the pass was made and ran back to her own half to receive the pass. Rotate your arm up and over an imaginary line.

The *Guide to Procedures* says, "Other signals or methods of communication intended to supplement those described here are permitted only if they do not conflict with established procedures and only if they do not intrude on the game, are not distracting, are limited in number and purpose and are carefully described by the referee prior to the commencement of a match."

The referee might appreciate that signal from you, especially if players begin to question the decision. The referee can say with certainty, "Your teammate came from the other half to play the ball. She was over there when the pass was made." That should quiet most dissent.

The National Federation rulebook dictates that referees calling National Federation (high school) contests use the signal shown in the PlayPic to denote offside. Typically used for American football games, spectators may understand the reason for the whistle more readily if you use that signal.

Do not use the signal during NCAA or USSF contests.

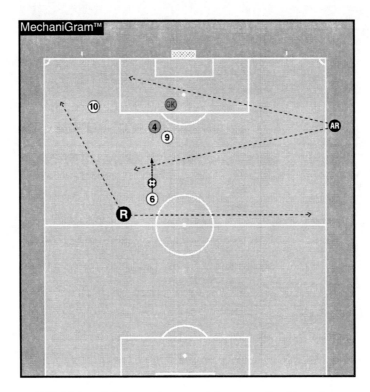

Offside position — player not in area of active play

Action on the field:

As the attackers advance on goal, there is a player in an offside position. The referee has the proper perspective to see which direction the ball is traveling but may not know which player is in an offside position. The assistant knows which player is in an offside position but may not have the perspective to know which direction the ball is traveling.

Referee Responsibilities

You have to make the final decision based on the information available to you. If you trust your assistants to carry out your pregame instructions, and you told them, "It's better to pause and come up a split-second later with a correct flag than to be early with a wrong flag," you'll get better information. The assistant will pause, read the direction of the pass and make a better decision.

You may get an early flag. You then have to decide if ⑨, the player about to receive the ball, was in an offside position at the time of the pass. From the MechaniGram above, clearly ⑩ is well outside the active zone of play. If you judge ⑨ was even with or behind ④, or if you judge ⑩ wasn't involved, allow play to continue and wave your assistant's flag down.

Assistant Referee Responsibilities

When the pass initially comes off ⑥'s foot, you might be inclined to snap the flag up to indicate the offside position. Wait. Be patient. Let the play develop. See where the ball is going. You know ⑩ is in an offside position. If the wind or a deflection from ④ pushes the ball toward ⑩, you can still raise the flag because it is only then that law 11 is being violated.

However, if your first reaction is to raise the flag, and the ball proceeds to ⑨, you'll likely kill a valid attack and draw comments from the forwards, team bench and spectators. Even if the referee waves your flag down, you've opened room for doubt on future decisions. Let the play develop.

Offside position — player not in area of active play

In the PlayPic, you are viewing a playing situation that confuses many assistant referees. Many assistants feel compelled to quickly pass some information — at the moment ⑥ struck the ball, ⑩ was in an offside position. While that is good information, it is not what the referee needs at that moment.

It's all about angles. The DSC works because officials view plays from various angles and communicate with each other about what they see.

It's clear to the assistant that ⑩ is in an offside position as the ball is about to be kicked. ⑨ is not. If the assistant raises the flag immediately, without waiting to see where the ball is going, it may stop the attack. The ball's path dictates the area of active play.

The referee has the clearest view of which angle the ball is going after leaving ⑥'s foot. But if the referee does not have good depth perception, the relationship between ❹, ⑨ and ⑩ may be unclear. That's why the referee checks with the assistant to assist with the offside decision. But the assistant may need half a second to determine the flight of the ball.

Players will yell that you can't penalize the infraction that late — they're wrong. What they tend not to realize is that you are waiting with the thought you will not penalize the team for the offside position of one of their players — but if that player interferes or gains an advantage, you must.

As the assistant, pause for a split second until you can read where the ball is going. A chip shot over the keeper's head? No flag. A pass to the near side for ⑨ to collect? No flag. A pass to the far side of the field to a wide open ⑩? Clearly a flag for the offside violation. A pass to the goalkeeper's right, halfway between ⑨ and ⑩? Now you will have to wait some more to see what ⑩'s reaction is to the pass. If he sprints to space to collect the ball, flag the infraction. If he stands by and watches ⑨ out sprint ❹ to the ball, do not raise the flag. Instead, move laterally to stay even with the second-to-last defender or the ball.

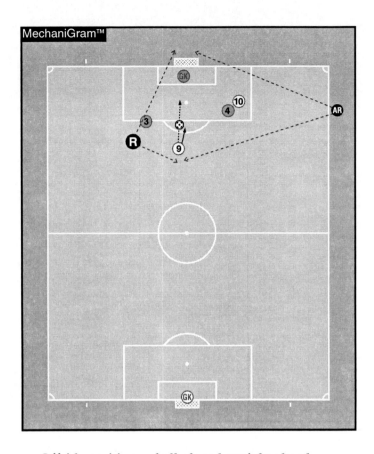

Offside position — ball played straight ahead

Action on the field:

⑨ has the ball about 30 yards from goal. ⑩ is standing in an offside position when ⑨ pushes the ball about 12 yards in front of himself, planning to run onto the ball and take a shot.

Referee Responsibilities

That is a very difficult judgement with a great possibility for things to go wrong. Because of the angle, expect the assistant referee to flag the offside position by ⑩. Read ⑨'s intentions carefully and if ⑨ pushed the ball ahead and then continued to run forward to play it, wave the flag down. Also, expect contact between ⑨ and the goalkeeper. Both will have enough time to gain full momentum, so you should expect contact — you have to decide if any of the contact was illegal. If the goal is scored and allowed, expect comments from the defensive team and bench.

Assistant Referee Responsibilities

Move laterally to stay with the second-to-last defender. Read ⑩'s body language and reactions. If ⑩ does not move aggressively toward the ball, keep the flag down. Take the time needed to read the play.

If the goal is scored, since the player who scored the goal was not the player in the offside position, do not raise the flag. A top referee will be aware of ⑩'s offside position, smile at you and give you a thumbs up for not flagging the offside position. If you feel compelled to tell the referee about ⑩'s offside position, stand at attention and make eye contact with the referee, with the flag at your side. Should the referee need additional information, explain the facts when the referee comes to you.

Offside position — ball played straight ahead

A very challenging decision for the referee team. ⑨ has the ball about 30 yards from goal. ⑩ is standing in an offside position when ⑨ pushes the ball about 12 yards in front of himself, planning to run onto the ball and take a shot. Because of the angle, expect the assistant referee to flag a potential offside by ⑩.

Upon discovering that he is in an offside position, ⑩ must do everything possible to avoid coming into the area of active play or having the area of active play overtake him. If the avoidance is unsuccessful, the offside penalty applies. But, ⑩ can redeem himself if he quickly and unambiguously performs some act which indicates an intent to be uninvolved. The burden shifts to ⑩'s shoulders.

Not knowing he is in an offside position is not enough. Knowing it but being unaware of being in the area of active play is not enough. Knowing it and being aware of being in the area of active play but doing nothing is not enough. Doing something which doesn't clearly communicate the intent of uninvolvement to the referee is not enough. All attackers in an offside position and in the area of active play should be deemed as involved in play regardless of what they are doing — unless what they are doing is deliberately and publicly taking themselves out of the active play.

If you are the assistant referee in the PlayPic, take the time needed to read the play. If the goal is scored, since the player who scored the goal was not the player in the offside position, do not raise the flag.

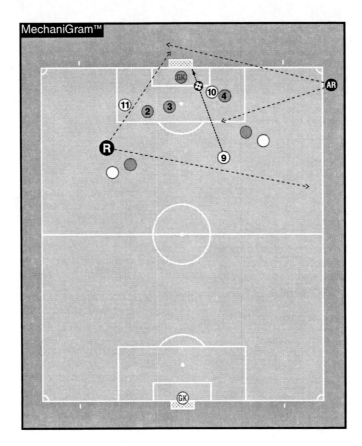

Offside position — shot taken to near post

Action on the field:
⑨ has the ball and rips a shot from 26 yards. With ⑩ standing in an offside position, the shot goes to the near post and enters the goal.

Referee Responsibilities
Many things influence the size of the area of active play. Among the factors are age and competition level of the players. If U-17 players are ripping shots from 25-30 yards and have enough skill to judge a shot that's going near post or far post, you are at an advanced level of play.

Since the player aims the shot near post and the ball passes close to ⑩'s shoulder you should judge that ⑩ interfered with an opponent and is guilty of an offside infraction.

Advice to Referees 11.4 defines interfering with an opponent as "preventing an opponent from moving towards the ball." Had ⑩ not been standing there, ④ may have been able to get to the ball and play it out of danger.

Assistant Referee Responsibilities
Move laterally to stay with the second-to-last defender. Read the player's body language and reactions. Notice that ④ did actually attempt to move to the ball but was blocked by ⑩.

Since the player who scored the goal was not the player in the offside position, do not raise the flag. Stand at attention and make eye contact with the referee, with the flag at your side. Should the referee need additional information, explain the facts when the referee comes to you.

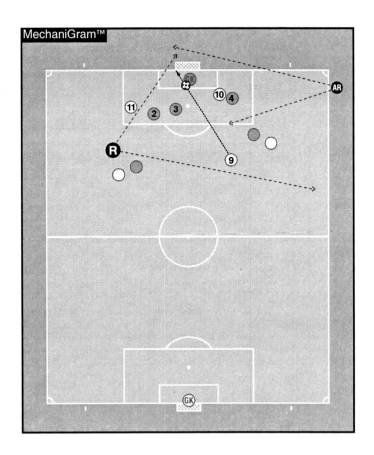

Offside position — shot taken to far post

Action on the field:
⑨ has the ball and rips a shot from 26 yards. With ⑩ standing in an offside position, the shot goes to the far post and enters the goal.

Referee Responsibilities
Since the shot is aimed far post and the ball passes far from ⑩'s shoulder, you should judge that ⑩ did not interfere with an opponent, did not interfere with play, did not gain an advantage and is not guilty of an offside infraction.

Advice to Referees 11.3 details the area of active involvement. When dealing with older age competitors with a high skill level, the area of active involvement is more narrow than youth U-10. Allow that spectacular shot to stand. There was no infraction that prevented a defender from reaching that ball.

Assistant Referee Responsibilities
Move laterally to stay with the second-to-last defender. Read the player's body language and reactions. ④ made no attempt to play the ball — it was just a great shot that could not be defended from that angle.

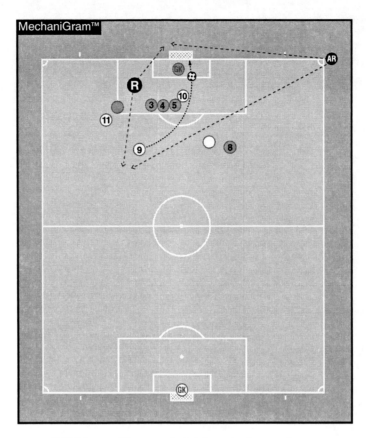

Offside position — shot taken to far post

Action on the field:

⑨ has the ball and rips a direct free kick from 30 yards. With ⑩ standing in an offside position at the far end of the wall, the shot goes to the far post and enters the goal.

Referee Responsibilities

Many things influence the size of the area of active play. Among the factors are age and competition level of the players. If U-17 players are ripping direct free kicks from 30 yards and have enough skill to judge a shot that's going near post or far post, you are at an advanced level of play.

Since the player aimed the shot far post and ⑩ is standing in an offside position between the defender and the path of the ball, you should judge that ⑩ interfered with play and is guilty of an offside infraction.

Advice to Referees 11.5 details interfering with play as "moving towards the opponent or the ball and thereby affecting how play develops. It is not necessary for a player to make contact with the ball or with an opponent to be judged as interfering with play."

Assistant Referee Responsibilities

Move laterally to stay with the second-to-last defender. Read the player's body language and reactions. Notice that ⑤ attempted to play the ball but was blocked by the offside ⑩.

Since the player who scored the goal was not the player in the offside position, do not raise the flag. Stand at attention and make eye contact with the referee, with the flag at your side. Should the referee need additional information, explain the facts when the referee comes to you.

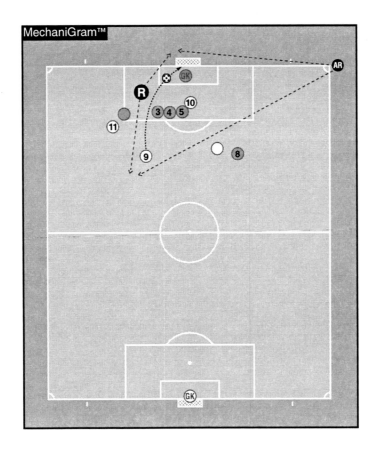

Offside position — shot taken to near post

Action on the field:

⑨ has the ball and rips a direct free kick from 30 yards. With ⑩ standing in an offside position at the far end of the wall, the shot goes to the near post and enters the goal.

Referee Responsibilities

Since the shot is aimed near post and the ball passes far from ⑩, you should judge that ⑩ did not interfere with an opponent, did not interfere with play, did not gain an advantage and is not guilty of an offside infraction.

Advice to Referees 11.3 details the area of active involvement. When dealing with older age competitors with a high skill level, the area of active involvement is more narrow than youth U-10. Allow that spectacular shot to stand. There was no infraction that prevented a defender from reaching that ball.

Assistant Referee Responsibilities

Move laterally to stay with the second-to-last defender. Read the player's body language and reactions. ⑤ made no attempt to play the ball — it was just a great shot that could not be defended from that angle.

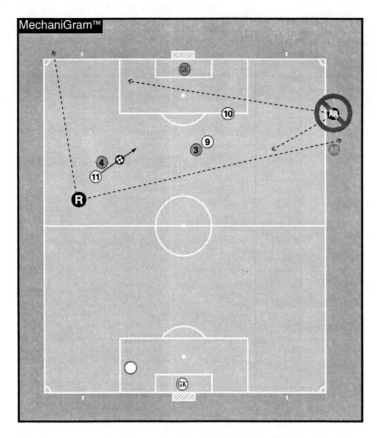

Improper mechanic — staying with the lead attacker

Action on the field:

The white team is attacking and has two players in an offside position. At the moment the ball is passed, both ⑨ and ⑩ are nearer the goalline than the second-to-last defender. The assistant referee has improperly chosen to stay level with the lead attacker rather than the second-to-last defender.

Referee Responsibilities

If you are able to pick up on other clues that ⑨ is also in an offside position, that is going to be a difficult decision for you. Protests from the defense, superb peripheral vision or a sudden sprint to be in line with the second-to-last defender may allow you to make the right choice.

Failing that, your partner's poor positioning might lead to a poor decision and some dissent from the defense. Learn from the experience and turn it into a teaching point at halftime or at full time.

Assistant Referee Responsibilities

You chose to stay with the leading attacker. Although contrary to USSF guidance on positioning, there are referees who believe that is the best way to referee. The MechaniGram shows that ⑩ has pulled you seven yards from your proper position. Because you are seven yards ahead of where you should be, from your improper vantage point, it will appear as though ⑨ and ③ are level. ⑨'s entire torso is in front of the second-to-last defender and thus in an offside position at the time of ⑪'s pass. While ⑨ should be flagged for an offside infraction upon becoming involved in active play, improper positioning will lead to the wrong decision.

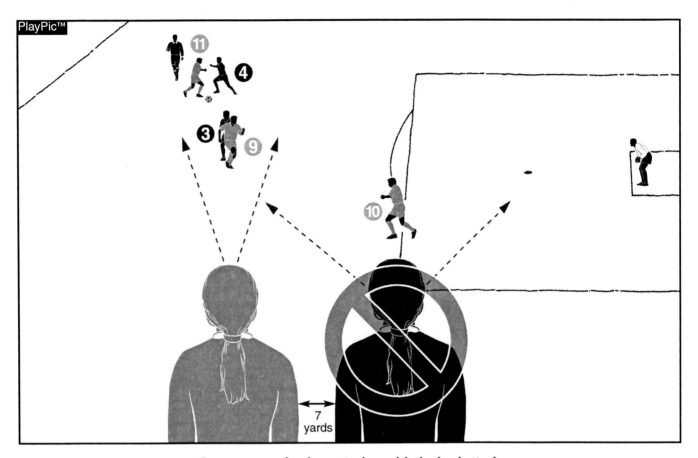

Improper mechanic — staying with the lead attacker

The light-colored team is attacking and has two players in an offside position. At the moment the ball is passed, both ⑨ and ⑩ are nearer the goalline than the second-to-last defender. The assistant referee has improperly chosen to stay level with the lead attacker rather than the second-to-last defender.

The MechaniGram shows that ⑩ has pulled you seven yards from your proper position. Because you are seven yards ahead of where you should be, from your improper vantage point, it will appear as though ⑨ and ❸ are level. Actually, ⑨'s entire torso is in front of the second-to-last defender and thus in an offside position at the time of ⑪'s pass. While ⑨ should be flagged for an offside infraction upon becoming involved in active play, improper positioning will lead to the wrong decision.

To less-experienced referees, it seems like such a minor point: "Give me a break, it's only a yard or two." But those few yards alter your sight lines significantly, giving false impressions. Mix that with the speed of today's game and developing tactics and the potential for improper decisions is magnified.

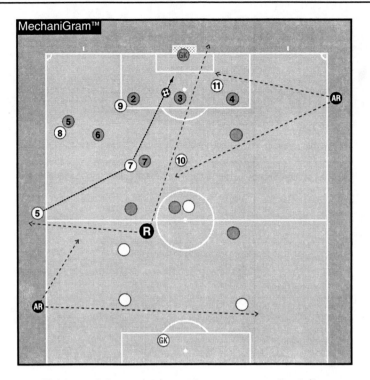

Offside position — referee does not see raised flag

Action on the field:

Playing one-touch soccer, ⑤ throws the ball in to ⑦, who left foots the ball toward the penalty mark. ⑨ is onside at the time of the kick but ⑪ is in an offside position. The assistant quickly raises the flag to indicate the offside position and infringement.

Referee Responsibilities

Referees should not automatically accept flags raised by the assistant referee. You must evaluate the player's actions and decide for yourself if the player is interfering with play, interfering with an opponent or gaining an advantage. But first, you must become aware the assistant has raised the flag.

The referee was poorly positioned at the restart for a team that plays one-touch soccer. The ball traveled almost 70 yards in less than two seconds and the referee's field of view did not contain all the needed elements: ball, assistant referee, attacker and defender.

When the referee finally hears enough players scream and looks to see the raised flag, the referee might unfairly penalize ⑪ who had turned away from play or was kneeling down to show non-involvement with the play.

Assistant Referee Responsibilities

Be patient before raising the flag for an offside infraction. If you are in doubt, do not raise the flag. Once you decide to raise the flag, leave it up until one of five things happen: the referee stops play, the referee waves your flag down, the defense controls the ball without pressure, the ball goes out for a defensive throw-in or the ball goes out for a goalkick. Quickly raising and then lowering the flag (called a phantom flag by some referees) confuses everyone.

The *NISOA DSC Instructional Manual* recommends collegiate referees hold the flag for a slow count of "1000, 2000, 3000" and then drop the flag and proceed to the normal position on the pattern and resume normal play. If a goal is scored directly by the offending team, stand at the corner area, make eye contact with the referee and if the referee comes over, tell the referee about the incident. Referees should discuss that during pregame discussions.

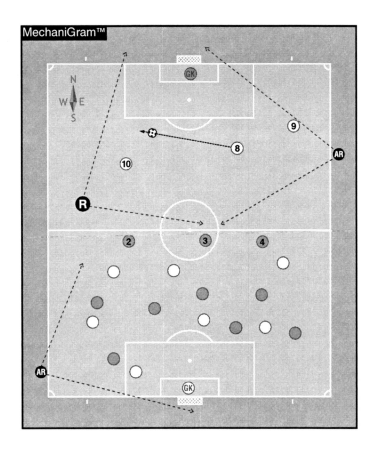

Offside position — not involved in active play

Action on the field:
From a scene replicated in the 1971 Football Association Cup between Leeds and West Bromwich Albion, WBA was on the attack toward the south end. A Leeds attacker stole the ball and began a counterattack with three players as the WBA defense stood flat-footed. **⑧** carried the ball down the center with teammates to both sides. **⑨** was in an offside position to the right as **⑧** made a square pass to the left. **⑩** struck the ball into the net for the deciding goal.

Referee Responsibilities
Culturally, different national associations perceive that call differently. Also, in 1971, the general interpretation was different. While all profess to adhere to FIFA law, the onfield interpretation by referees in diverse nations differs radically.

The USSF guidance is clear. Since **⑨** was not involved in active play, do not punish **⑨** simply for being in an offside position. Since **⑩** was well behind the ball at the time of the pass, **⑩** is not in an offside position. The goal counts.

Assistant Referee Responsibilities
Do not flag the offside position. Regardless of anyone's earlier training, whether in the U.S. or some other nation, that is not an infringement of the *Laws of the Game*. Allow play to continue and allow the goal to stand.

Indirect free kick

• Indirect free kicks are awarded to the opposing team after a technical violation is committed.

• If an indirect free kick is awarded to the attacking team within a goal area, the special circumstances in law 8 require a specific location for the restart. The restart must take place along the goal area line that runs parallel with the goalline, six yards from the goalline. You should move the ball perpendicular to the goalline from the location of the restart.

• An offside violation is punished by awarding an indirect free kick to the opposing team.

Quiz

Without referring back, you should be able to answer the following true-false questions.

1. Defenders cannot be closer than 10 yards of the restart for an indirect free kick if the attackers choose to require enforcement of the limit, unless an indirect free kick is awarded to the attacking team within 10 yards of the goal.

2. The referee should hold the indirect free kick signal from when the ball is put into play until it touches another player or goes out of play.

3. The referee should hold the indirect free kick signal from when the ball is put into play and touches another player or the ball goes out of play.

1 - True, 2 - False, 3 - True

Chapter 15

Penalty Kick

When a defender commits any of the penal fouls inside the penalty area against an opponent while the ball is in play, the restart is a penalty kick to the offended team.

Surprised spectators

Many who view a soccer game are amazed to see a referee award a penalty kick when a defender strikes an attacker in the penalty area while the ball is in play at midfield. Teammates, coaches and fans will howl abuse at the referee for the "mistake." That is not a mistake. That is the correct interpretation. Be strong.

Quick penalty kick — no such thing

Look for cunning players who attempt to take a quick penalty kick, hoping to catch the goalkeeper off guard. It should be a given that a penalty kick takes time to set up, clear players out of the arc, etc. Look for verbal sparring between opponents if a player kicks the ball early.

A number of things prevent a quick penalty kick, including the need for the kicker to be properly identified and the players to be properly positioned. However, the main thing preventing it is the law 14 provision: "The referee does not signal for a penalty kick to be taken until the players have taken up position in accordance with the law."

Effectively using assistants

Here is a recommendation from an emeritus National Referee on what to tell your assistant during a penalty kick: "If the ball hits the frame of the goal or the goalkeeper and rebounds back into play, you are to remain in position and be a goal judge. You are not to try to run back to cover the offside. It's hopeless; you're in no-man's land if you try and you'll be of no use to me to judge offside or the goalline. So stay on the goalline with only that single responsibility."

As the referee, it's your responsibility to cover the offside if there is a rebound on the penalty kick. Tell your assistant that you'll take the offside and that they are not to move back to the touchline until it's safe to do so (i.e., ball out of play or counterattack and the ball goes toward the other end).

Deal with emotions

Perhaps because players view televised matches and see big stars cluster around the referee, sharing their opinions as to why a mistake is being made, they feel obligated to share their wisdom with you. It would be the rare decision that is not greeted by at least minor levels of dissent. Understanding that emotion is natural helps you deal with it when you hear it. There is a

limit. When players shout or gesture in such a way that it becomes demeaning to your office as a sports official, or accuse you of cheating, they overstep their bounds. Use your personality and distance to decrease some of the comments.

Don't stay on the mark

You need to signal toward the penalty mark to convey the next restart. It is a mistaken impression that you must run to the penalty mark to give that signal. It is poor mechanics to remain on the penalty mark after you've given that signal. It's logical for players to run to you and surround you if you mistakenly stand on the mark.

Balance

Now is a good time for you to read the tenor of the game. While the difference is only a few seconds, you need to find the right balance between getting the ball in play (usually the best recommendation) and slowing things down with an extended ceremony. Read the players and their emotions. Perhaps taking an extra 10 seconds to walk over and triple check something may allow that simmering pot to cool off a bit. Read and evaluate.

Tricks

As young players come into their first referee training classes, they seem eager to know if the tricks they've thought up or been taught by their coaches are legal. "Can I tap the ball ahead to my teammate who will run up and score?" Yes, but why would you want to? On average, you stand an 82 percent chance of scoring off the kick. Why go through all those extra steps with the inevitable likelihood of inducing errors. Goalkeepers will attempt to move off the goalline early. Non-kicking field players will attempt to rush the penalty area, some with a running head start. Not all of them time their entry well. Some kickers hesitate during their kicking motion, just after they place their plant leg on the ground and before they begin their kicking motion.

Discuss those tricks with your mentors, instructors and senior referees during your scheduled meetings. Role-play what you've seen. Demonstrate it repeatedly until everyone can differentiate between legal and illegal. Some goalkeepers attempt to break the kickers concentration by coming out to shake hands or congratulate them on a well-deserved penalty kick. There is little or no good that can come from letting the goalkeeper come out to talk to the kicker. Intercede.

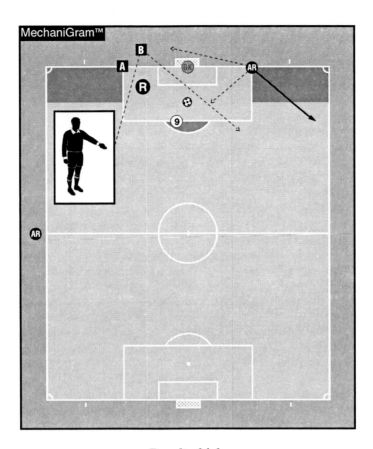

Penalty kick

Action on the field:
The referee awards a penalty kick to the white team and signals the decision.

Referee Responsibilities
Unless needed at the spot of the foul for game control, move to location A to avoid confrontation and dissent. Stop the clock if playing under Federation or NCAA rules. Use your personality and hand gestures to dissuade players from arguing to overturn your decision. If players persist, some referees move several yards off the field to position B, which gives players two detrimental choices — leave the field of play without your permission or dissent more loudly so you (and everyone else) can hear the dissent. If players make either of those choices, the reason behind the caution is more evident.

Players must vacate the penalty area and the darkened areas on the MechaniGram. Identify the kicker and have the kicker spot the ball on the penalty mark. As a courtesy, tell the goalkeeper which opponent will take the kick. Move to position R, check with your assistant referee, double check player positioning and signal for the kick to be taken.

Assistant Referee Responsibilities
Move to the intersection of the penalty area and goalline. Perform those duties that the referee assigned during the pregame discussion, usually acting as goal judge only. If you agree a valid goal is scored, follow the normal goal procedure and regain a position level with the second-to-last defender.

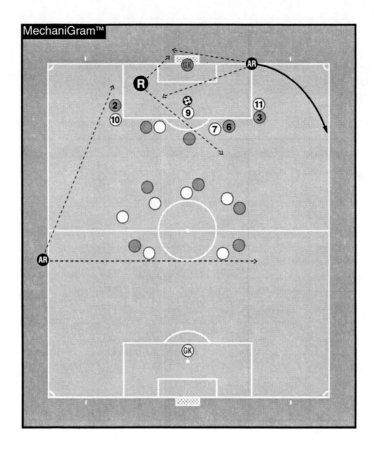

Penalty kick

Action on the field:
The referee awards a penalty kick based on a penal foul committed by a defender within the penalty area.

Referee Responsibilities
The referee stops play with a whistle, gives a strong signal to indicate a penalty kick and moves to the edge of the penalty area to limit those who might dispute the decision. Stop the clock if playing under Federation or NCAA rules. Identify the kicker and watch as the kicker places the ball on the penalty mark. Double check to see that all other players are properly positioned, including the requirement that ② and ⑪ to be at least 12 yards from the goalline, and that the assistant referee is prepared. Signal for the kick, traditionally with a whistle.

Assistant Referee Responsibilities
Move quickly to the intersection of the goalline and the penalty area. Prepare for the duties assigned by the referee in the pregame. Without getting in the way of continuing play, cut across the field to resume your position: along the touchline with the second-to-last defender. If a goal is scored, observe the players as the other assistant referee records the goal. If a goal is not scored, keep play in view for possible offside infringements.

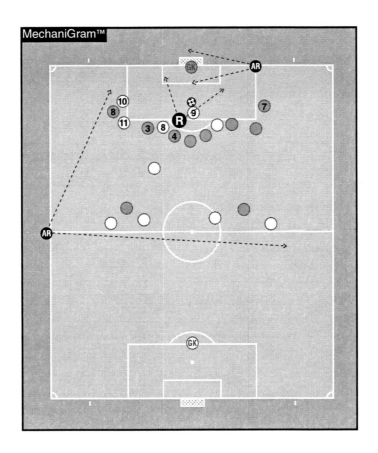

Penalty kick — problems between opponents

Action on the field:
The referee awards a penalty kick based on a penal foul committed by a defender within the penalty area. There have been ongoing behavioral problems between ⑧ and ④ — untoward comments, bravado and snide remarks.

Referee Responsibilities
The referee has a responsibility to control the game. The referee must be in position to see all the critical elements of the kick: the assistant referee, the kicker, the ball and the goalkeeper. By moving to the position shown, within the D, or penalty arc, the referee has overview over all the essential elements and is nearby to hear comments made between the antagonists. Your presence on the scene may prevent the problems during that emotional stage of the game.

Although not a standard mechanic, the position is used by some officials. Check with the appropriate governing bodies to see if you can use it.

Assistant Referee Responsibilities
Move quickly to the intersection of the goalline and the penalty area. Prepare for the duties assigned by the referee in the pregame. You may want to watch the referee's back a bit more than usual since the referee is close to upset players. Remember your primary focus is to act as goal judge.

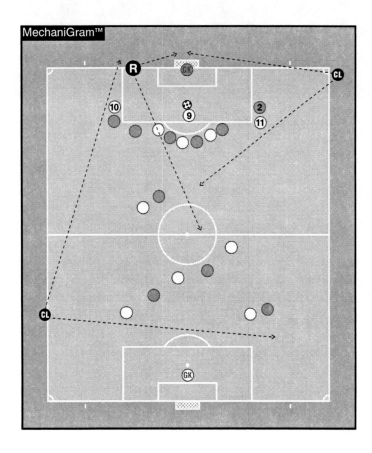

Penalty kick — club linesman

Action on the field:
The referee awards a penalty kick based on a penal foul committed by a defender within the penalty area. The referee is working alone. There are two club linesmen to assist with balls crossing over the touchline.

Referee Responsibilities
All other aspects of the penalty kick remain the same, except for the referee's position. You must also act as goal judge in addition to all the other duties, so you will need to move to the goalline to properly view that important decision. From that position, it is harder to judge if ⑩ and ❷ remain at least 12 yards from the goalline until the kick is taken. You sacrifice something in the one-referee system but it is more important to prioritize the important decisions.

Assistant Referee Responsibilities
Not applicable. You do not want a club linesman making that vital call. Go there yourself and be ready to hustle on a counterattack.

KEY

Ⓡ Referee   ⒶⓇ Assistant Referee   ④ Fourth Referee   ⒸⓁ Club Linesman   Ⓐ Optional Position   ●⸱⸱⸱ Coverage Area   ◯ Offense   ⬤ Defense

→ Movement   Initial Position ⒶⓇ ➝ ⒶⓇ Current Position   ⬤ Ball   --- ⊡-▸ Ball Movement   Goal

182 *Soccer Officials Guidebook*

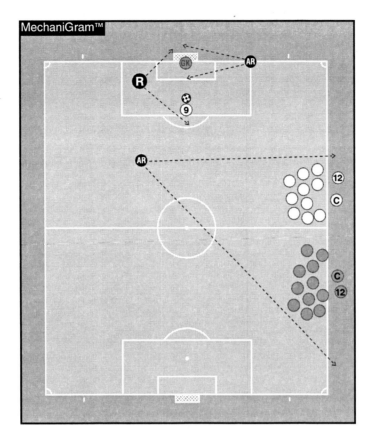

Penalty kick — after time has expired

Action on the field:

The referee awards a penalty kick based on a penal foul committed by a defender within the penalty area. Before the kick can be taken, halftime or full time (including an allowance for time lost) expires. The penalty kick proceeds.

Referee Responsibilities

Inform both team captains that there will be no more playing time in the half or in the game, but that the penalty kick will take place in extended time. Allow a substitution for the goalkeeper if the defensive team wishes, and they have not used their allotted substitution quota. (Note: For games played under Federation rules, do not allow that substitution unless the goalkeeper was injured or cautioned.) Allow the defensive team to switch the goalkeeper with any player on the field. Remind both teams that all players must remain on the field. *Advice to Referees* 14.8 reminds you that referees have no authority to make the players leave the field or the vicinity of the penalty area.

Referee recommends you blow your whistle strongly as soon as you decide the penalty kick has been completed, unless it is obvious the ball entered or did not enter the goal.

Assistant Referee Responsibilities

Most players will want to get some water and huddle up near their coach. Allow that, but supervise to make certain they remain on the field until all playing action is complete. If opposing players get near each other outside the penalty area and penalty arc, monitor their actions closely. The other assistant acts a goal judge.

Penalty Kick

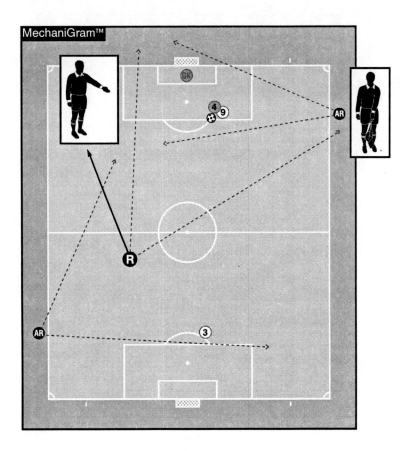

Penalty kick — referee caught on counterattack

Action on the field:
One of the 10 penal fouls takes place near the penalty area line and the referee whistles to stop play. The referee was caught in a counterattack and needs help to determine if the foul occurred inside the penalty area.

Referee Responsibilities
Continue to sprint hard, and blow an extended whistle, so it gives the appearance you were closer to the play than you were. Establish eye contact with your assistant referee who gives a subtle signal to indicate the foul occurred inside the penalty area. Once you see the signal, sell the penalty kick decision with a strong arm signal and keep moving through the penalty area to the intersection of the goalline and the penalty area. Stop the clock if playing under Federation or NCAA rules. Conduct the penalty kick in the standard fashion.

Assistant Referee Responsibilities
Move to stay with the second-to-last defender. Once you hear the referee's whistle and know the foul occurred inside the penalty area, come to a stop. If the referee makes eye contact with you for help, face the field of play and hold the flag straight downward in front of your body. Once the referee signals the penalty kick, move quickly to the intersection of the goalline and the penalty area. Perform those duties as assigned by the referee in the pregame discussion.

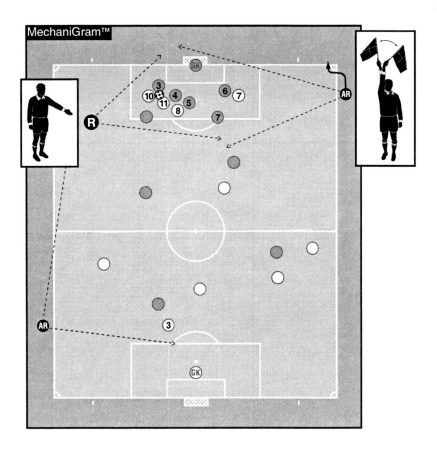

Penalty kick — indicated by the assistant referee

Action on the field:
The referee focuses intently on the action around the ball while the assistant referee observes **6** pull **7** to the ground inside the penalty area. The assistant referee determines that the infringement was not seen by the referee (the contact was not trifling and would have caused the referee to stop play if seen, based on the prior pattern of referee decisions) and signals the foul.

Referee Responsibilities
Observe the assistant referee's signal and whistle to stop the game. Watch what the assistant does next. If the assistant begins moving toward the corner flagpost, give a strong arm signal to indicate the penalty kick and follow the normal procedures for a penalty kick. Stop the clock if playing under Federation or NCAA rules.

Assistant Referee Responsibilities
Signal with the flag straight up in your right hand until the referee recognizes your signal. Once you establish eye contact, give the flag a slight wave. Having the flag in your right hand alerts the referee to the fact that you are calling a foul against the defense. If the referee honors your request for a stoppage in play and blows the whistle, lower the flag and walk briskly to stand in front of the corner flagpost. Follow the normal procedures for a penalty kick.

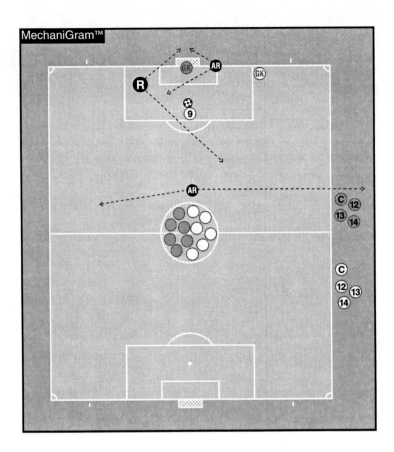

Kicks from the penalty mark — by the book

Action on the field:

The full time (including an allowance for time lost) expires, as well as periods of extra time. Both teams scored an equal number of goals (or no goals), so the match is a draw. The competition rules declare that a winner must be determined for advancement to the next round.

Referee Responsibilities

Choose the goal where the shots will be taken, factoring in sunlight, wind, field conditions and spectators. Conduct a coin toss to determine which team shoots first. If playing under the *Laws of the Game*, the winner must shoot first. Under Federation and NCAA rules, the captain has a choice. Alternately have the teams kick until a winner is determined. Keep all others, including coaches, off the field. Have players not involved in the kicks remain within the center circle. Players on the field must continue to meet all other law requirements, i.e., shinguards on, uniforms worn properly, etc.

Assistant Referee Responsibilities

The position for the lead assistant referee is different from a standard penalty kick. Move forward until you are at the intersection of the goalline and the goal area line, six yards from the goalpost. The trail assistant must closely supervise the remaining 19 players, tightly packed into the confined area of the center circle.

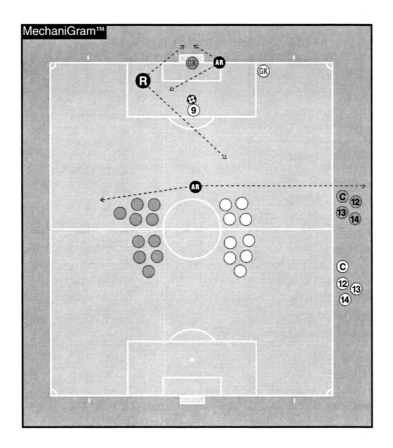

Kicks from the penalty mark — a realistic departure

Action on the field:

The full time (including an allowance for time lost) expires, as well as periods of extra time. Both teams scored an equal number of goals (or no goals), so the match is a draw. The competition rules declare that a winner must be determined for advancement to the next round.

Referee Responsibilities

Choose the goal where the shots will be taken, factoring in sunlight, wind, field conditions and spectators. Conduct a coin toss to determine which team shoots first. Alternately have the teams kick until a winner is determined. Keep all others off the field.

You want the next kicker immediately available to speed the process, so keep both teams near the halfway line. The few minutes it takes to conduct those kicks are an emotional time. Packing opposing players into a cramped space leads to unwanted comments and retaliatory barbs. A suggestion — air it out a little. Ask the teams to step apart just a bit. Do not yield to the coach's desire to enter the field.

Assistant Referee Responsibilities

The position for the lead assistant referee is different from a standard penalty kick. Move forward until you are at the intersection of the goalline and the goal area line, six yards from the goalpost. The trail assistant must supervise the remaining 19 players, preparing the next kicker to move to the penalty mark as soon as the outcome of the shot is determined.

Penalty kick

• If a defender commits one of the 10 penal fouls within the penalty area, while the ball is in play, award a penalty kick.

• Identify the kicker and have the kicker spot the ball on the penalty mark. Inform the goalkeeper who will take the kick. Move into position, check with your assistant referee, double check player positioning and signal for the kick to be taken.

• Penalty kicks are defining moments for the referee team. Opponents are in close proximity, there are many restrictions on positioning and movement and everyone is testing the envelope for just a slight advantage.

• *Referee* recommends you verbally tell the kicker to wait for your whistle. Show everyone the whistle and tap it with your other hand as you instruct the kicker to wait for your signal.

Quiz

Without referring back, you should be able to answer the following true-false questions.

1. After awarding a penalty kick, you should stop the clock if playing under Federation or NCAA rules.

2. It is acceptable for a club linesman to act as a goal judge during a penalty kick.

3. Referees have the authority to make the players leave the field or the vicinity of the penalty area when a penalty kick is being taken in extended time.

1 - True, 2 - False, 3 - False

Chapter 16

Dropped Ball

"A dropped ball is a way of restarting the match after a temporary stoppage which becomes necessary, while the ball is in play, for any reason not mentioned elsewhere in the *Laws of the Game*." While injury tends to be the most common reason for such a stoppage, inadvertent whistles, burst balls, toddlers and animals are possibilities during your games.

Historical look at injury management

Denis Howell was a Football League (England) referee for almost 20 years, and in 1955, was elected to Parliament. In 1964, he was appointed his nation's first Minister of Sport. Howell wrote *Soccer Refereeing* (© 1968, Pelham Books, London). In that book, he described the days leading up to the 1966 World Cup, held in England: "Another subject that came up early, following incidents on the field of play, concerned injured players. At first a host of officials would charge onto the field, but with Mr. (Ken) Aston in the chair (of the FIFA referee committee) the referees decided they would agree to two attendants coming on to the field, and FIFA then dispatched a telex containing this decision to each of the teams at their various headquarters throughout the country."

Many years after that historic World Cup, the guidance remains much the same. Quoting a Memorandum on instructions for referees and resolutions affecting team managers and players from *In the Eye of the Whistle II: The Refereeing at the 1990 World Cup*, page 143 says:

"Coaches, Trainers, Doctors

• Coaching of players during a game is permitted only from the team's bench. (*Editor's note:* Currently, under National Federation rules, neither team may coach during an injury stoppage.)

• Only two team officials may enter the field when called upon by the referee in the case of injury of a player.

• An injured player may not be treated on the field of play. If necessary, he shall be removed by stretcher.

• The two officials are permitted to enter the field of play solely for the purpose of assessing an injury — not to treat it — and to arrange for his removal, if necessary. In these circumstances, only a minimum of first-aid equipment should be carried onto the field."

Common sense

You are not going to stop the mother of a small child from entering a field, even if she is the third representative of that team to step onto the field. The guidance shown is for major competitions: first division matches, state cup contests, professional divisions, etc. On local parks, it is wise to know what the guidance is so you can prevent an excess by calling upon the guidance but do not get heavy-handed during a recreational game when there is the possibility of serious injury. Err on the side of safety.

Extracts from the USL handbook – 1999 version
Injured player removal

"It is important that player injuries are dealt with as expeditiously and efficiently as possible. Nevertheless, nothing should be done that would potentially cause further or permanent injury to a player.

• Team trainers or other medical personnel may not enter the field until summoned by the referee but shall always be summoned before calling for a stretcher.

• A stretcher or spine board shall be kept at the fourth official's table. If a spine board or stretcher is called for, the player is required to leave the field, unless the player is the goalkeeper and is otherwise able to continue.

"Under no circumstances shall a player be moved or removed if there is an injury to the head, neck or back, until it can be accomplished without risk of further or permanent injury."

Injuries

Many referees misunderstand dealing with an injured player. Many referees do not properly manage that aspect of the game because of their lack of concentration on play and the game. There are obvious differences in dealing with injured players at professional levels, school levels and at youth play.

For example, two players bang heads in mid-air in the penalty area. As soon as they fall down, blow the whistle, stop play and summon help. If you don't stop the contest and one player is down but the opponents continue to play, look for a very angry teammate to come down hard on the ankles of an opponent to cause a foul. In the mind of the player committing the foul, at least that stops the game for the teammate to be tended to.

Act as if you are in charge of the game. There is no one answer to dealing with sensitive aspects of game management. Some signs, if observed, could enhance your image.

• What caused the player to go down? Was it a collision with a teammate, an opponent, a goalpost or the advertising boards? Was there a fair or foul tackle or challenge? What is the location of the incident? What is the location of continuing play? What is the score? What is the style of play? All those and more play a crucial role in determining the way you act when a player goes down.

There is no single answer to the complex web of scenarios. The generally acceptable guidelines:

• The higher the level of play, the more likely you might wait a few seconds for the players to kick the ball out. The farther the ball is from the penalty area, the faster the stoppage comes.

• The younger or less skillful the players, the faster the whistle needs to be blown. Since most referees are involved in youth soccer, it is safer to hit the whistle and summon the coaches to do their part.

The parents and coaches will forgive you if a decent scoring chance was wasted due to your prompt stoppage. Watch parents and coaches react to both options: rarely will parents and coaches disagree with the immediate halt to play. On the other hand, watch referees get screamed at, even by the injured player's coaches and parents for allowing their team to play and score while their own player is down in pain.

Special circumstances
A dropped ball is one of two cases when a ball is moved to a location six yards from the goalline when the restart was within the goal area.

Ball in play
The dropped ball is the only one of the eight restarts that is not restarted by a player. The referee starts the play and the ball is not in play until it touches the ground. If a player touches the ball before the ball strikes the ground, the ball must be redropped.

Number of players involved
Since equality is one of the tenets of the spirit of the game, it is customary to have one player from each team participate in the dropped ball. However, it is a mistaken assumption that all dropped balls must be conducted in that manner. *Advice to Referees* 8.5 points out that, "There is no requirement that players from both teams — or that any player — must take part at a dropped ball." Be fair but do what you think is right, given the circumstances.

The National Federation dictates that, "The ball is dropped by an official from waist level to the ground between two opposing players."

Dropped balls

Inadvertent whistles, outside agents, burst balls and injuries — those are common reasons to restart play with a dropped ball.

Law 8 says, "A dropped ball is a way of restarting the match after a temporary stoppage which becomes necessary, while the ball is in play, for any reason not mentioned elsewhere in the *Laws of the Game*."

Federation 9-2-1a even allows for a dropped ball based on simultaneous touches by opposing teams that cause the ball to leave the field. If you aren't certain which team should be awarded the throw-in based on that simultaneous touch, you could drop the ball. While technically correct under Federation rules, it's better to make a decision and stick to it rather than appear indecisive. If you were to give the dropped ball in that instance, coaches and fans would criticize many of your later decisions. You may not restart with a dropped ball under the *Laws of the Game* under those circumstances.

There are many odd variations of the dropped ball, including improperly throwing the ball at the ground with great velocity so it bounces 25 feet into the air (imagine the calamity when it comes down). One referee started by holding the ball in front of his body but released it behind his back. That's just not fair to anyone.

Most referees place one hand under the ball and drop it as shown in the PlayPic. That is one method to execute a dropped ball.

Dropped balls — safer for the referee

To increase the chances of the ball hitting the ground and increase your own personal safety, put one hand under the ball and the other hand over the ball, similar to the PlayPic. As shown, stand back and lean forward as you prepare to drop the ball. Move the top hand dramatically above the ball. Get the players focused on that hand. Start talking to them by saying, "Remember, the ball isn't in play until it hits the ground." About halfway through that sentence, without moving the top hand, let the ball drop to the ground. If you've done a good job of having the players focus on your upper hand or your voice, they won't notice the ball dropping and it gets to the ground before they react.

Additionally, if one of the players pops the ball straight up toward your nose, there is some chance it will be deflected by your top hand, which you've left out there for that reason. If you're slick, you'll continue to talk even as you drop the ball. That's tough, so practice that technique a couple of times before trying it in a game.

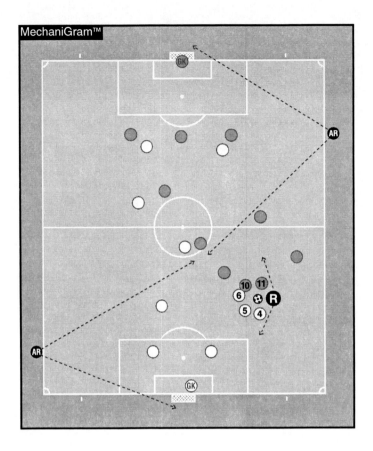

Dropped ball

Action on the field:
An incident leading to a dropped ball (serious injury, outside agent, misconduct off the field of play, etc.) takes place.

Referee Responsibilities
Deal with the incident that forced the stoppage in play — have a coach or trainer treat the injury, have security escort the parent off the field or wait until the animal is removed from the playing area. Since equality is one of the tenets of the spirit of the game, it is customary to have one player from each team participate in the dropped ball. However, it is a mistaken assumption that all dropped balls must be conducted in that manner. Here, three white team players are participating with two dark-shirted opponents. That is legal. *Advice to Referees* 8.5 points out that, "There is no requirement that players from both teams — or that any player — must take part at a dropped ball." Position yourself so you are facing the assistant referee on the opposite side of the field.

Federation rules offer a slightly different view. "The ball is dropped by an official from waist level to the ground between two opposing players. Other players may be positioned anywhere on the field of play provided they do not interfere with the drop-ball procedure."

Assistant Referee Responsibilities
Move laterally to stay even with the second-to-last defender.

Dropped Ball

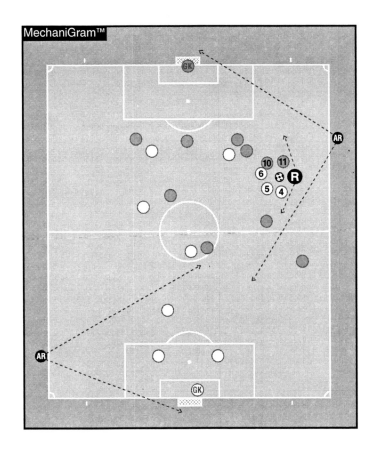

Dropped ball — in front of an assistant referee

Action on the field:
An incident leading to a dropped ball (serious injury, outside agent, misconduct off the field of play, etc.) takes place directly in front of one of your assistant referees.

Referee Responsibilities
Deal with the incident that forced the stoppage in play. It is a mistaken assumption that all dropped balls must be conducted like an ice hockey faceoff. Here, three white team players are participating with two dark-shirted opponents. That is legal.

Your positioning is well off the standard diagonal. Both you and the assistant have the same view of play and a large quadrant of the field has no official. Drop the ball and make certain it touches the ground. Then you should break behind the players as the ball moves to regain a position more in line with the diagonal.

Assistant Referee Responsibilities
Move laterally to stay even with the second-to-last defender.

KEY · **R** Referee · **AR** Assistant Referee · **4th** Fourth Referee · **CL** Club Linesman · **A** Optional Position · ●⋯→ Coverage Area · ○ Offense · ⬤ Defense

→ Movement · Initial Position **AR** ——● **AR** Current Position · ✪ Ball · ⋯⋯✪→ Ball Movement · ▨ Goal

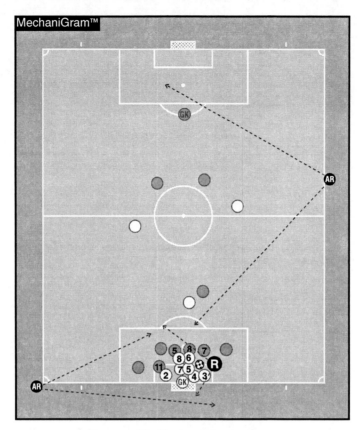

Dropped ball on goal area line

Action on the field:

An incident leading to a dropped ball (serious injury, outside agent, etc.) takes place within the goal area. The special circumstances in law 8 dictate the ball be moved to the goal area line parallel to the goalline, six yards from the goalline.

Referee Responsibilities

During those tense moments, expect much physical contact as opponents scramble for an advantageous position. Position yourself so you are facing your lead assistant referee. Drop the ball from your hands at waist level and make sure the ball touches the ground before it is touched. If it does not, redrop the ball.

The goalkeeper may participate in the dropped ball and may handle the ball immediately after it touches the ground. If it appears the goalkeeper may participate, watch closely for dangerous situations.

Assistant Referee Responsibilities

Attackers may not be offside directly from the dropped ball, so assist by watching for physical contact with so many players in close proximity. Be alert for a short pass to an attacker in an offside position. Concentrate to determine that the pass came from an attacker and not a defender trying to back-heel the ball to the goalkeeper. Goalkeepers may not handle a ball deliberately kicked to them by a teammate, but commonly, referees reserve that decision for themselves rather than seek assistant referee input.

If you are serving as an assistant and become aware that ⑧ and ⑤ or ⑥ and ⑧ have been annoying each other earlier in the match, keep a watchful eye on them as they are in close proximity. The referee has many other tasks with higher priority and may miss misconduct committed by those players. It's important for game control that the misconduct is seen and dealt with properly.

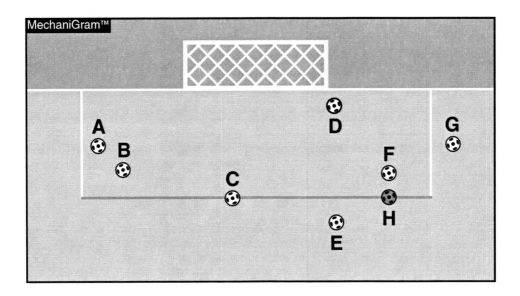

Ball location — dropped balls

Action on the field:
The referee stops play while the ball is in the goal area. The restart is a dropped ball. The special circumstances in law 8 require a specific location for the restart.

Referee Responsibilities
The restart must take place along the goal area line that runs parallel with the goalline, six yards from the goalline (darkened in the MechaniGram above). You should move the ball perpendicular to the goalline from the location of the restart. An example: If the ball were in location F when you stopped play, you should restart with the ball in location H. Similarly, balls in locations A, B and D need to be moved. Ball C is already at the proper location. Balls E and G would not be moved.

The goal area will be tightly packed with players trying to score or defend. Be aware of increased emotional play.

Assistant Referee Responsibilities
Move laterally to stay even with the second-to-last defender. Assist the referee with game control. Be aware of players on the fringes taking unfair advantage of the referee's diverted attention.

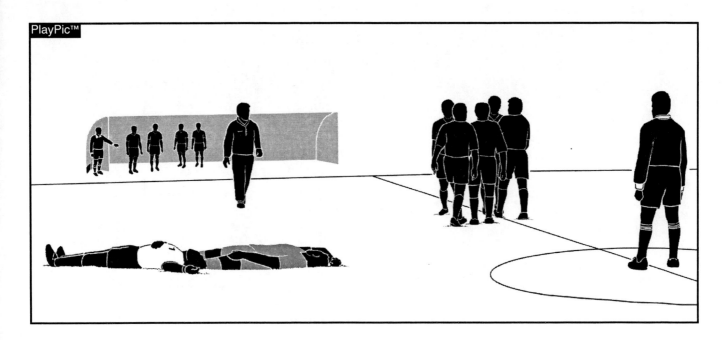

Get away from injured players

Law 5 gives you the power to allow play to continue until the ball goes out of play if a player is only slightly injured. Of course, you have the duty to stop play if a player is seriously injured.

There are a few essential indicators to assist you in deciding when to stop play. The younger the players, the quicker you should stop play. Adults are used to the scrapes and bruises that go along with competitive sports; U-8 players are not. The closer the injury is to the head or spine, the quicker you should stop play. Respiratory problems, cardiac problems and spinal injures are potentially life threatening and need quick care. Lastly, any time you spot blood, it should be an indicator to stop play. Blood pathogens are too dangerous to allow taking unwarranted chances. Thus, a U-19 player may have to walk off that ankle sprain but a U-7 player getting hit in the face with a ball gets a quick whistle and a coach to render care. There is a common misconception that a player must "go down" as an indication of a game-stopping injury. That is neither necessary nor a sufficient condition.

Here obviously, both players are seriously injured and need medical attention, which has been motioned onto the field. In cases where players are less seriously injured, jog over to the player and ask, "Do you need me to bring the coach on the field." Base your decision on not only what the player says, but also such variables as alertness, strength of voice, eye contact and hand gestures. You are probably not a medical expert, so err on the side of caution.

As soon as you call for medical attention, move well away from the injured player. Here our referee has taken up a position in the center circle, about 15 yards from the prone players. If you need additional information, walk over to discuss what happened with your assistant referee. If teammates gather to discuss strategy, that's fine, but if opponents cluster to discuss the incident, move to that trouble spot quickly.

Be careful. In a 10/97 interview in *Referee Soccer Extra*, then-FIFA assistant referee Steve Olson was asked: "Has humor ever backfired on you?" His answer is a lesson to us all in injury situations: "Sure, but the most memorable was having an injured player tended to by his trainers. After I made sure everything was all right, I was talking with a few of the other players. We laughed over a one-liner and the next day's newspaper had a photo of me laughing with an injured player in the same frame."

During your pregame discussion, explain to your partners that when your attention is diverted elsewhere by injuries or player misbehavior, they "have the whistle" and should expand their field coverage areas for indicating fouls or misconduct.

Dealing with injuries — the wrong way

Injured players are not uncommon. The action-filled, contact sport of soccer is going to have fouls, misconduct and wrecks that lead to players being injured. Occasionally, players will be injured seriously enough that coaches and trainers must come onto the field to deal with them, soothe them or treat them.

Assess the seriousness of the injury and if the player requires a trainer, call the trainer onto the field. Then get away from the injured player. Your task done, you have a bigger job to do. While sweeping your eyes across the area where the injured player is down, you have to manage the rest of the game. Now is an excellent time to discuss a point with your assistant referees or clear up a misunderstanding with the official scorer.

If opponents gather to confront one another, either about the situation that led to the injury or some earlier matter, either go over there and monitor the discussion or ask them to step apart.

Many times coaches instruct players to come to the touchline for water and added advice. Allow that but remember the players must stay on the field of play. Federation rule 3 prohibits the coach of either team from coaching during injury treatment.

By not stepping away from the injured player, the referee above has stepped into a quandary. Two trainers and the coach entered the field. While the two trainers are assessing and working on the athlete, the coach discusses the decision with the referee. The coach is emotional because one of his young charges is injured. That emotion is going to come out in the discussion. In far too many cases, coaches have to be disciplined simply because the referee took an improper position. Get away.

If you are 30 yards away, and the coach passes the injured player to discuss a matter with you, simply say, "Coach, your player needs your attention now. Please attend to her." If the coach continues to approach, as you draw away from the coach toward the nearest assistant referee, say more loudly, "Coach, please tend to your injured player." If the coach persists, advise the coach you will report his misconduct. Under NCAA and Federation rules, display the yellow card.

Dropped ball

• Deal with the incident that forced the stoppage in play — have a coach or trainer treat the injury, have security escort the parent off the field or wait until the animal is removed from the playing area.

• To increase the chances of the ball hitting the ground and increase your own personal safety, put one hand under the ball and the other hand over the ball.

• It is customary to have one player from each team participate in the dropped ball. However, it is a mistaken assumption that all dropped balls must be conducted in that manner.

Quiz

Without referring back, you should be able to answer the following true-false questions.

1. The ball is in play from a dropped ball as soon as the referee releases it.

2. Federation rules require a dropped ball between two opposing players.

3. It is legal for three white team players to participate in a dropped ball with two dark-shirted opponents.

4. An incident leading to a dropped ball (serious injury, outside agent, misconduct off the field of play, etc.) takes place within the goal area. The special circumstances in law 8 dictate the dropped ball be conducted at that location.

1 - False, 2 - True, 3 - True, 4 - False

Chapter 17

Pregame

The pregame discussion between the referee and the assistant referees is their chance to get it right before events unfold. Paul Tamberino, FIFA assistant referee, MLS referee and referee instructor at the first National Referee Academy, told his 11 charges that, "A good referee is not going to be surprised during a game."

Experience
Some of what Tamberino mentioned goes back to experience. A 23-year veteran who has attained the grade of State Referee will be surprised less often than a six-year recreational referee. If you've had events happen to you before, or to your crew, you learn from the events and mistakes. Share those during your recertification training, during your regularly scheduled meetings and during your pregame.

Meet
Arrive at the field in a timely manner to allow the proper time for a pregame. Laugh, share a joke, ask about the families and then get down to business.

What might be discussed
In the fourth edition of their book, *Fair or Foul: The Complete Guide to Soccer Officiating*, Paul and Larry Harris, (© 1983, Soccer for Americans, Manhattan Beach, Calif.) mention a number of topics.

"The referee and [assistants] should discuss all matters involving mutual cooperation. The following referee instructions should be fully covered (takes about 20 minutes).

a. [Assistant]'s duties prior to the game (field inspection, etc.)

b. Who shall be senior [assistant] in case of need (Red flag — NASL and ASL)

c. The side and end of the field each [assistant] will take during each half of the match.

d. The positions taken for various types of play resumptions.

e. Signals to be used

f. Watch synchronization."

This book offers three versions of a pregame outline, including a quick pregame that might be useful in a tournament setting. Experiment with each variation and tailor the pregame to meet your needs.

Know why you ask for certain items in a pregame
Think through what you are going to say before your pregame. Let's take the example of placing your assistant referees along each touchline. Think about why you are placing that assistant on that side (speedier assistant on the downwind side, problems

with coaches in the past, the assistant who requires prescription sunglasses looking into the sun). Discuss the possibility of switching diagonals during play (bench problems, players opposite your diagonal are causing grave game control problems, the sun).

Security dealing with a player sent off
Most referees don't work in stadiums with a security staff to handle problems. What should you do at your field? You must know what actions to take based on the rules you are playing under. The biggest concern you have is that the sent off (disqualified under Federation rules and ejected under NCAA rules) player not unduly influence the game or present safety problems to anyone at the game site. If you have those concerns, temporarily suspend the game and solve that problem.

Ideally, you will speak with security, or the host management, before the game and discuss possible situations. Know where they will be during the game. If you expect problems, discuss solutions before the game.

Playing under Federation rules, the disqualified player is under the direct supervision of the head coach. Unless you feel absolutely compelled for safety reasons, do not send the player from the team bench area. In that rare case, force the head coach to assign an assistant coach to accompany the student-athlete. For legal purposes, you might record a note regarding the incident at the time you make that decision. If you disqualify a coach, the coach "shall leave the vicinity of the playing area immediately and is prohibited from any further contact, direct or indirect, with the team during the remainder of the game." Traditionally, you may hear referees refer to that as "sight and sound."

Under NCAA rules, ejected players are restricted to the team area. Coaches "ejected from the game, shall leave the premises of the field of play. ..."

In USSF youth matches, use common sense. You do not want to be responsible for sending a youth player "sight and sound" away from a soccer field only to have that youth commit or be the target of violence. If the youth communicates a threat you believe to be viable, disrupts the match with unseemly comments or other actions that require removal, ensure the coach assigns an adult to supervise the youth for the duration of the match.

Starting the game
Under NCAA and FIFA laws, the referee determines if the game will start when the field conditions are poor. Federation rule 1 gives that responsibility to the host institution, up until the moment the game begins. Then the decision belongs to the referee.

Pregame

A. Official's pregame duties
1. Position during warmups
2. Check equipment, including uniforms
3. Check field and nets
4. Watch both teams for clues about playing styles, key players

B. Scorer/timer duties
1. Establish rapport with table personnel
2. Check players' passes or team rosters
3. Check clock, if used
4. Ask scorer to help hold substitutes for official's beckon
5. Inform table personnel of pertinent rule changes, timing concerns, etc.

C. Captain's meeting
1. Keep it brief
2. Flip coin and monitor selection
3. Meet coaches prior to start

D. Kickoff
1. Position, mechanics

E. Field coverage
1. Any differences from *Guide to Procedures*

F. Throw-ins
1. Eye contact
2. Which official watches what aspect of throw
3. Step goal-side of thrower

G. Foul call
1. Use advantage/disadvantage principles in contact situations. See the entire play
2. Mechanics:
   a. Proper signals
   b. Point direction
   c. Reporting to table/fourth official
      1. Stationary
      2. Eye contact with scorer
      3. Clear signals
3. Mechanics: Assistant referees
   a. Dead-ball officiating
   b. Help if necessary
   c. Watch players at throw-in or restart

H. Misconduct administration

I. Timing

J. Points of emphasis
1. Rough play
2. Taunting
3. Special situations

K. Bench decorum

L. Establish tempo — let the game come to you

Halftime

A. Meet as a trio on the field

B. Relax

C. Discuss concerns/problems

D. Adjustments, if necessary
1. Field coverage
2. Philosophy: Are the points of emphasis under control?

E. Review overtime procedure, if needed

F. Remind each other of the things done well in first half

G. Return to field
1. Watch players
2. Just before restart, check with table personnel

Postgame

A. Leave field together

B. Relax

C. Review game
1. Points of emphasis?
2. Tempo?
3. Bench decorum?
4. Strange plays, rulings?

D. Solicit constructive criticism — "What could I have done better?"

E. Leave field area together — safety in numbers

Quick pregame
by Ken Loomis

Here is a pregame that you can use if you don't have a lot of time to speak with your assistants prior to the game, perhaps in a tournament setting. It quickly gets to the most important points without leaving anything out. Try it as is or make minor adjustments to fit your personal style. Notice the reminder letters spell offside.

O: Offside. Stick with the second to last defender and run all balls down to the goalline. Signal for involvement only, but if because of your view, you cannot tell and signal by mistake I may overrule you. Don't be offended.

F: Fouls. Don't call fouls that I can see, I'll take care of them. If I cannot see it (like a handling or shirt pull on your side of the player) give me a flag and direction.

F: Free kicks. On free kicks close to the goal, stay with the offside line. I'll be the goal judge. Keep the defenders honest on corner kicks.

S: Substitutions. All substitutes come in from the halfway line. They must be ready before the stoppage or they don't come in. Keep strict account of the number of players on the field. The senior assistant referee may need to come to the halfway line to manage the substitution process. I don't want to have to deal with any situations.

I: Into touch. Give me direction on balls that go into touch. If you don't know the direction, put the flag straight up and I'll call it. In my half of the field, if I look to you for help, give me a flag straight up and hold it in the hand of the direction the throw should go. If you can't do that, just show direction in the normal way.

D: Deportment. Don't comment to the crowd or the coaches on the calls. Support my calls, even if I have to overrule you. Make sure the coaches and bench people behave and give me a flag if you need any help. If you want somebody cautioned, point to your badge.

E: Eye contact. Let's make eye contact on every stoppage. If I forget, give me a subtle reminder with a hand gesture such as pointing to your eye.

Until the pregame becomes second nature to you, this mnemonic device helps you make sure to cover the vital points. The most important aspects are that your assistants understand you, are comfortable with what you want and that you begin the match as a team.

(Ken Loomis, Lexington, Mass., is a USSF referee. Loomis, a 5-year veteran is also a USSF D-licensed coach and a league administrator. This article first appeared in the 8/99 Referee Soccer Extra.)

Another pregame option

Day prior to game
- Call your partners
- Verify the time and place
- Agree on uniform
- Check local playing rules

Forty-five minutes prior to the game
- Confirm start time
- Receive payment
- Check the field
- Look for wet or bare spots
- Check markings/net
- Check both goalkeeper's colors
- Check game balls
- Verify local rules

If working with partners
- Talk about how they can assist game control
- They always have offside decisions
- Establish default position for free kicks near goal
- Eye contact
- One assistant always watches field
- Hustle to goalline
- Don't chase the ball
- Advantage not used much in first 15 min.
- Count 11 players, then unfurl the flag
- Allow no dissent or delay

Refereeing team signals
- *Guide to Procedures* signals
- A foul occurs behind referee's back
- Offside, not offside position
- Referee overruling

Position
- *Guide to Procedures* locations
- Any differences
- Wall situations

- Throw-in (feet)
- Second-to-last defender
- Which diagonal will be used

Back-up watch
- Time left – 5/4/3 … patch

Designate the senior assistant
- Discuss philosophy of working together
- Handling the ball
- If there is a fight, only get jersey numbers
- Third player into the fight is gone

Captains pregame meeting
- Introduce
- Number of minutes per half
- How to break a tie/overtime
- Number of substitutions allowed
- Toss the coin

Players
- Equipment and passes

Halftime
- Time interval (not more than 15 min.)
- Take the ball with you

Immediately after the game
- Shake hands with your partners
- Ask if they have any feedback to improve your game
- Give them feedback if they ask for any
- Return the ball to the home team captain
- Make any notes needed to write the game report
- If needed, call your assignor on any send offs or problems

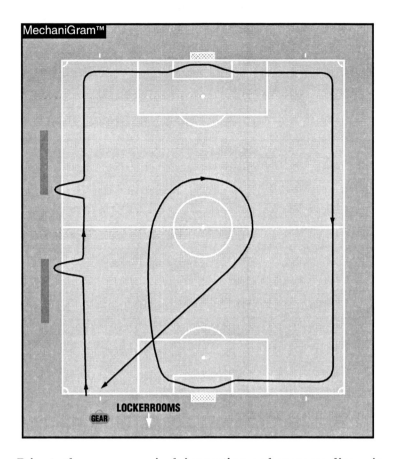

Prior to the game — arrival, inspection and pregame discussion

Action on the field:
The referee team arrives at the field at least 30 minutes before kickoff. Professional division matches require referees at the game site earlier than 30 minutes, so know the requirements for your league. While some referees prefer to store their kit between the team benches, *Referee* recommends you keep your kits along one goalline near where the assistant referee patrols. Some facilities have dressing rooms and secure storage areas for referee kits. Carefully inspect the field, markings, playing conditions and the balls.

Referee Responsibilities
While each referee chooses different styles for their review of the field, the path shown above is complete and comprehensive. Walk to one team bench, secure the team roster, introduce the referee team to the coach and repeat that same procedure at the other team bench. While making an outer loop along the perimeter of the field, discuss instructions with the fourth official and both assistants. Check goalposts, crossbars and nets as you come to them. Discuss any mechanics or signals you want used that are not mentioned in the *Guide to Procedures for Referees, Assistant Referees and Fourth Officials*. Fully cover special rules of competition, such as what to do in case of a tie. Identify the senior assistant referee. Watch players warm up to help determine key players and to assist you in reading the game. Continue to make an inner loop so you cover the complete field. Return to your kits and drink plenty of fluids to hydrate for the game. Jog, stretch and warm up off the field and out of view of the players and spectators.

Assistant Referee Responsibilities
Be a full participant in the referee's pregame discussion. Ask questions to clarify any points you do not understand. Jog, stretch and warm up. When directed by the referee, check player equipment, player passes and team rosters. Approach each team with a pair of referees — both assistants or an assistant and the fourth official.

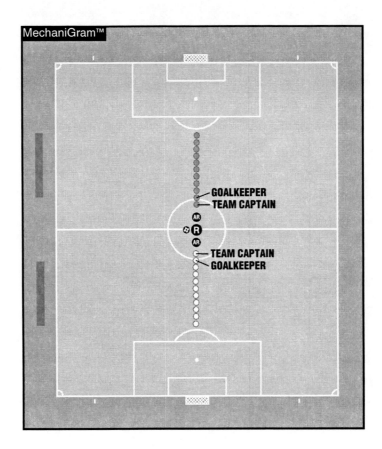

GOALKEEPER
TEAM CAPTAIN

TEAM CAPTAIN
GOALKEEPER

Prior to kickoff

Action on the field:
Several minutes before the kickoff, the referee team enters
the field together. If the game is not in a stadium or formal
setting, move directly from your kits to the center circle. If
there will be a "World Cup-style" walk-in, move to the
halfway line and gather each team, placing the captains
first, the goalkeepers next and the rest of the team. Walk to
the center of the field; allow player introductions and the
national anthem.

Referee Responsibilities
Some referees prefer to do the coin toss along the touchline
before the game and have the teams enter on the side they
will defend first. The referee carries the game ball.

Assistant Referee Responsibilities
Keep your flags furled until you are ready to start. Walk
out alongside the referee until you reach the center mark.

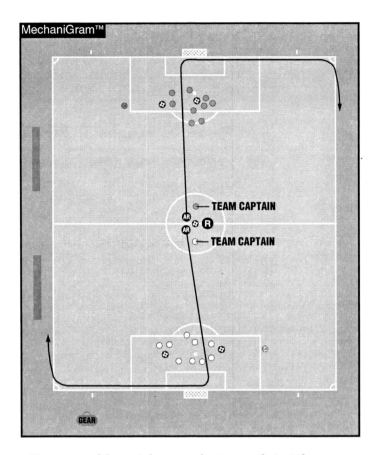

Pregame with captains — coin toss and start the game

Action on the field:
To determine which end of the field the teams will attack, the referee must conduct a coin toss with the team captain from each squad. Under Federation and NCAA rules, the captain winning the toss may choose to kick off or choose which end to attack. Under FIFA laws, the captain winning the toss chooses which end to attack and the other team kicks off.

Referee Responsibilities
Introduce the referee team to both team captains, and as a gesture toward sportsmanship, ask the captains to introduce themselves to each other and shake hands. Traditionally, the visiting captain calls the toss. Referees differ as to whether they allow the home team to actually toss the coin, or, if they do the toss, whether to catch the coin in the air or let it fall to the ground. In case more than one player represents the team, make sure you identify who will call the toss. Under Federation and NCAA rules, the visiting team shall call the coin. Record the results of the coin toss. Make eye contact with both assistant referees and look for their unfurled flags. Start your watch and make sure it is working before whistling to start the game.

Assistant Referee Responsibilities
When the captains gather for the coin toss, move opposite from the referee so you may clearly hear all the referee's instructions. In a stadium field, put your backs to the pressbox so the referee may face the pressbox. Record the results of the coin toss. Make a final check of the net and move to the touchline, level with the second-to-last defender. Unfurl your flag to show the referee you are ready. Make eye contact with the referee.

Not ready for the start of play

Ready for the start of play

Assistant referees are to carry their flags from the moment they enter the field together with the referee. A furled flag indicates the assistant is not ready for the start of play, for whatever reason. Before the flag is unfurled, the assistant must make a final check of the net at that end of the field, check to make sure the goalkeeper is ready to play and wearing a properly identified uniform, silently count 11 players on that end of the field, move to the touchline in line with the second-to-last defender, set the stopwatch to 0:00 and make sure that no outside agents are on the field of play. While making eye contact with the referee, each assistant unfurls the flag and prepares for the kickoff.

That is repeated to start the second half and for any extra periods of play.

At the start of each half of play and any period of extra time, the referee checks each assistant referee to see if they are prepared to start. An assistant who is ready will unfurl the flag, hold the flag straight down in view of the referee and make eye contact with the referee after doing several things: make a final check of the net at that end of the field, check to make sure the goalkeeper is ready to play, silently count 11 players on that end of the field (less in a short-sided game), move to the touchline in line with the second-to-last defender, set the stopwatch to 0:00 and make sure that no outside agents are on the field of play.

The referee simply checks to see if both assistants are ready with unfurled flags and then whistles to start the match.

The *NISOA Assistant Referee Duties & Responsibilities* offers a slight mechanics addition: "Should anything go wrong at the start of play, the assistant referee raises the flag straight up (do not wave the flag) to indicate to the referee."

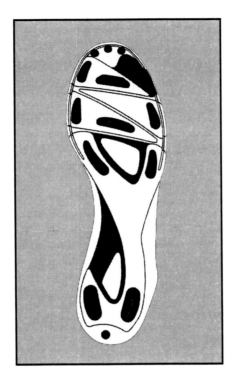

Player's equipment — shoes

The technological advancement in player equipment is astounding. Nowhere is that more evident than in shoes. A hundred years ago, shoes had bars and studs that had to be limited in length and width. With the 1990 changes to the *Laws of the Game*, the process is much simpler for referees — the player must wear shoes. The shoes cannot be dangerous to the wearer or another player.

As technology advances further, new stabilizing soles are developed. Quoting from a 1/99 news article in *Referee Soccer Extra*, "Many inquiries are received at the USSF national office regarding the soccer shoe developed by adidas with an outsole called 'Traxion.' Other makers such as Diadora and Nike have a similar cleat pattern.

"Apparently some game officials have been reluctant to let players wear those shoes on the field. To answer the question of the shoe's safety, Alfred Kleinaitis, USSF manager for referee development and education, shared a letter from FIFA regarding the shoe. The letter states that the shoe with the 'Traxion' outsole is no more dangerous than any other traditional shoe on the market and the referee should recognize it as such. He asked that we pass that information to all concerned. However, it is still the responsibility of the referee to see that a player does not wear anything which could be dangerous to another player."

The shoe, as manufactured, is safe. If someone intentionally files away a portion of the cleat or outsole, it has the potential to be dangerous. If there is any question as to the shoe's safety, run your hand along the shoe's bottom. If you feel sharp edges or altered cleats, inform the players they cannot play with shoes in that condition.

If a player asks you to check an opponent's cleats, do so at the next stoppage. If one player is wearing dangerous equipment, you want to discover it promptly, not wait until after it causes injury.

Should a shoe come off during the course of play, *Advice to Referees* 4.5 says, "It is within the referee's discretion to allow such a player to continue playing for a short while until he can recover his shoe and put it back on." That applies even to the phase of play just before scoring a goal (unless, of course, the shoe went flying directly at the goalkeeper and, as a result, the goal was scored). In an interpretation difference, when that same question was put to Cliff McCrath, secretary-rules editor for NCAA soccer, the interpretation is that the goal would not count. Under NCAA rules, the referee should not allow players to participate in action without footwear. Federation rules offer no specific guidance or play rulings. Apply common sense such as noted in *Advice to Referees* 4.5. Federation 4-3-1 Penalty says, "Play shall not be stopped immediately for an infringement of this rule except that the referee may stop play immediately when there is an immediate dangerous situation."

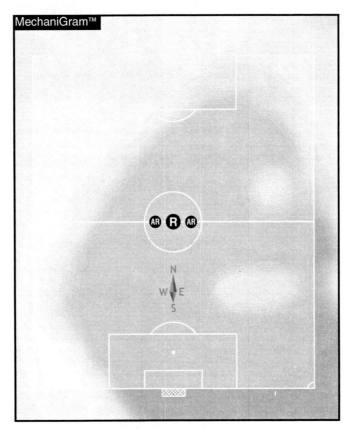

Weather considerations — fog, lightning, ice

Action on the field:
The field is partially shrouded in fog 10 minutes before the game start time. The referee must decide to start the match or cancel the game. The referee might decide to wait 15-30 minutes to see if conditions improve or call the weather bureau to determine if conditions are expected to improve.

Referee Responsibilities
There are no hard and fast rules. General guidelines evolved over time based on the three guiding principles of safety, equality and enjoyment.

For fog, if the referee, standing in the center circle, can see both goalposts, the game should start. In the MechaniGram above, if the whole field were as clear as the south end of the field, play the game. However, in the case pictured, goalkeepers and defenders at the north end are severely hampered in their ability to see crosses and corner kicks. Assistant referees on the northern end could only guess as to offside positioning. The game would be a farce.

Lightning presents a serious health hazard for referees, players and spectators. Lightning is deceptively destructive. You may observe flashes miles away and the next flash may pass along unseen paths to strike someone on your field. Do not take chances. Many leagues or tournaments now have detectors to aid you — use them.

Ice presents some problems for players. Instead of falling to the cushioning safety of a grass field, players fall on a rock-hard surface. Games played the previous day on a muddy field may have left small ridges of mud as players slid and turned. An overnight freeze turns those ridges into razor-sharp protrusions that slice into exposed thighs and calves.

There are dozens of factors to consider: age, skill level, traveling distance, tournament progression. A team owner of an Atlanta A-League franchise is not going to want to pay to travel to Milwaukee a second time due to a few thunderbolts. Therefore, you wait. You telephone the local weather station to get the forecast. You consult the local television station that is aware of weather patterns. Considering all of that, you make a decision. Err on the side of safety.

Assistant Referee Responsibilities
If you have more experience in those matters than the referee, draw the referee off to the side and offer advice. The referee is the game manager and makes the final choice. You are a trusted advisor who may know the local conditions better than a referee who traveled hundreds of miles to be at your local tournament. Offer advice and assist by going to reliable resources at your disposal.

Arrive at least one-half hour before game time

You should be at the game site at least one-half hour before the game, at a minimum. Pregame preparations, paperwork, checking the field and players' equipment, discussing match control with your partners, stretching and warming up take at least 30 minutes.

Some youth leagues have adopted a policy that if you have not checked in to the referee area 20 minutes before game start time, you lose the right to officiate that game and a standby referee is given your game. Other associations include statements in their bylaws that if you are not at the field within specified time limits, you will be fined. As always, valid emergencies and reasons are acceptable.

You do not want to gain a reputation for being late. A Midwestern tournament referee director was waiting anxiously for a referee to arrive for a 1 p.m. game. At 12:50 he asked another referee to get suited up and go to the field. As the referee was changing shirts, he asked who was late. When he heard the name, he said, "Oh, that makes sense. He's always late." At 12:53 when the tardy referee finally showed up claiming he didn't have good directions to a field within his own home city, the out-of-town tournament referee director chose not to use his services on either game. The referee lost two games fees, the right to work highly competitive regional level soccer and established a blemish on his reputation with an influential assignor.

Professional division games have added requirements for showing up early — 90 to 120 minutes before kickoff. Know your requirements — and meet them.

Pregame

• Discuss any mechanics or signals you want used that are not mentioned in the *Guide to Procedures for Referees, Assistant Referees and Fourth Officials*. Identify the senior assistant referee.

• Fully cover special rules of competition, such as what to do in case of a tie.

• Introduce the referee team to both team captains, and as a gesture toward sportsmanship, ask the captains to introduce themselves to each other and shake hands. Traditionally, the visiting captain calls the toss.

• A furled flag indicates the assistant is not ready for the start of play, for whatever reason. Before the flag is unfurled, the assistant must make a final check of the net at that end of the field, check to make sure the goalkeeper is properly uniformed, silently count 11 players on that end of the field, move to the touchline in line with the second-to-last defender, set the stopwatch to 0:00 and make sure that no outside agents are on the field of play.

Quiz

Without referring back, you should be able to answer the following true-false questions.

1. Referees should watch players warm up to help determine key players and to assist them in reading the game.

2. During the pregame equipment check, approach each team with a pair of referees — both assistants or an assistant and the fourth official.

3. Under Federation and NCAA rules, the captain may choose to kick off or choose which end to attack.

4. Some referees prefer to do the coin toss along the touchline before the game and have the teams enter on the side they will defend first.

1 - True, 2 - True, 3 - True, 4 - True

Chapter 18

Substitutions

Oddly enough, the original *Laws of the Game* made no provision for substitutes. Eleven players started the game and those same 11 iron-men finished the game.

1999 law change allows reentry

It was not until the IFAB meeting on Feb. 20, 1999, that players had written permission under the *Laws of the Game* to reenter once they departed. And not all players — only children below the age of 16, women and veterans (usually designated as more than 35 years old.) When you hear the term "flying substitution," think of it as free substitution, with the right of reentry.

Free substitution

The NCAA and Federation allowed free substitution, as well as youth games played in the U.S. under the *Laws of the Game.*

Potential problems with substitutions

While you may monitor thousands of substitutions in your career without any problems, when something goes amiss, it creates a major problem. Doing the right thing by the letter of the law goes against what feels right under the spirit of the law. It places referees in a very undesirable spot. Read page 222. Think about what you would do in that situation.

Below highly competitive and professional levels, weight the additional playing time gained by the players against the possible consequences. In the professional divisions, follow the letter of the law.

Fourth official

Although still a luxury for many, the assignment of a fourth official to your game is a great aid. Include the fourth official in your pregame discussion and go over their specific duties. To the degree that you are able to, and still complete all your pregame duties, spend extra time with officials serving in that role for the first time.

Local referee associations and referee mentors do not need to wait for professional division assignments or playoff contests to train fourth officials in their duties. There should be no problem with either coach if you use the opportunity during a U-15 league game to train a younger official on what is expected of a fourth official. Train them during one game and sit back and watch them during a second game. Use those teaching moments to give them confidence. When their first official

assignment as a fourth official comes, they are ready to step up to the role with complete knowledge and an understanding of what is expected.

Assistants mirror the substitution signal

Top referees make eye contact with both assistant referees during every stoppage in play. If you are serving as the assistant referee on the side away from the team benches and notice the other assistant is signaling for a substitution that goes unobserved by the referee, mirror the signal. The referee will notice your flag, turn and initiate the substitution process.

Substitute must be ready

Before a fourth official or assistant referee signals for substitutions, the substitutes must be ready. They must be properly uniformed, near the halfway line and have their player passes available.

Field exit by player being replaced

To increase playing time, referees should encourage players being replaced to exit the field at the closest point. As soon as the player being replaced is off the field, the substitute may enter. It is becoming commonplace for departing players to come touch the hand of the entering substitute. There is no need for such action. Do not allow a team with a slim lead to waste time using that technique.

When the substitute becomes ready

Use common sense. If the substitute enters during a defensive corner kick, you might allow them to jog to a proper defensive position. Referees are not obligated to wait for a player to get into position to signal the restart. That is a courtesy many referees extend but do not allow a team with a slim lead to waste time using that technique. If a substitute walks toward a defensive position rather than jogs into place, while sitting on a 2-1 lead, call for the restart. They certainly can't say they're tired, can they?

Substitution placard by fourth official

If asked to serve as a fourth official in a competition, one of your responsibilities will be to monitor a substitute's entry into the contest. After checking the player's equipment, check the player's pass (or substitution ticket), alert the nearest assistant referee and, with both of you well back from the touchline, watch for the next stoppage in play. (Under the *Laws of the Game*, substitutes may enter at any stoppage. The competition rules may have special provisions, so know what those provisions are and follow them.) If the referee makes eye contact with the assistant referee first, the assistant gives the substitution signal and the referee will make eye contact with you. After you have eye contact, raise the placard showing the number of the departing player high above your head so it is clearly visible for all to see. Angle it so the referee has a clear view of it first, and then angle the placard so it is most visible to the departing player. Once the player is aware, slowly turn the placard so everyone can see it. As soon as the player being substituted departs the field, allow the substitute to enter. Record the entering and departing players' numbers and the game time on the fourth official's log.

Substitution

Raise the flag horizontally, well above your head, between both hands. Lower the flag as soon as the referee acknowledges your signal. If you are working without a fourth official, jog to the halfway line to supervise the player coming off the field and then allow the properly equipped substitute to step onto the field to become a player, or otherwise as instructed in the pregame discussion with the referee. Collect the player pass if appropriate.

The *NISOA Assistant Referee Duties & Responsibilities* says, "When a substitution is about to be made, both assistant referees shall indicate to the referee by raising their flags over their heads as shown. The flags shall be lowered simultaneously when the referee signals the substitutes to enter the field of play. Again, this indicates *teamwork* and gives the referee the freedom to observe the field as desired."

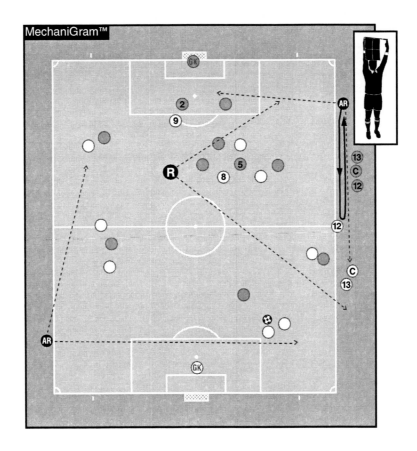

Substitution

Action on the field:

The white team desires to substitute ⑫ for ⑧. Under the *Laws of the Game*, substitution is allowed at any stoppage, with a maximum of between three and seven (depending on the rules of competition) substitutions per team.

Referee Responsibilities

Strictly adhering to the requirements in the laws prevents any problems: the referee is informed before any proposed substitution is made, the substitute enters the field after the player being replaced has left, and, upon a signal from the referee, the substitute enters at the halfway line during a stoppage in play.

Assistant Referee Responsibilities

The *Guide to Procedures* calls for the assistant referee to move to the halfway line to supervise, if instructed in the pregame discussion. If a fourth official is available, the fourth official prevents the substitute from entering the field until the player being replaced has departed the field.

    The lead assistant referee signals to the referee that the white team desires a substitution. Once the referee recognizes the signal, the assistant lowers the flag and moves to the halfway line. Inspect ⑫'s equipment and take the player pass. Once ⑧ departs the field, allow ⑫ to enter. Return to your position level with the second-to-last defender. A hint: Don't take the substitute's pass or substitution ticket until after the player being substituted departs the field.

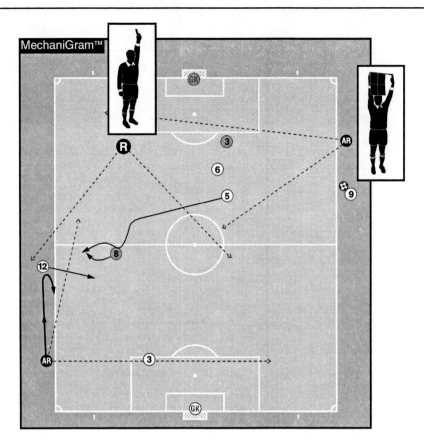

MechaniGram™

Problems with a substitution

Action on the field:

With play stopped, the white team requests a substitution, replacing ⑤ with ⑫. The trail assistant referee moves toward the halfway line to monitor the substitution but in violation of procedures, allows ⑫ onto the field before ⑤ departs the field. ⑧ taunts ⑤ as ⑤ departs the field and ⑤ pushes ⑧ to the ground with two hands. ⑧ regains his feet, runs after ⑤ and punches him from behind.

Referee Responsibilities

You display red cards to both ⑧ and ⑤ for violent conduct. Because proper procedures were not followed, the dark team continues with 10 players while the white team has 11 players. Law 3 states "a substitution is completed when a substitute enters the field of play." Once ⑫ stepped onto the field, ⑤ is no longer an acknowledged player according to law 3, which states "from that moment, the substitute becomes a player and the player he has replaced ceases to be a player." So the team who initiated the physical misconduct benefits from that referee team error.

Assistant Referee Responsibilities

Allowing ⑫ onto the field before ⑤ stepped off the field created a major game-control problem for the referee. Following the letter of the law creates an inequality in the number of players. Demanding that ⑫ depart the field so the teams play with equal numbers is in violation of law 3 regarding substitutions. Players, coaches and spectators will not understand the former course of action (11 versus 10), while the latter course of action is a technical violation of the laws leading to a protest that should be upheld.

   While that scenario is rare, the consequences are extraordinary. Establish the habit pattern of not allowing substitutes onto the field until the player being replaced has departed.

UNITED
SOCCER
LEAGUES

Substitution Pass

TEAM
EQUIPO _____

PLAYER IN
JUGADOR ENTRA _____ # _____

PLAYER OUT
JUGARDOR SALE _____ # _____

COACH
DIRECTOR _____

REFEREE
ARBITRO _____

DATE
FECHA _____ GAME TIME _____

USL substitution ticket

The United Soccer Leagues, as with many professional leagues around the world, control entry into the game by using a substitution ticket. Some youth and amateur leagues attempt to do that with the player's pass. The substitution ticket is a more definite method of control.

You can see that name and number designate the player coming off. You can also see where the team's coach must sign the ticket. Until those areas are completed, the officiating team does not activate the substitution process.

The USL allows four field players and one reserve goalkeeper to substitute in during a match. Thus, the fourth official before the game would give each team five tickets. (Hint: Initial the tickets in red or blue ink before giving them to the team. That way you know you'll only get the maximum allowed from each team.) Know the requirements for your league before the game.

Look at the ticket to be certain it is properly completed. Do not take the substitution ticket at that time. Verify the name and jersey number of the substitute is on the team roster of eligible players, given to you before the game. Check the player's equipment and uniform and make any needed corrections, such as asking the player to tuck in the jersey. Prepare your substitution placard by displaying the number of the player coming off the field. Then, get the attention of the senior assistant referee (the one on your side of the field) and notify her that one team desires a substitution at the next opportunity. Ask the substitute to join you near the halfway line, about one yard away from the touchline.

As soon as a stoppage occurs, you, the assistant and the referee will make eye contact. Following an approving signal by the referee, you'll raise the placard and the substitute will want to run onto the field. That's the reason you didn't take the substitution ticket before, and why you shouldn't take it now. Let the player coming off the field get all the way off the field before you take the ticket from the entering player. Now the substitution is complete and you may record the needed information on the fourth official's game log.

Substitutions

• Establish the habit pattern of not allowing substitutes onto the field until the player being replaced has departed.

• Strictly adhering to the requirements in the laws prevents any problems: inform the referee, the substitute enters the field after the player being replaced has left and, upon a signal from the referee, the substitute enters at the halfway line during a stoppage in play.

• Let the player coming off the field get all the way off the field before you take the ticket from the entering player. Now the substitution is complete and you may record the needed information.

• The *Guide to Procedures* advises that the assistant referee move to the halfway line to supervise, if instructed in the pregame discussion between referees.

Quiz

Without referring back, you should be able to answer the following true-false questions.

1. Once the referee recognizes the assistant's substitution signal, the assistant keeps the flag in the raised position until the substitute enters the field.

2. For a substitution signal, the assistant raises the flag horizontally, well above the head and holds the cloth portion of the flag.

3. As the fourth official, raise the substitution placard showing the number of the departing player high above your head so it is clearly visible for all to see. Angle it so the referee has a clear view of it first, and then angle the placard so it is most visible to the departing player.

1 - False, 2 - False, 3 - True

Chapter 19

Lessons Learned

"Indeed, the young referee might be well advised to look as though he knows what he is doing even when he doesn't. And the senior referee will be well advised to remember it, too." That quote, from *Soccer Refereeing* by Denis Howell summarizes our role on the field.

Training

You've been through 16 hours or more of intensive training to start your career. You attend five hours of recertification every year. The high school state association has mandatory training sessions each season to brief you on the new rules and improve consistency. You are as well versed on the laws and the proper interpretation of those laws as anyone on the soccer field. Referees in their second season, for the most part, know the rules and application of the rules better than coaches who have been around the sport for decades. Act the part.

Dress and appearance

The cliche still rings true. You only get one chance to make a first impression. If you show up at the field looking like the PlayPic at the right, what do you think the players and spectators can expect?

Errors due to lack of communication

Most errors are because referees do not communicate well. If there is any eye contact, errors happen because of poor signal technique. Most often, there is no eye contact.

Another short quote from *Soccer Refereeing* sums up the point. "Even here, when the (assistant) is certain he has seen an infringement deserving redress, he should still hesitate before waving his flag. Has the referee seen something else? Or has he seen it and intends to play the advantage? Or perhaps the referee thinks it is not an intentional foul but something incidental to the run of the game. All these are perfectly proper considerations. So, too, is the desire to interrupt the flow of the game as little as possible.

"All this is summed up in the question the good (assistant) asks himself: does the referee want my flag?

Shirt untucked, shoelaces untied and socks down around the ankles as this referee walks onto the field for the first time — what sort of performance can the players expect?

There are still too many (assistants) who never stop to ask themselves that question. I repeat, the golden rule should be: Never wave until you have first looked for the referee.

"In that fleeting moment you will have time to resolve the questions that should be asked. A great asset of the good (assistant) is to know when to stay out of the game, which is of equal importance to the ability to come into the game, though the latter virtue seems to have more adherents than the former.

"It follows from all this that the referee must have signals he can return to the (assistant), and this is something even less practiced than those from the line to the middle. If we can get (assistants) to look for the referee, then so much can be said by either a nod or a shake of the head.

"I remember running in the line at Leicester one day to Bill Ling, a commanding referee. An incident occurred which I thought was a penalty. I looked up and was about to flag but there was Bill, smiling broadly and shaking his head. He had not only seen the incident but anticipated a reaction from me too. A fine piece of refereeing! In most other cases a slight gesture with his hand will be sufficient to tell the (assistant) 'Thank you, I saw it, but we are playing on.'"

Talk too much

Most referees have a tendency to talk too much during play. A quiet word with a single player, asking play to be held up while an injured player is attended to or a single word or two to an irate coach along the touchline is helpful to game control.

Far too many referees seem like they are doing simultaneous duty as a television broadcaster — shouting out what the foul was (or worse, demonstrating it with hand gestures), why they chose to award the free kick and lengthy monologues about what might happen upon repetition. Keep it short, if words are needed at all. In many cases, those words come back to haunt you.

Improper mechanic — ball watching

Referees tend to create their own mistakes, in many cases. Players commit fouls; the ball does not commit fouls. Why do referees watch the ball?

As players and spectators, people get in the habit of watching the ball and watching action around the ball. Referees need to break that habit and focus on action ahead of the ball. Look for where the next significant action is going to take place. Referee the defense.

What clues do you need to figure out where the next significant action will take place? As soon as the ball goes high in the air, sweep the field to look for contact situations. If there are none, say a small prayer and sneak a quarter-second look at the ball; just enough to gauge the ball's direction and distance. That look should allow you to find where the ball will land, within 15 yards. Then sweep that area, looking for contact situations.

If you focus on the ball, as the referee is doing in the PlayPic, you miss significant action, such as ⑩'s arm to ❺'s throat. Spectators and teammates might see that action and scream for justice — you'll be wondering why all the commotion. After all, you didn't see any foul.

Ball watching has no benefits, only drawbacks. Break that bad habit now, if you have it.

Improper mechanic — touching players

The well-intentioned referee is committing one of the cardinal sins. Do not touch players. ⑨ reacts strongly to a foul committed by ❻, possibly by retaliating and striking ❻. The referee figures he has done well and saved a red card.

Do not open the door for any physical contact between referees and players. Let's imagine you grab ⑨ in the 16th minute of play when he is hot over a supposed foul. Later, you call a foul on him and he reacts angrily with a finger poked into your chest. Since you overlooked that one, in the 80th minute, with the score tied, you call a penalty kick against ⑨ and he comes over to you and pushes you to the ground. At the appeal hearing, ⑨ is dressed in a suit and tie and calmly explains to the board members that he thought it was OK for him to push you. After all, you pulled him by the arm earlier in the game. Six teammates come in as witnesses verifying that you pulled him by the arm. It doesn't matter what the reason is, you opened the door. Instead of the six-month suspension ⑨ should have gotten, the board considers your actions and only suspends him for one game.

Let's suppose ⑨ and ❻ are U-12 players. In a very competitive league and in a hard-fought game, you pull ⑨ by the arm. His mother sees that action and screams at you. Minutes after the game ends and you are doing your postgame with your partners, ⑨, his mother and his coach all approach you. They say they plan to file both civil and criminal charges because they all witnessed you commit child abuse and ⑨ now has unspecified nerve damage in his arm. Far-fetched? Why even open the door?

Want another example? It's 20 minutes before the game. You and your partners conducted your pregame discussion and are walking the field. You get near the home team coach, a nice person you've known for 15 years or more. You put your arm around him. You chat for a few moments and move on. You pass by the visiting coach and simply say, "Coach, your number four needs to take his earring out." How are the visiting spectators going to feel about your impartiality? Right decisions or wrong, what is the visiting coach going to think if the first two decisions go against his club? With a simple misapplied gesture, you've set yourself up for problems.

Law 18: common sense. Use it.

Dealing with injuries — the wrong way

Injured players are not uncommon. The action-filled, contact sport of soccer is going to have fouls, misconduct and wrecks that lead to players being injured. Occasionally, players will be injured seriously enough that coaches and trainers must come onto the field to deal with them, soothe them or treat them.

Assess the seriousness of the injury and if the player requires a trainer, call the trainer onto the field. Then get away from the injured player. Your task is done. You have a bigger job to do. While sweeping your eyes across the area where the injured player is down, you have to manage the rest of the game. Now is an excellent time to discuss a point with your assistant referees or clear up a misunderstanding with the official scorer.

If opponents gather to confront one another, either about the situation that led to the injury or some earlier matter, either go over there and monitor the discussion or ask them to step apart.

Many times coaches instruct players to come to the touchline for water and added advice. Allow that but remember the players must stay on the field of play. Federation 3-3-2 prohibits the coach of either team from coaching during injury treatment.

By not stepping away from the injured player, the referee in the PlayPic has stepped into a quandary. Two trainers and the coach entered the field. While the two trainers are assessing and working on the athlete, the coach discusses the decision with the referee. The coach is emotional because one of his young charges is injured. That emotion is going to come out in the discussion. In far too many cases, coaches have to be disciplined simply because the referee took an improper position. Get away. Plus, you've allowed the coach to distract you from your other duties. Inventory the field. Look at both assistant referees. Hydrate yourself.

If you are 30 yards away, and the coach passes the injured player to discuss a matter with you, simply say, "Coach, your player needs your attention now. Please attend to her." If the coach continues to approach, as you draw away from the coach toward the nearest assistant referee, say more loudly, "Coach, please tend to your injured player." If the coach persists, advise the coach you will report his misconduct. Under NCAA and Federation rules, display the yellow card.

Lessons learned

• Players commit fouls; the ball does not commit fouls. Why do referees watch the ball?

• Referees need to break the habit of watching the ball while high in the air and focus on action ahead of the ball. Look for where the next significant action is going to take place. Referee the defense.

• Do not touch players.

• In far too many cases, coaches have to be disciplined simply because the referee took an improper position. Get away. However, at some point, you have to stop "getting away" and stand your ground when the coach commits misconduct.

Quiz

Without referring back, you should be able to answer the following true-false questions.

1. Referees tend to create their own mistakes, in many cases.

2. It's OK if you get near the home team coach, a nice person you've known for 15 years or more and put your arm around him. You chat for a few moments and move on.

3. Assess the seriousness of the injury and if the player requires a trainer, call the trainer onto the field. Then get away from the injured player. Your task is done.

1 - True, 2 - False, 3 - True

Chapter 20

Reading Play

Continue to be a student of the game. Learn what techniques coaches are showing players. Attend coaching clinics to hear what coaches discuss. Watch televised and professional matches to pick up on key decisions being made by top referees.

Clinics and camps

There are a growing number of camps and clinics being offered around the country. The AYSO has an annual Super Camp in the Chicago area simply to improve refereeing at all levels from Area Referee to AYSO National Referee. NISOA has its annual camps in Elizabethtown, Pa. The USSF had its first National Referee Academy to train 11 elite referees for further work in professional soccer. Each region runs an ODP camp and brings referees in to work with mentors, instructors and assessors to improve your skills. Go.

Read books

In a sampling of books that have been in print, here are a few stories that bring to life incidents that happen on soccer fields. Reading about them ahead of time may allow you to contemplate what you might do in similar circumstances. From *The Inner Game of Soccer*, "The goalkeeper invites a particularly swift and dangerous charge if he rolls the ball in the vicinity of an opponent who will understandably grow frustrated at being teased or taunted and will try to catch the goalkeeper off guard with a quick and unexpected tackle or shoulder charge. Furthermore, it can be disastrous. I have seen at least one instance in which the forward stole the roll-out from the goalkeeper and scored."

In The Eye Of The Whistle, II: The Refereeing at the 1990 World Cup has a chapter written by former FIFA referee David Socha. In it he said, "Early in my career, a colleague explained to me that (soccer) is first of all for players, then for the spectators, clubs and leagues and, lastly, for the referee. Nobody pays to see the referee. Like any sporting event, the competition and thrill of the game is the reason why it is played. Hence, the individual who assumes the role of 'official' must acknowledge that his position is important insofar as making sure that the laws and guidelines are obeyed by the players; but it goes no further. When he lets his authority become an attitude which influences his style of officiating, he will tend to forget why he is there. Should it not be for the love of the game and the opportunity to partake in that rather than the futile attempt to display a personal need for authority? When I look back to the World Cups of yesteryear, the games were officiated by referees who truly let their individual style, personality and love for the game

guide them. Of course they were not infallible. For the most part though, they were not affected by the problem of today, where professional success and status supersedes the personal desire to obtain gratification from what gives true pleasure.

"For some, all (soccer) officials must look and act alike in order for there to be consistency. However, while general laws must be followed the applications of those laws need not be mimicked. When a referee performs to the best of his ability, and does so in a way that reflects his personality as it would be on or off the field, he will be better accepted by those involved in the game."

Quoting from the same book, Algerian ex-FIFA referee Ahmed Khelifi has written an excellent study on referees and refereeing, entitled *L'arbitrage a travers les caracteres du football*.

"At all levels of play, when it comes to dealing with situations and making decisions not in contravention of specific laws, the game would be better served by a flexible referee who is strong in psychology and player management and who makes some marginal mistakes in judgment calls but maintains game control than it would be by a rigid by-the-book automaton who makes no errors in interpretation but loses control of the match."

As Khelifi has said — among his many gems of wisdom — "The impartial referee is admirable to the extent that he permits every player to distinguish himself according to his own potential without having to be subject to violence or unsportsmanlike play. ... The impartial referee must know how to distinguish the intentional foul from an instinctive mistake if he is to intervene with authority."

Tactical awareness

You are doing yourself and the game a disservice if you do not develop a tactical awareness. That sense of the game will help your foul recognition, your positioning and your game control.

Field awareness

Know what else is going on around the field. Broaden your horizons. Eye contact with both assistants when the ball is out of play is a giant first step. When an unusual situation develops, for example, a star player suddenly is agitated after no contact, look around the field to determine the reason why — spectators shouting abusive comments, the coach is preparing a substitute to take his place in the next few minutes, etc.

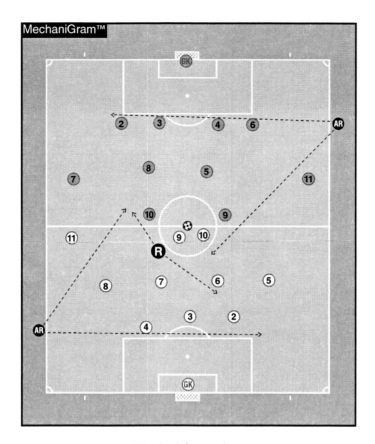

Tactical formations

Action on the field:

At the start of the game, opposing teams are lined up in different tactical formations. The dark team is in the 4-4-2, while the white team is in the more offensive 3-4-3 formation. Starting from the back, the formation numbers tell you the number of defenders, the number of midfielders and the number of strikers. Of course, the positions are not static so defenders may make runs forward and participate in the attack.

In addition, the dark-shirted team is in a flat-back four defense while the white team has a sweeper-stopper formation.

Referee Responsibilities

As a referee, if you are able to spot the team's formation, you gain valuable insight into their orientation and mindset. Carefully watch substitutions — a team with a one-goal lead late in the game is liable to substitute a defender for an attacker. That is a strong clue to you to vary your positioning.

Assistant Referee Responsibilities

Assistant referees should determine a team's defensive posture and note which defender is leading the offside strategy. If a team is playing a flat-back four, look for them to constantly challenge the offside positioning. A team with a sweeper-stopper set may go 20-25 minutes without rushing forward to create an offside-position decision and lull you into a false sense of security. When the sweeper rushes forward, you must anticipate the move and react instantly, focusing on all the relevant points in making the offside determination: respective positioning of the attacker and defender, the moment the ball is played and who played the ball.

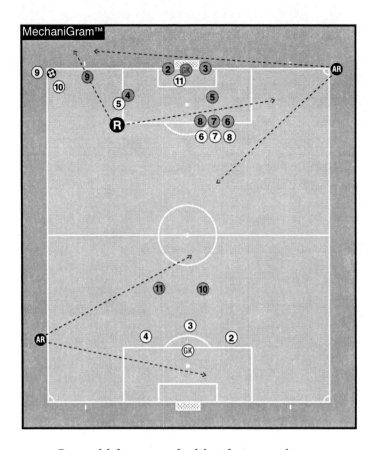

Corner kick — complexities that can arise

Action on the field:

A player takes a corner kick from the referee's side of the field. ⑩ has come over to assist, opening the possibility of a "short corner." ⑨ is defending against that and will attempt to move within 10 yards of the ball before the kick is taken. ⑤ and ④ are bumping one another as the attacking team opens the possibility of a flick-on. ⑪ is fronting the goalkeeper, often with an amount of body contact as both jostle for position. ⑥, ⑦ and ⑧ are lined up to make crossing runs to the near post, far post and penalty mark to confuse the defenders and possibly create contact situations that will leave a player unguarded.

Referee Responsibilities

This variation of the normally simple corner kick can place you in task overload due to the attacking team's strategy to complicate the defense. There is simply too much activity for you to see all in one glance, so you must prioritize your focus and react to the most probable plays. Good referees read what the players offer them — use those clues to help you successfully position yourself for the optimum view of the next significant action.

Become unpredictable in your positioning while maintaining oversight over all the essential elements: your assistant referee, the ball, the goalkeeper and those players who participate in action around the ball.

Assistant Referee Responsibilities

Attackers cannot be offside if they receive the ball directly from a corner kick. The other assistant referee must be ready to observe a counterattack. Federation assistant referees should move down the goalline to a position approximately where it intersects with the penalty area line. Move laterally to stay even with the second-to-last defender.

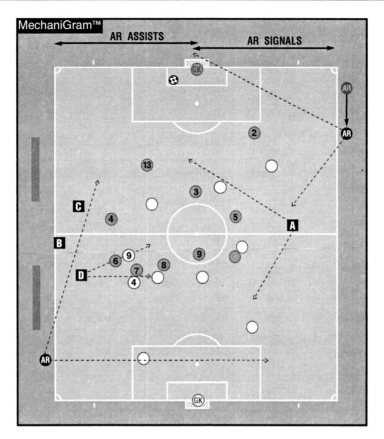

Goalkick

Action on the field:

The goalkeeper is taking a goalkick in an older-age game.

Referee Responsibilities

Read the play and find the dropping zone. Anticipate where the ball will land and get a proper angle to look through the players rather than looking at player's shoulders or backs. Positions A, B, C and D are good candidates but adjustments might be needed based on the flight of the ball. If the ball goes to **5**, **7**, **8** or **9**, position D works effectively. If the ball goes to **6**, you are looking directly into **6**'s back as **6** and **⑨** jostle for position; in addition, you are too close to the play. Moving a few steps toward the center of the field opens that angle and you have a clear view between the players.

A suggestion to assist in positioning: Stand on the side of the center circle away from the side where the goalkick is to be taken. If the goalkeeper moves the ball to the far right corner of the goal area, position A is a good starting point for most goalkicks. Increasingly position A is being recommended for all goalkicks, especially if you believe the team taking the goalkick will continue the attack. That places you on your diagonal.

Assistant Referee Responsibilities

Move to the top of the goal area to check proper ball placement. If players are near the top of the penalty area, observe the ball wholly cross outside the penalty area before it is touched. Move laterally to stay even with the second-to-last defender. If the referee has not read play well and you determine that an infringement was not or could not be seen by the referee, signal an infraction.

For games played under Federation rules, the assistant referee moves in line with the penalty area line after checking placement of the ball. Remain there to see that the ball leaves the penalty area before it is played a second time.

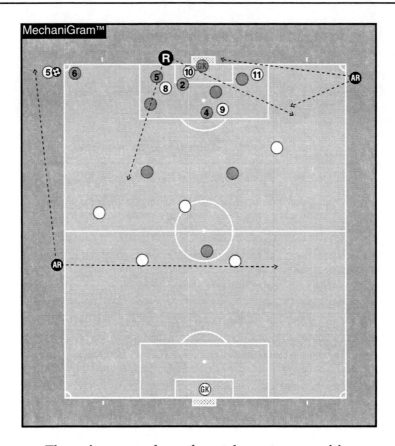

Throw-in near goal — referee takes extreme position

Action on the field:

A team uses a throw-in as an attacking weapon. A skilled player with a long throw-in can be as effective as a corner kick. Look for two types of long throw-ins: a high looping throw that a tall attacker tries to drive directly into the goal, and a line drive that an attacker at the near post tries to flick on to a teammate on the far post.

Referee Responsibilities

You might read that a long throw-in is about to take place when a particular player moves out of normal position to take the restart. Listen for a coach to call a certain player to throw. Look for the cluster of offensive players (or the target person on a line drive throw) and position yourself so you have a good angle on the next significant action.

From position R, you have an excellent view of a line drive throw to ⑧, who has three choices to flick the ball: ⑨, ⑩ or ⑪. An airborne ⑧ may fling arms and elbows into the defenders or may be pushed or pulled as the ball draws close. You have a superb, close view to see if ⑩ impedes the goalkeeper and your goal/no-goal decision will not be disputed if the ball hits the woodwork and rides the goalline. Perhaps most important, by being across the goalline you are not in the way of a shot on goal or a clearance.

The one drawback is the same as any time you take an extreme position — in case of a counterattack, you may be an extra 10-15 yards behind play and must sprint in a straight line to catch up. That straight sprint causes you to follow play and you get straightlined or flat, not being able to see diagonally through the players.

Assistant Referee Responsibilities

Be aware that a player who receives the ball directly from a throw-in, even though in an offside position, cannot be offside. Move laterally to stay even with the second-to-last defender.

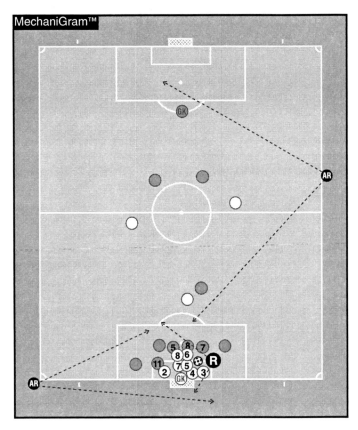

Dropped ball on goal area line

Action on the field:

An incident leading to a dropped ball (serious injury, outside agent, etc.) takes place within the goal area. The special circumstances in law 8 dictate the ball be moved to the goal area line parallel to the goalline, six yards from the goalline.

Referee Responsibilities

During those tense moments, expect much physical contact as opponents scramble for an advantageous position. Position yourself so you are facing your lead assistant referee. Drop the ball from your hands at waist level and make sure the ball touches the ground before it is touched. If it does not, redrop the ball.

The goalkeeper may participate in the dropped ball and may handle the ball immediately after it touches the ground. If it appears the goalkeeper may participate, watch closely for dangerous situations.

Assistant Referee Responsibilities

Attackers may not be offside directly from the dropped ball, so assist by watching for physical contact with so many players in close proximity. Be alert for a short pass to an attacker in an offside position. Concentrate to determine that the pass came from an attacker and not a defender trying to back-heel the ball to the goalkeeper. Goalkeepers may not handle a ball deliberately kicked to them by a teammate, but commonly, referees reserve that decision for themselves rather than seek assistant referee input.

If you are serving as an assistant and become aware that ⑧ and ⑤ or ⑥ and ⑧ have been annoying each other earlier in the match, keep a watchful eye on them as they are in close proximity. The referee has many other tasks with higher priority and may miss misconduct committed by those players. It's important for game control that the misconduct is seen and dealt with properly.

Improper mechanic — turning away from taunting opponents

During an emotional game, opponents say things to each other that further escalate bad feelings. There may be holdover feelings from a previous meeting. Several examples: One player that was on team A may be making the first appearance for team B; in the last meeting, ❺ may have faked an injury that caused ❽ to be sent off and serve a one-game suspension.

Your awareness of actions going on around you adds to match control. Opponents gesturing to each other, finger pointing, chest pounding and taunting words like, "You want some of me. Come on over here and get some," have no place in a soccer contest. Someone must observe those actions on the officiating crew. You cannot simply turn your head and walk away as opponents draw close to one another with some possibility of physical confrontation. Keep looking around. Even more challenging is when the players are speaking a language you do not understand. In such cases, it is important to watch closely the body language reactions of those who hear the words and know what they mean. Constant eye contact with your partners helps identify some of those essential match-ups early.

Inject humor into a tense situation. During the 1998 collegiate season, an assistant referee quietly passed to the referee the information that numbers 14 and 9 are jostling one another when in proximity and making comments that inflame each other. The referee hears the information clearly but says loudly, "Do you want me to watch no. 9 and no. 14?" Much more loudly the second time, the referee asks, "Are you saying you want me to watch no. 9 on the red team and no. 14 on the green team? Is that what you said?" As numbers 9 and 14 shrink in embarrassment, several players start to chuckle and the referee screams, "Are you saying that no. 9 and no. 14 are pushing each other and saying naughty things to each other. OK, I'll keep an eye on no. 9 and no. 14." Those 10 seconds broke the tension, the referee used humor to gain match control and no. 9 and no. 14 were exceptionally well behaved during the remaining 20 minutes.

Preventing the goalkeeper from releasing the ball

Goalkeepers are notorious for wasting time by holding the ball. All codes have cracked down by imposing time limits on how long a keeper may control the ball. The objective is to get the ball to the feet of the 20 field players and let their skills determine the outcome of the game. Referees are encouraged to speed play, because that makes it more enjoyable and more entertaining.

Players who attempt to block goalkeeper distributions hinder that objective. Tempers flair as goalkeepers and defenders yell at those offenders. Time ticks by as defenders yell to you to protect their keeper. The keeper holds the ball until the attacker clears away. All that yelling and no playing.

Here is where smart referees think before they act. The law is clear and specific: "An indirect free kick is also awarded to the opposing team if a player ... prevents the goalkeeper from releasing the ball from his hands." Does the defensive team want an indirect free kick from deep in its own penalty area? No. That kick puts them at a severe disadvantage. The goalkeeper loses the flexibility of rolling or throwing the ball and must kick the stationary ball from the ground instead of a punt or drop kick. That might cut 20-25 yards off the distance of a kick. Referees who automatically whistle the infraction and award the free kick, without at least warning the attackers, place undue hardship on the defense.

Communicate with the players. Without blowing your whistle, run to the players and say to the goalkeeper, "Keep, I'll give you an extra few seconds while I talk to ⑩. Don't put it in play yet." Then turn to the attacker and say, "OK, ⑩. My job is to keep the ball in play. You're preventing that. Let's see that nobody wearing a dark-colored shirt does that again today." Sprint toward midfield and call for the keeper to play the ball. With an effective warning, ⑩ will not go near the keeper and if a teammate wanders in that direction, you have an ally in helping you. ⑩ should speak up, "John, the ref said we can't do that. You better back off." Caution players who do not heed that advice.

Dummy

That tactical moves create space and time for the team with the ball. A defender guarding ⑨ assumes ⑨ will trap the ball and either begin to dribble or pass to a teammate, so the defender stops and cuts off the passing lanes. If ⑨ lets the ball run through his legs to teammate ⑦, then the defender must start from a standing stop to chase ⑦. If ⑨ lets the ball run through his legs and then chases the ball himself, ⑨ has a running start and is 15-20 yards away by the time the defender realizes it was a dummy and begins the chase.

Referees who read dummies before they happen are in much better position for the ensuing play. If you read the play will happen in front of ⑨ and alter your run or stop because you think you have reached the proper position, you will be 25 yards from the next significant action. If you are able to read the dummy and continue your run to a position behind ⑨, the play comes to you and all the angles to see between players open up for you.

How do you know if a team will use the dummy? Watch their pregame warmup. Look for the various tactical and technical skills exhibited.

Reading play — sensing a foul before it happens

At certain levels of play, you must become aware of what is going to happen and react to the next significant action. That is the moment of truth. The referee in the PlayPic is about to face a moment of truth, and from his body posture and the fact that he is walking toward play, does not know it.

Let's read what has happened so far. ⑩ has dribbled past ❾ with a sudden burst of speed, cross-footed ❼ so badly she fell down, put on a cha-cha move to get past ❺ and is riding off an aggressive challenge by ❹. What do you think ❸ is going to do when ⑩ comes a few steps closer?

There is likely going to be a foul. Clear and simple. ⑩ beat four of her teammates, ❸ knows she is the last line of defense except for the goalkeeper, knows she is outside the penalty area and knows her team has a slim lead. ❸ is going to foul ⑩. Knowing just that little, the referee ought to be jogging or sprinting toward where the foul may occur.

More than likely, ❸ is going to send a message. The message will be along the lines of, "You embarrassed four of my teammates and thought you could bring the ball in here. My coach will make me run laps until I drop if I let you through. You are going to remember this hit."

Read the tactical play and react to the situation. Tactically it makes sense to foul in that portion of the field. ❸ has to stop ⑩. If you are in ❸'s peripheral vision, it may only be a careless foul. If you are standing well away from the area of contact, the foul is likely to be much more aggressive.

Shot taken — assistant referee follows the ball to the goalline

Action on the field:
The attacking team takes a hard driven shot from a long distance.

Referee Responsibilities
Observe the shooter to make sure no defender kicks the plant leg just as the shot is being taken. Quickly glance at the assistant referee to see if there was an offside infraction. If the goalkeeper has a pattern of not cleanly catching the ball, close in toward the goalmouth to observe goalkeeper/attacker interaction.

Assistant Referee Responsibilities
Make the offside infraction judgement. Sprint toward the goalline to make goal/no-goal decisions. Watch for physical play between the goalkeeper and attackers if the ball is not cleanly held. Continue to watch as the goalkeeper distributes the ball to make certain the whole ball does not pass entirely beyond the goalline.

At top competitive levels, when you sense that a hard shot will be taken and no attacking players are close to being in an offside position, you can release a split second early to cover the more important goal/no-goal decision. You may only gain five yards in that time but the better angle allows you more credibility in selling the call.

Reading play

- As a referee, if you are able to spot the team's formation, you gain valuable insight into their orientation and mindset. Carefully watch substitutions.

- Good referees read what the players offer them — use those clues to help you successfully position yourself for the optimum view of the next significant action.

- A suggestion to assist in positioning: Stand on the side of the center circle away from the side where the goalkick is to be taken.

Quiz

Without referring back, you should be able to answer the following true-false questions.

1. Assistant referees should not concern themselves with a team's defensive posture or note which defender is leading the offside strategy.

2. Read the play and find the dropping zone. Anticipate where the ball will land and get a proper angle to look through the players rather than looking at players' shoulders or backs.

3. There are no drawbacks to taking an extreme (off the field or ahead of play) position.

4. Your awareness of actions going on around you adds to match control.

1 - False, 2 - True, 3 - False, 4 - True

Chapter 21

Foul Recognition
Indirect Free Kick

For the most part, referees easily recognize indirect free kick infractions. They are technical in nature and tend to be violations that do not involve physical contact.

Steps and seconds

Goalkeepers are allowed to take four steps, while controlling the ball with their hands, before releasing it from possession. An IFAB decision says goalkeepers are guilty of timewasting (and therefore an indirect free kick should be awarded) if they hold the ball in their hands or arms for more than five to six seconds.

No contact situations

Many violations that lead to an indirect free kick had no contact between opponents. Goalkeepers who pick up the ball after it was deliberately played back to them by a teammate's foot or who catch a ball thrown in by a teammate violate a technical aspect of the game. When a player who restarts the game (via throw-in, corner kick, kickoff, etc.) touches the ball directly after the restart, award an indirect free kick. Successive touches that include the restart are not allowed. But again, there has been no contact between opponents.

With contact, the nature of the foul changes

It is an indirect free kick to prevent goalkeepers from releasing the ball from their hands. If an opponent blocks or impedes them, you would award the indirect free kick. But if the opponent holds the goalkeeper to prevent the release, you would call holding and award a direct free kick. If a forward raises a leg to chest level to play the ball, while an opponent who was trying to chest trap the ball is nearby, you might consider the action dangerous play if the opponent is prevented from playing the ball by the forward's actions. But if the forward kicks the opponent in the chest, the nature of the foul has changed to kicking. Award a direct free kick in that contact situation.

Read the play — it varies with level

Most of you started out refereeing U-8 and U-10 games. They were recreational and they were fun for you and the participants. Given that competitive level, an extra stoppage or two for a mistakenly called dangerous play did not hurt the outcome of the game. Most coaches and parents were happy to hear your whistle on those dubious decisions. They could use your whistle as a teaching point to train the youth what the allowable limits to the game look like in execution.

With advancing age and skill level, your whistle on a doubtful dangerous play situation becomes a distraction, an irritant. As you progress in levels, your ability to separate the truly dangerous from the category of, "Gee, that looked bad," becomes more important. Read these next few pages carefully. They may open a new vista to your foul recognition skills. If you disagree vehemently with what is written here, it shows you care enough to dissect the game. Discuss your questions with a senior referee, a mentor or an instructor until you understand the points that go into picking up the elements of each infraction.

Learning what not to call

As you progress in soccer officiating, you are increasingly defined by your ability to decide quickly which actions are not a foul, which actions are doubtful or trifling fouls, which actions are fouls but play should not be stopped (advantage) and when to stop play immediately. That is known as "call sorting" and is a critical element in assessing your ability to perform at higher competitive levels. Often, newer officials refer to that as knowing when to make no-calls but experienced referees understand that every decision about which player actions fall into which of those four categories is in fact a call. Would you punish a goalkeeper for not releasing the ball after 6.1 seconds? At the professional level, I hope not. Get the message passed to that goalkeeper that play needs to speed up. Perhaps at the next corner kick opportunity, as one team is running to fetch the ball, you might jog by the keeper and say, "When you hold the ball that long you're asking me to make a decision. If you get rid of it quickly, I've got no decision to make."

Use your personality. Use humor. Make deals and bargain with players to not commit those technical violations. Use tools you pick up inside referee tents at tournaments. Use whatever you can to prevent those interruptions in play. Get on them the first time they occur and wipe them out of your games.

Are you coaching? No. You will do the same for the other team as well. You are not creating an imbalance between the teams via your comments — you are increasing the playing time by preventing interruptions and adding to game flow.

Even the experts disagree

Denis Howell, a veteran of the Football Association, says in *Soccer Refereeing*, "Some referees I know look for fouls early on so that they can clearly demonstrate who is in charge. I myself liked to get the feel of the game, like a goalkeeper who is on edge until he has played the ball, but in my view a referee has no more right to create a foul in the opening stages of a match in order assert his authority than he has at any other time." *Fair or Foul* offers these words, "Look carefully for that first foul. How and when you see it and how you handle it will make a difference for the remainder of the game. You should be the first one on the field to anticipate that foul. If you referee like [former professional player and NASL referee] Gordon Hill, you will know a lot about fouls before they happen. Once Hill even stopped an important match because he knew what a player was *thinking* of doing."

Dangerous play
Straight-legged tackle — no contact

Various cultures react differently to what you see in the PlayPic. Some say ❺ is aggressively playing for the ball. Most will say that even if there is no contact, ❺ is committing a serious infraction.

Analyzing the PlayPic, we see ❺ is coming toward ❷ with cleats up, a raised leg and the knee locked. ❷ is swinging his leg from right to left across his body to play the ball, probably with great momentum if that is a shot, cross or clearance. If there is contact, what's going to happen?

❷ will kick the upraised cleats. Assuming it hits a hard surface like the bottom of ❷'s shoe or shinguards, the contact will cause discomfort. If contact is on the shoe top or above or to the side of the shinguard, the injury potential is high. If ❷ has significant momentum in his leg swing, a lot of force must be overcome. Since ❺ has his knee locked, is there any give? None. That means ❷ must overcome ❺'s entire body weight. That is also unlikely, so the most likely scenario is for ❷ to get a compound fracture of the lower leg. What you are seeing is a very dangerous situation.

During my tenure in semi-professional soccer in Germany, if any player on the field used that technique, 21 players on the field would yell — teammates as well as opponents. Latin players will comment to you if you do not penalize that infraction — contact or not. Since the potential for a season-long or career-long injury is so high, you must blow the whistle every time you see a leg in that position, going toward an opponent.

Do not confuse legitimate attempts to defend against a shot with the PlayPic above. If players are side by side and ❺ raises a leg to defend against a cross, there would be no danger to ❷. Even if ❺ stretched as far as possible and locked his knee, the parallel angle of the legs minimizes danger.

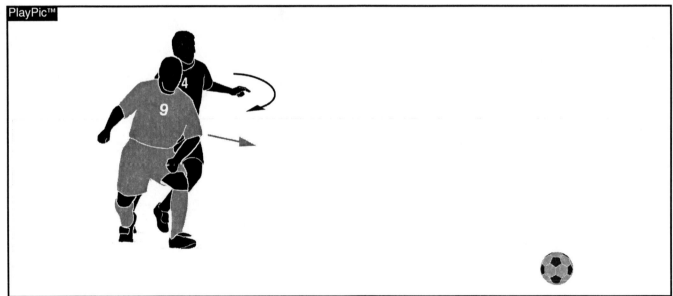

Impeding an opponent

In a scene replicated hundreds of times during a soccer match, opponents use their bodies to attempt to gain an advantage, keep possession of the ball and create time and space. In attempting to distinguish fair from foul, there are a few essential points you must observe.

Is the ball within playing distance? *Advice to Referees* 12.15 provides a guideline of two strides at the speed ⑨ is moving. In the PlayPic, ⑨ is almost five yards from the ball, clearly outside playing distance.

Is there physical contact? ⑨ moves back and forth, moving slowly to keep his body between the ball and the opponent. At that point, ⑨ is obstructing, interfering with and blocking the path of ❹. Once physical contact occurs, initiated by ⑨, you should consider the direct free kick offense of charging an opponent. *Advice to Referees* 12.22 allows you to consider an offense written into older versions of the *Laws of the Game*, charging an opponent away from the ball.

What you see in the PlayPic, with the ball five yards from the players, is an illegal act. If ❹ reacts to the impeding by charging recklessly or violently into ⑨'s back or uses both arms to throw ⑨ to the side, then the impeding foul will be on ⑨ and you should caution or send off ❹, depending on the level of violence in his actions.

Goalkeeper possession

As little as a single finger is sufficient for goalkeeper possession of the ball. Even though the goalkeeper is at full extension and has only one hand or arm on the ball, if the attacker kicks the ball out of the keeper's possession, award a direct free kick to the defense. Law 12, IFAB decision 3 and *Advice to Referees* 12.16 include parrying the ball, bouncing the ball and throwing the ball in the air as possession.

Law 12 restricts goalkeepers to five-to-six seconds before they release the ball into play. In the PlayPic above, do not begin timing those seconds the instant the keeper controls the ball. To be fair, allow the goalkeeper to attain an upright position before timing the release.

It is USSF policy that no hand gesture or verbal count signify how much time has passed. Normally you will warn the keeper once before awarding an indirect free kick for the technical violation. You will see referees in the National Professional Soccer League (NPSL) make obvious hand gestures marking the seconds. Unless you are refereeing in the NPSL, make no such gestures.

Dangerous play

Mistakenly called high kicking by many, the potential for injury exists whenever feet come in close proximity to heads. It may also occur when heads sink too low to the ground, trying to play the ball in an area where most players would use their feet. Since safety is one of the three major tenets of the spirit of the game, you must stop play and penalize the person who creates the dangerous situation.

Advice to Referees 12.13 lists three important criteria to help you determine if dangerous play should be whistled: the action must be dangerous to someone, it was committed by an opponent close by, and the dangerous nature of the action caused the opponent to cease active play for the ball or be otherwise disadvantaged.

As ❺ realizes ❽'s leg is coming up, ❺ reacts by drawing her arm in to protect her body and retracts her head and neck to avoid injury. Had ❽ not lifted her foot so high, ❺ would have headed the ball toward the goal or a teammate. ❽'s actions put ❺ and the dark team at a disadvantage, so you must stop play and award an indirect free kick.

That points out a rule difference between the various codes of play. Under the *Laws of the Game* and NCAA rules, if ❺ and ❽ were teammates, there would not be a stoppage. Under Federation rules, that is an offense and the opposing team would be awarded an indirect free kick.

PlayPic™

Dangerous play

In the late stages of a tie game, ⑩ will do almost anything to put the ball into the goal, including sacrifice his body. That desperation leads to unthinking acts, such as placing himself in danger of being hurt.

❽ readies himself for a long clearance hoping to get the ball away from his own goal and start a counterattack. He focuses solely on the ball. He may not even be aware of ⑩ coming in from the side. The thought is: "Kick it and kick it hard." If a head appears at the last second, ❽ may or may not be able to stop his kicking motion.

If you witness ❽ withhold his kicking motion because of ⑩'s actions, based on the criteria on the preceding page, ⑩ committed an illegal action. You must restore the balance by allowing the dark-shirted team an indirect free kick.

Foul recognition — indirect free kick

• Various cultures react differently to the cleats up, raised leg and knee locked tackle. Whistle it at every opportunity, contact or not, if the leg is coming toward an opponent. If the players and legs are parallel, there is little chance of danger or injury.

• Goalkeeper possession includes parrying the ball, bouncing the ball and throwing the ball in the air.

• It is USSF policy that no hand gesture or verbal count signify how much time has passed while the goalkeeper is holding the ball. Normally you will warn the keeper once before awarding an indirect free kick for the technical violation.

Quiz

Without referring back, you should be able to answer the following true-false questions.

1. To help decide playing distance situations, *Advice to Referees* provides a guideline of four strides at the speed a player is moving.

2. Opponents may not use their bodies to attempt to gain an advantage, keep possession of the ball and create time and space.

3. As little as a single finger is sufficient for goalkeeper possession of the ball.

1 - False, 2 - False, 3 - True

Chapter 22

Foul Recognition
Direct Free Kick

Awarding a direct free kick to a team restores the balance created by an opponent's unfair actions. If you are aware of the situations when an illegal action creates the imbalance, and act to undo that wrong, you will perform you job as requested. Sometimes, more than a simple direct free kick is required but those instances will be covered in Chapter 25, Misconduct.

Sensitivity

All phases of the game are not the same. Games played by the same team demand different referee styles. For example, you might referee the same team two weekends in a row. The first weekend they are mannerly and compliant as they lose, 1-0. The next weekend, playing their bitter crosstown rivals, they pull out all the stops and are cumbersome, crude and vicious in their physical play. You need to be sensitive to those differences. Likewise, you need to be aware that fouling patterns change during the game.

Extracted from *In The Eye Of The Whistle, II: The Refereeing at the 1990 World Cup*, "It is obvious that, in the 52 matches taken as a whole, the 20 to 30 minute span was the most critical moment in the first half, in the sense that the greatest concentration of misconduct incidents occurred in that period."

"Were the outbursts caused by players straining every muscle to score or to prevent opponents form scoring, or did they occur because referees tired and/or relaxed too soon before terminating play?"

"For their part, having contained the customary explosions, referees may have relaxed too soon or they may simply have tired, with the result that they were not as able to contain late offenses as they ought to have been.

"Did goals, fouls, penalty kicks, etc., have a significant effect on the conduct of players as time started to run out? Was the effect greater on teams that were facing elimination from the tournament?"

"Did the apparent leniency of referees early in each half lead to a build-up of tensions and feelings that surfaced in the final five minutes of that half? Expressed another way, how effective were some of the early warnings and cautions in preventing subsequent more serious incidents?"

"Did playing conditions sometimes deteriorate in the second half, thus affecting the poise and control of players? On this question, one should note that many of the games in the tournament were played on very hot days when the humidity was also uncomfortably high, and that three players were dismissed between the 83rd and 89th minute, whereas one was ordered off in the 109th minute."

New tricks

Instead of performing the usual and easily spotted forward dive, attackers are attempting an interesting ploy. In a run for the ball against a fast defender, and once they realize they are not going to win the foot race, they grab the defender's shirt. They then thrust their own body against the defender's body hard enough to get slammed to the ground — hoping to get the call. It's extremely difficult to spot on the field. The result is a very advantageous direct free kick just outside the penalty area.

The speed of play

Interviewing FIFA and National Referees, the theme I hear most often is how they had to adjust to the speed of play. While foot speed is an important aspect in the speed of play, it is more the decision-making that separates the upper levels of play. Top players guess whether they can toe-poke a ball away and either attack or fall back to yield space slowly. Whereas youth players may have to take four moves and three seconds to settle a cross, look up, knock the ball out in front of themselves and cross the ball, a skilled professional does that in two touches in less than a second.

In defense, a youth player might challenge in a clumsy manner and it is obvious to everyone there was an unfair challenge for you to whistle. At the professional level, a fast-moving blur simultaneously bumps the plant leg to throw off the opponent's timing, gets a small grab on the shirt to unbalance the opponent and while falling, gets an outstretched leg on the ball, knocking it toward a teammate. The youth example took 1.3 seconds to develop, the professional example is over in .6 seconds. If you are not used to seeing that speed of play, those .7 seconds spell trouble for you.

Focus

Many referees focus too high. Drop your focus to mid-thigh and you will see more of the playing action that needs your attention. Watch for little flicks of the foot that strike an opponent's heel. Watch the play after the ball goes away. The ball won't foul anyone.

If you don't see the foul, you can't recognize it. If you are already looking upfield by the time the foul takes place, you will miss the illegal action. If you miss too many, tempers flare and you might lose game control.

Kicking

As 🄼 throws his body into defense in a desperation slide tackle, the potential for serious injury exists. 🄼 started his tackle too late or too close to 🄼. 🄼 has strong lateral momentum and will not contact the ground until he is under where 🄼 is standing now. The wide expanse of 🄼's body leaves 🄼 little escape. All 🄼 can hope to do is get airborne before contact to minimize injury. If 🄼's cleats are buried in the grass as 🄼 makes contact, the torsion on the ankles and knees is extreme.

That mis-timed tackle is at least reckless (unnatural movement designed to intimidate an opponent) and might be an example of a player using excessive force (placed the opponent in considerable danger of bodily harm). The key to watch for in determining excessive force is to watch 🄼's hips as he starts the tackle. If he throws the hips upward, into the opponent, he is after the opponent's body. If the hips drop toward the ground, where the ball is, he simply mis-timed the tackle while playing for the ball.

Referees no longer judge a player's intent. We don't know if 🄼 wanted to hurt 🄼 or just clumsily started the tackle one step too late. You simply make your judgement based on what you see the player do. Here, 🄼 was high and late and that is a foul. The determination that the foul was reckless or used excessive force leads to the display of a misconduct card.

Inevitably, players will exclaim, "But ref, I got the ball." *Advice to Referees* 12.8 is clear: "Making contact with the opponent after touching the ball while performing a tackle does not necessarily mean that a foul has not been committed. *The declaration by a player that he has in fact played the ball is irrelevant if, while tackling for the ball, the player carelessly, recklessly or with excessive force commits any of the prohibited actions."*

Unfair charge — jumping at an opponent

Fouls occur when one player is playing the ball and the opponent is playing the man. The PlayPic shows the dark-shirted player focused on the airborne ball, going straight up to play the ball. ❹ has his head down, focused on ❾'s torso and jumping into ❾ at an angle.

If ❾ is contacted before the ball gets there, his header will be misdirected, causing him a disadvantage. If ❾ is contacted after he heads the ball away, he still has his ribs and torso exposed to the onrushing opponent, potentially causing injury. In either case, it is a foul (jumping at an opponent), so award a direct free kick.

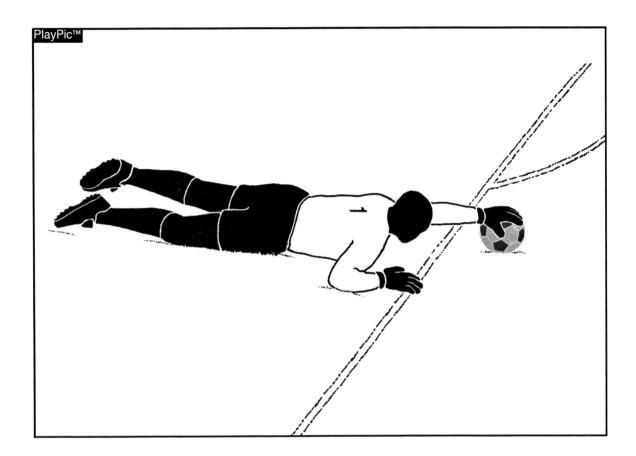

Goalkeeper within penalty area reaches outside to play a ball

The position of the player does not matter. The only consideration you judge to determine if the goalkeeper commits an infraction is the position of the ball with respect to the line. If the ball wholly crosses outside the penalty area line, whether on the ground or in the air, and is then touched by the goalkeeper, it is deliberately handling the ball. Award a direct free kick to the attacking team from outside the penalty area.

The fact that the goalkeeper is mostly inside the penalty area does not allow him to play the ball. The assistant referee must also get an angle to view the play. Do not let the player's body block your view. Do not guess that the ball is wholly outside the penalty area — if you are not certain it is outside, allow play to continue.

Handling the ball

An airborne ⑩ does not have the confidence in his skill to cleanly chest trap the ball, so he extends his right arm to engulf and cradle the ball so it falls to the ground within playing distance.

That is an advantage not allowed under the *Laws of the Game*. Penalize it with a direct free kick. Some players, to prove their innocence, will point to a muddy spot on the center of their chest. If you had watched pregame warmups, you would know that spot came from five minutes before kickoff.

Chest trap — deliberately handling the ball

Some younger players have not yet developed the skill to cleanly chest trap a ball and have it fall to their feet. Some skilled players in tense situations feel compelled to make a well-executed trap, so they forget the basic techniques. Some coaches teach the technique demonstrated in the PlayPic. What you see is a deliberate handling of the ball.

Advice to Referees 12.9 says deliberate handling "means that the player could have avoided the touch but chose not to, that the player's arms were not in a normal playing position at the time or that the player deliberately continued an initially accidental contact for the purpose of gaining an unfair advantage." Here we see ❻ having his arms in an unnatural playing position to funnel the ball to the ground. Whistle a direct free kick in favor of the opponents.

Unnatural arm motions

Players in a wall are there to defend against goals. Staring down the barrel of a direct free kick from 10 yards away brings fear to many. Both male and female players will station their arms to protect vulnerable body parts. That pre-positioning is unlikely to produce an infringement.

Using the definition of deliberate contact in *Advice to Referees* 12.9, it "means that the player could have avoided the touch but chose not to, that the player's arms were not in a normal playing position at the time or that the player deliberately continued an initially accidental contact for the purpose of gaining an unfair advantage."

If ❺ or ❾ are struck by that direct free kick in the arms, it should not be whistled. However, if ❻ were struck anywhere along the hands or arms, it would be the offense of deliberately handling the ball because the arms are not in a normal playing position. ❼ and ⓫ form the middle ground — parts of their arms are in a normal playing position, but their forearms are thrust out to the side to make their bodies wider.

Coaches are teaching that technique and referees need to be aware that players willfully try to take advantage. Here the dark-shirted team has made a wall that is six bodies wide with only five players. The defenders fill the gaps and creases with hands and forearms. That leaves one extra defender available to cover an attacker, giving a significant advantage.

Handling the ball — unnatural hand position

Very young players may react instinctively to protect themselves as a ball moves in their direction. Referees should evaluate that reflex action in judging deliberate handling offenses.

The PlayPic above shows experienced, amateur players with years of playing experience. ❸ has seen hundreds or thousands of balls come at him, so any hand or arm movement on his part is intentional. In this example, ❸ knows he does not have the skill to cleanly thigh trap the ball and have it fall within playing distance. He also started to raise his leg a bit late as ⑨ made his crossing kick. ❸ needs help not intended by the laws. He's smart enough not to handle the ball directly but if he can get a thigh on it and rebound it up to his arm, he can claim he didn't mean to handle the ball. Don't fall for it.

Advice to Referee 12.9 gives three essential considerations to help you judge the deliberate actions by players. Could the player avoid the touch? Were the arms in an unnatural position? Did the player continue accidental contact to gain an advantage?

❸'s arm should be going much higher to steady his balance. Try this. Whistle the infraction once early in the game against ❸. Then watch to see how he adjusts on a similar play later in the game. ❸ will make the needed adjustments to defend against the cross without handling the ball. He knows you caught him at his first trick, so he will work harder to play the ball fairly.

Striking or attempting to strike

Airborne battles between opponents are exciting to watch. Players who are strong in the air are a valuable commodity to a team. Lightning quick goals can result from a single cross to a well-placed header to the back of the net.

Players who are less skilled in the air resort to various tactics to counter such opponents. In our PlayPic, ❺ goes up with an elbow into ㉑'s ribs. Even the attempt to strike is punishable by a direct free kick. If you deem the act reckless, award the direct free kick plus a caution. If the act uses excessive force, award the direct free kick plus a send off.

❺ is also demonstrating another tactic used by defenders to deny space and punish airborne players. See how his right leg is well forward of his body. ❺ might be lucky enough to trick the referee into calling a foul on ㉑. ❺ is hoping that some contact with that leg is enough to throw off ㉑'s timing and cause the header to miss the target. At a minimum, ㉑ will not have sufficient space to land without contacting ❺'s leg, which will cause ㉑ to fall and contact the ground. There is the potential that after a couple of those, ㉑ may lose the resolve to go airborne if ❺ is in the area. Thus, the light-colored team loses a potent offensive weapon — because you did not do your job and protect the skills of an attacking player playing fairly.

Goalkeeper — jumping at the opponent

All too often, the scene looks like the PlayPic above. Changing any one of a number of elements can create that picture. The attacker puts on a late burst of speed, the attacker changes the angle of the attack at the last moment, the keeper is wrong-footed and has to take an extra step to dive to the proper side, the keeper's reactions just aren't fast enough to cope with the attack — any of those elements can create the scene in the PlayPic.

In looking at the PlayPic, a moment frozen in time in a dynamic play, hopefully you agree it is careless and thus, a foul. Most will agree it is reckless and thus misconduct meriting a yellow card. The arguments start when you consider if that is excessive force, or using intentional violence. If you decide it is excessive force, then it is serious foul play (the ball is in play, the foul is against an opponent while challenging for the ball and the foul occurred on the field) and a sending off is called for.

What factors can you look for to help you decide? Players' age and competitive level. Weather conditions. Past meetings between those teams and their record of misconduct when playing each other. Comments made earlier in the game between the keeper and opponents. Score. For example, if the ball that is rolling into the goal makes the score 4-0, and the keeper figures by wiping out one opponent, the next time down they'll be less likely to take him on, it can be argued he used excessive force.

Trying to decide from one PlayPic is exceptionally difficult. You need to evaluate the whole play and be a part of the action from start to finish to know exactly what to do. That needs to run through your mind when you see that scene happen on a field: "I know I'm going to caution the keeper. What else has he done so far to help me decide if he should stay in the game?" It's a difficult choice you have to make. Many will say leave him in the game, he's only doing his job. Others contend his actions injured the opponent who must miss next week's game — maybe the keeper should miss next week's game also.

The classic 8 versus 5 header

Certain national styles of play dictate a large number of headers in the midfield area. The ball is whacked long toward the corner flag, a winger tries to chase it down before it goes over the goalline and the attacker's job is to whack a cross into the mixer. Tall teammate ❺ waits there to knock it into the net while his nemesis ⑧ is there to prevent the score. When two teams play that same attacking style, it is not unusual to see that situation many times in a match.

Look at the PlayPic. It's nearly impossible to judge who commits an infraction, isn't it? Often, there will be no infraction, just two players going hard to the ball. However, what are we faced with here? ⑧ is still on the ground while the ball is almost two feet above his head. ⑧ is not looking at the ball but is instead focused on his opponent's torso. ❺ has jumped straight up to where the ball will be and focuses intently on the ball. But ❺ has let his hands wander over 8's shoulders. ❺, with even the slightest forward momentum, will crash into ⑧'s back, possibly causing ⑧ to fall to the ground.

If you struggle with those situations, do not feel alone in your dilemma. The key is to watch the defense and watch the player's eyes. Too many referees watch the flight of the ball. The ball will not foul anyone. By watching the ball, you are missing critical information. Did ⑧ try to jump for the ball but ❺'s early leap prevented the play on the ball? Foul on ❺. Was ⑧ watching the flight of the ball the entire time and only stayed on the ground because ❺'s hands on his shoulders kept him on the ground? Foul on ❺. Did ⑧ look to see where ❺ was, then stay on the ground and move his hips back just slightly to "bridge" or trip ❺? Tripping foul on ⑧. Did ⑧ mistakenly leap too soon and returned to the ground as ❺ plays the ball cleanly? No-call.

Look for those situations on crosses into the mixer, corner kicks and long throw-ins. Be especially alert as tall defenders come forward or coaches scream for certain position changes on set plays. Run harder to see through the players in the dying seconds of a close game as a team tries to score the tying or go-ahead goal goal.

Tripping

A commonly missed infraction upsets skilled players and may lead to a loss of game control and dissent. A tall player goes airborne to head the ball to a teammate or into goal and a shorter player moves under the opponent and uses his body to upset or upend the taller opponent. Known as "bridging" or "making a back," that infraction is actually tripping, as much as reaching out a foot and contacting an opponent's leg while running.  ⑤ will fall awkwardly with large torsion forces on his back. The potential for serious injury is great.

Until referees gain enough experience to recognize that foul, what they see is a large player above a smaller player. When both players hit the ground, they mistakenly award a direct free kick to the dark-shirted team.

Let's analyze the PlayPic to look for several key points: ⑤ is looking directly at the ball and has already played the ball, ❽ is turned away from the ball; ⑤ went straight up in his own vertical space, ❽ is off balance and will fall down if ⑤ is not there to block his fall; ⑤ has control over his body, ❽ is flailing his arms to keep from falling; ❽ hooked ⑤'s arm in one more effort to throw off the timing and have the header go off target. Seeing each of those aspects frozen in time, you can understand why ⑤ might dissent if you award a direct free kick to ❽ and the dark-shirted team.

Making a back, bridging or tripping

Those who have played the game call it making a back, those who follow the *Laws of the Game* call it tripping, but everyone should call it unfair. That is a particularly dangerous foul for, as you can see, ⑧ is in for a hard landing.

⑧ simply went airborne to head the ball. He had some awareness that a defender was nearby and was prepared for some shoulder-to-shoulder contact just as the ball was coming in. That is the way to play the game, challenging for the ball.

❺ chose a different route. He knows he's not capable in the air, knows he's shorter than ⑧ and realizes he doesn't have the better angle. So rather than challenge fairly by jumping to play the ball, he shuffles his feet six inches to the rear to make sure of a couple of things. ❺ wants the referee to give his team the ball even if ⑧ scores off the header, wants ⑧ to be distracted on every future header and wants ⑧ to have to play with a sore shoulder or hip because of the fall.

All too often, when the whistle blows, getting exactly what he wants rewards ❺. If you referee the defense, you saw that ❺ made no effort to play the ball, ❺'s eyes focused solely on the attacker and ❺ shuffled his feet six inches to the rear to guarantee contact.

It is a hard call to sell. Every player in a dark jersey will scream incredulously, coaches and spectators will go frantic and openly question your sanity. The correct call can be even harder to sell if ⑧ acts to prevent falling. Once airborne and tripped, ⑧ is going to reach out for anything that will break the fall. The first thing available is ❺'s back. Therefore, to everyone else, it appears that ⑧ is pushing ❺ in the back. If ❺ is smart enough, he will crumble in a heap and feign a near-death experience. Now it's really a hard call to sell.

Can you understand why it has become so popular to call the foul against ⑧? Be strong. Don't do it.

Pushing — making a back

Young players tend to commit that foul. They fear that if they defend while facing the player, they might get hurt. Many players simply turn their back and push the opponent with their lower back, while a smaller percentage will thrust their lower legs toward the opponent and make contact with the feet before pushing with the lower back.

When ❻ drops her right leg and pushes rearward with her lower back, there is going to be significant impact from the momentum. In a small percentage of cases, it knocks the wind out of the opponent.

A couple of calls early in the game and early in the season will prompt the coach to work intensively with any youngsters still committing that foul. It soon cleans itself up as players move up in age brackets and competitive levels.

Recognizing that foul may cause an adjustment in your game. Many referees do not watch for that action so it will be a change to what they are currently doing. There is one other complicating factor — ⑧'s reactions to ❻ moving toward her. If you notice the first instance in the match, you might see ⑧ put her arms on ❻'s back to absorb some of the shock. You might also see a small retaliatory shove after the initial contact. Most likely, you won't see the first incident in the game and ⑧ will remember the first contact. She'll be more aware of ❻'s play and prepare herself for the contact. The foul is still on ❻, in most cases, with ⑧ just preparing to absorb some of the force. Of course, supporters of the dark-shirted team won't see it that way. In some small percentage of cases, ⑧ will be the player responsible for the contact or will recklessly drive her arms into ❻'s back.

Tackle from behind, which endangers the safety of an opponent

⑳ is about to suffer the worst of all possible fouls. He is about to feel ❺'s cleats in the unprotected flesh of his upper calf, with no awareness that the contact is about to occur. That is potentially a career-ending injury. At a minimum, there will be pain from the resulting contact. Nevertheless, with ⑳'s forward momentum, and the momentum added by ❺, he will fall heavily on his sternum and face. If he twists to avoid such a hard landing, he subjects himself to broken arms and collarbones. None of those is a pleasant prospect.

Stop the thuggery. Be absolutely certain it does not happen a second time in a game you are refereeing. It's bad enough that a player may contemplate doing it once, but if you show everyone that the consequences are severe, and that you are upholding the law as written, you will red card the first offender.

As a result, players respect you more. Even ❺'s teammates may have a kind word for you after sending him off for a foul of that nature. Your games will be more flowing. You will have more creative runs by skilled players. You find the average goals per game increases. Games are more fun if you take care of business and send off players who commit fouls of the sort pictured above.

Foul tackle

If a player tackles an opponent to gain possession of the ball but makes contact with the opponent before touching the ball, award a direct free kick. The referee is perfectly positioned to see ❺ sweep the legs out from under ⑧ without making any contact with the ball. That is not one of the fouls that you must decide was done in a careless or reckless manner or with excessive force. *Advice to Referees* 12.2 says referees "need only decide if the act occurred."

❺ was alongside ⑧ when the tackle began, so it is within ⑧'s peripheral vision. Although that may be characterized as a hard tackle, it should not be construed as a tackle from behind which endangers the safety of an opponent. You should be aware of the cultural differences regarding player's acceptance of those heavy tackles. As you begin to move up to more competitive levels of adult play, discuss those differences with a trusted referee, mentor or instructor.

The referee should continue running until he arrives at the spot of the foul. That helps prevent retaliation and gives ⑧ the feeling that you are nearby to offer protection. Perhaps a quiet word to both players as they untangle their legs and get up might be in order.

Tripping — the need to watch the whole play

Slide tackles are an exciting element of a well-played soccer match. In the PlayPic, the attacker has broken away, has some real estate in front of him to execute his magic and a defender races in to make a last-ditch effort. Law 12 is clear on two important points: a tackle from behind, which endangers the safety of an opponent, must be sanctioned as serious foul play (red card); and, while tackling an opponent to gain possession of the ball, making contact with the opponent before touching the ball is a direct free kick offense.

A vital skill to develop as you move to more competitive levels of play is to watch the whole play. In the PlayPic above, many referees would follow the path of the ball, missing the foul that is going to occur almost four-tenths of a second later.

❹ came in with a perfectly executed slide tackle with his right leg and just nicked the ball, pushing it slightly to the left, away from his goal. So far so good. If the referee looks away now, the referee will have a picture in his mind of ⑨'s right leg on the ground in front of ❹, ❹'s right leg on the ground having pushed the ball away and the goalkeeper rushing out to clear the ball.

In a typical example, ❹ has been trained to stop attackers from getting to his goal. The last time an attacker got through to score, the coach substituted and benched him. The time before that, an attacker timed a perfect leap, got over ❹, and scored the tournament-winning goal. No one is getting past ❹. He thinks he got the ball but it was with the bottom of his cleat, so he may not have felt the slight touch. As ⑨ lifts his left leg to step over ❹, ❹ also lifts his left leg, hooking ⑨'s instep and causing the catastrophic flight you see here.

Focus on the play until the play is over.

Tripping

The governing bodies are trying to make soccer more attractive by allowing more attacking play and restricting crude defensive play. Under the mantra that "Defense wins championships," coaches and skilled players are learning new techniques to make sure that defenders stop strikers before they reach their target. At the youngest ages and in recreational play, obvious fouls are clear. Referees whistle those infractions. Most contact comes because of clumsy play from players still learning how to perfect their techniques.

Competitive play brings new challenges for referees with experience. The tackle above by ⑯ starts out clean — the tackle with the left leg. ⑯ made first contact with the ball and ⑨ is slightly off balance because of forward momentum. Watch the whole play.

Among the principles of soccer such as width and space, one principle is immediate re-attack — if you lose the ball, get it back right away. An off-balance ⑨ will recover and challenge ⑯ for the ball in the time it takes ⑯ to stand upright and make a pass. However, if ⑨ were also on the ground, ⑯ could stand, look for an open teammate and make a well-executed pass. For example, ⑯ could swing his right leg into the back of ⑨'s heels, with the scissors action of ⑯'s legs bringing ⑨ to the ground. Now ⑯ has the needed time and space. Watch the play after the ball leaves the area.

Only a referee who watches the whole play will catch that illegal action. Dark-shirted teammates will argue that ⑯ got the ball first. Agree with them. It's very disarming to attempt to argue with someone who agrees with you. Then simply say, "Did you watch his right leg? I did."

Kicking or attempting to kick

Various cultures react differently to what you see in the PlayPic. Some say ❺ is just aggressively playing for the ball. Most will say that even if there is no contact, ❺ is committing a serious infraction.

Analyzing the PlayPic, we see ❺ is coming toward ❷ with cleats up, a raised leg and the knee locked. ❷ is swinging his leg from right to left across his body to play the ball, probably with great momentum if that is a shot, cross or clearance. If there is contact, what's going to happen?

❷ will kick the upraised cleats. Assuming it hits a hard surface like the bottom of ❷'s shoe or shinguards, the contact will cause discomfort. If contact is on the shoe top or above or to the side of the shinguard, the injury potential is high. If ❷ has significant momentum in his leg swing, a lot of force must be overcome. Since ❺ has his knee locked, is there any give? None. That means ❷ must overcome ❺'s entire body weight. That is also unlikely, so the most likely scenario is for ❷ to get a compound fracture of the lower leg. What you are seeing is a very dangerous situation.

During my tenure in semi-professional soccer in Germany, if any player on the field used that technique, 21 players on the field would yell — teammates as well as opponents. Latin players will comment to you if you do not penalize that infraction — contact or not. Since the potential for a season-long or career-long injury is so high, you must blow the whistle every time you see a leg in that position, going toward an opponent.

Do not confuse legitimate attempts to defend against a shot with the PlayPic above. If players are side by side and ❺ raises a leg to defend against a cross, there would be no danger to ❷. Even if ❺ stretched as far as possible and locked his knee, the parallel angle of the legs minimizes danger.

Kicking — contact with the plant leg

A subtle foul can cause you enormous game control problems. ⑨ has already kicked the ball away and is slightly off balance. All his weight is on one leg, commonly referred to as the plant leg. The ligaments and tendons are stretched tight to hold up the entire body weight and perhaps even stressed, fighting to regain balance.

Even a light kick in the plant leg by ❹ is likely to cause pain and damage. Most often, the kick in the plant leg is in the unprotected rear of the leg. All too often, none of the referees saw the contact because they were all watching the ball.

Therefore, we have a hurt player lying on the ground, screaming dissenting comments and three referees wondering what he is yelling about on that play. Referee the defense. Only players commit fouls, not the ball. Watch the whole play, even if it means looking back over your shoulder as you run upfield.

Assistant referees offer a great service on a long clearance when they stay focused on that play. You do not need to watch the ball, there is another assistant referee focusing on the counterattack. Stay with that play. If the contact is significant enough to warrant a caution, initiate procedures outlined in *Guide to Procedures* 3N by raising your flag. If the contact was careless, be certain to pass the word to the referee as instructed in your pregame discussion. If you catch that once or twice early in the game, players stop doing it.

Pushing

Some aspects of pushing are very subtle. Much as you spent 16 hours in your entry-level training, attend recertification training each year and are reading this text to increase your awareness, players are still learning tricks of the trade. With the proper timing and angles, players can plant their forward leg just behind the path of a crossing attacker dribbling the ball. As soon as the weight shifts off that plant leg, the defender brings a thigh into the opponent's thigh.

Here **4** is acting innocent, even going so far as to show the referee his hands as he perfectly times driving his thigh into **9**. **9** may take another step of two before falling to the ground but still loses the ball due to **4**'s actions. *Advice to Referees* 12.3 defines careless as "indicating that the player has not exercised due caution in making his play." **4** carelessly pushed an opponent and you should award a direct free kick.

There are other forms of very subtle pushing. Here's an example. You referee the same U-19 team two weeks in a row. The first week, every head ball is within centimeters of where the header intends it to go. Three goals come from headers. Players head several excellent balls into space and start several give-and-go plays with headers. The same 11 players come together the next week against a different opponent. The first six headers spray all over the field. Several that should have been deflected off to the side pop straight up. Something is very odd. The referee alters her positioning slightly and catches the reason behind the sloppy play. She notices the defender waits until the opponent goes airborne and then touches the attacker inches below the numbers. The defender does not use much pressure, about enough to put a postage stamp on an envelope. That is enough to throw the attacker's balance off and a ball that should be hitting the hairline is now striking the top of the head. The ball that should have gone to **11**'s feet is now 10 yards in the air, with several players collecting underneath to fight for control.

If you call several such fouls in the first 10 minutes of the game, you may hear a comment from the touchline, "OK guys, let's go to plan B." It was a team tactic, the coach now knows you recognize the tactic and the coach is telling the team not to do it anymore. You won't see it the rest of the game, and probably will not see it any time you do that team in the future.

Tripping

The PlayPic above shows another look at the closely related foul of tripping. That is not an obvious trip, not the classical one-foot-hooks-an-opponent's-ankle trip. However, it is an unfair action. You must penalize that because ❺ won the ball by unfair means. ❺'s step with the right leg was performed carelessly. Focused concentration aids you in spotting those fouls.

Some referees miss that foul because their focus is too high on the bodies. Unless you learn where best to focus or learn through experience, the natural inclination is to watch around the waist level.

Some new referees, or referees who still play actively, tend to watch the ball exclusively. Their primary focus is on the ground, which is too low. They miss fouls committed by the upper body.

Your foul recognition will improve significantly if you look at the numbers on the shorts. That's where most of the action happens. If there is an obvious push at the shoulder level, you will catch that with your peripheral vision. Better game control comes when you catch the fouls at ankle level. The only way to catch those fouls is to watch for them. Focusing at mid-thigh assists you in spotting the fouls that hurt and disrupt.

Pushing

For the most part, players abide by referee's decisions. The occasional mistake happens or a player is unaware of a proper law interpretation, so a word or two of dissent creeps into the game from time to time.

There are times when you can help yourself out, if you recognize what is happening. In the PlayPic above, you are going to blow your whistle and award the dark-shirted team the ball. ⑫ is going to have a word or two to say because he knows ❻ pushed him in the back. If you take the time and effort to communicate with ⑫, the potential problem disappears quickly. Jogging toward the spot of the foul, simply say, "Surprised, huh? ⑩ 's left arm pushed him into you, so the foul is on ⑩ ."

A few kind words to players to help them understand what is going on in an unusual situation pays tremendous dividends. If the players know your reasoning behind your decisions in non-obvious situations, the emotional fire lessens.

Do not be confused — you can overdo it. Some referees verbalize on every decision, explaining every call as if they were the play-by-play announcer. That is inappropriate. Save it for those few situations each game where you need it.

Holding — creating space

Attacking players need time and space to work their magic. Defenders try to deny time and space. The battles rage on across the field. Your duty is to protect the balance the teams create for themselves and keep their actions within the boundaries allowed by the *Laws of the Game*.

⑲ may shield ❹ from getting to the ball — if she uses her body to do the shielding. By using her left arm to hold (or push, if you will) ❹ from playing the ball, ⑲ gains a significant advantage. That one-arm length is all ⑲ needs to work her artistry. However, she gained that space illegally. Your stopping play and awarding the dark-shirted team a direct free kick restores the proper balance.

Young players use their arms so much in pick-up contests and practices that it becomes an unconscious movement to them. Many will steadfastly deny they were holding their opponent. A few quick whistles early in the game focus their attention to their misdeeds and they concentrate on playing properly. Many skilled players can beat their opponents without resorting to those tactics but place their arms on opponents to ensure success.

Holding

If an opponent carelessly or recklessly holds an opponent, or an opponent's clothing, award a direct free kick.

Top referees withhold the whistle for a split second. Right now, the PlayPic shows what appears to be a 50-50 ball and both players are engaged in trifling holding. Based on the angles and running pattern, it appears that ⑥ should come away with the ball. If ⑥ is able to play the ball in spite of being held, the referee should swing both arms forward in an underhand motion and shout, "Play on! Advantage!" A quiet word to both players to leave the textile testing to the experts is in order.

The magic of allowing the advantage is knowing when not to stop play. For example, even if ⑥ does play the ball but reacts angrily to ⑪'s actions, the referee should blow the whistle, stop play and run to the spot of the foul to prevent retaliation. Even in a potential advantage situation, a stoppage is needed to let ⑥ know you caught the infraction and will protect him in future encounters. Game control may be more important than advantage, particularly in the middle third of the field. Quickly reading those subtle differences, and factoring in where the incident occurs on the field, become important in matches that are more competitive. Discuss any questions you have with a mentor or referee instructor.

The referee is well positioned to look through the play and is able to see both arms as the opponents hold each other. Too often, referees mistakenly focus their eyes on player's torsos and upper arms. If the referee pictured were to do that, he would call ⑥ for an infraction. Through experience, top referees shift their focus downward, toward player's thighs, because that allows a better perspective of where fouls normally occur. The referee should notice the twist in ⑥'s hips as ⑪ pulls his shorts and will properly award a direct free kick to the lighter-colored team.

Holding

World Cup '98 gained a label of the competition for textile testers. ❾ is showing that to an extreme in the PlayPic. Most of the holding you witness will not be that blatant.

④ is doing everything in her power to create offensive soccer. She is trying to put the ball in the net and arouse the passions of the crowd with a goal. ❾ is using "unnatural movements designed to intimidate an opponent or to gain an unfair advantage," the definition of a reckless foul. Show ❾ a yellow card.

If ④ is able to break free from the clutches of ❾, you may shout, "Play on! Advantage! Number nine, you're in the book." At the next stoppage, hold up play, walk to ❾, get the required information, display the card and restart play. Stop the clock if playing under Federation or NCAA rules.

Charging — two opponents

Advice to Referees 12.5 says, "It is a violation of law 12 to perform an otherwise fair charge against an opponent who is already being fairly charged by another player. Such an action is at minimum a careless challenge. It is also holding and is commonly referred to as a 'sandwich.'"

While refereeing in Germany, it was common to hear the words, *"Zwei gegner,"* when I was refereeing. I knew what the words meant, but I did not understand the concept. The German players were telling me that there were two defenders around the player with the ball. They wanted a free kick for that action, but no foul had been committed to that point. It was not until the publication of *Advice to Referees* that I found out my interpretation had been incorrect.

Just whistle the infraction and point the direction of the restart. Let the players figure out the specifics. If pressed for an answer as to who committed the foul, according to *Advice to Referees*, the player who fouls is the one who initiated contact second.

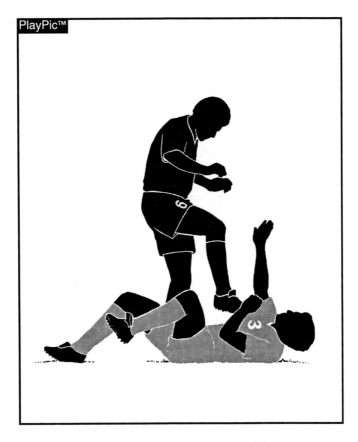

Kicking or attempting to kick

The PlayPic is one example of a number of actions that have no place in the game of soccer: spitting, striking with a closed fist, striking by elbowing, kicking an opponent lying helplessly on the ground, making a tackle from behind which endangers the safety of an opponent. All deserve a red card. Even when there is some degree of provocation, such as when U.S. star Tab Ramos was holding the Brazilian Leonardo's shirt during World Cup '94, that does not excuse the senseless violence that followed. Leonardo elbowed Ramos in the temple, knocking Ramos unconscious.

Actions which "far exceed the use of force necessary to make a fair play for the ball and place the opponent in considerable danger of bodily harm" deserve a red card. Stomping on an opponent's chest can create cardiac or respiratory problems leading to death. There is no place for that in soccer. Players who do that, even with some degree of provocation, should not take further part in the game you are officiating.

Goalkeeper becomes too aggressive

One of the great myths of soccer is that goalkeepers can do anything to prevent the ball from going into the goal. They seem to think that if they can look at the referee and say, "But ref, I was going for the ball," then all sins should be forgiven.

That is a myth. The fact is that goalkeepers have a special right to handle the ball legally within their own penalty area. That's it. They have several restrictions: must wear a distinctive uniform color, restricted to four steps and five-to-six seconds when possessing the ball, may not touch the ball with hands or arms in certain situations.

Under the guise of going for the ball, the keeper in the PlayPic above is committing at least a reckless act. Many would argue the goalkeeper is using excessive force. Stop play, award a penalty kick and show the misconduct card.

The keeper is well above where he needs to be to defend against the shot or the header. Referees must referee the defense. You would have seen the goalkeeper's eyes focused solely on ⑲ and watched the goalkeeper jump at ⑲.

Foul recognition — direct free kick

• Teams try to make a wall that is six bodies wide with only five players. The defenders fill the gaps and creases with hands and forearms. That leaves one extra defender available to cover an attacker, giving a significant advantage. Creating that wider wall is not illegal but it does have a bearing on what you might call if the free kick strikes the hands or arms that are filling the spaces.

• Very young players may react instinctively to protect themselves as a ball moves in their direction. Referees should evaluate that reflex action in judging deliberate handling offenses. Amateur players with years of playing experience have seen hundreds or thousands of balls come at them, so any hand or arm movement on their part is intentional.

• The key is to watch the defense and watch the player's eyes. Too many referees watch the flight of the ball. The ball will not foul anyone. By watching the ball, you are missing critical information.

• Focus on the play until the play is over.

Quiz

Without referring back, you should be able to answer the following true-false questions.

1. The position of the player does not matter. The only consideration you judge to determine if the goalkeeper commits a handling infraction is the position of the ball with respect to the line.

2. If you deem the foul reckless, award the direct free kick plus a caution. If the foul uses excessive force, award the direct free kick plus a send off.

3. If a player tackles an opponent to gain possession of the ball but makes contact with the opponent before touching the ball, award a direct free kick.

4. Some aspects of pushing are very subtle. With the proper timing and angles, players can plant their forward leg just behind the path of a crossing attacker dribbling the ball. As soon as the weight shifts off that plant leg, the defender brings a thigh into the opponent's thigh.

1 - True, 2 - True, 3 - True, 4 - True

Chapter 23

Referee Decisions

"The best calls you make are the ones you don't announce." Senior referees have been echoing those words to their less experienced partners for years. While not absolutely correct, there is a lot of simple wisdom in those words.

You are making a decision
When you watch playing action and decide to not whistle play to a stop, you are making a decision. That decision is just as much a part of the game as if you whistle a direct free kick. It sets the tone for what level of contact you allow. Giving advantage to a team is making a call. You've decided. But in this particular case, you've decided continuing play is the more fair thing to do, given the circumstances.

Law 18 — Common sense
Eric Sellin, in *The Inner Game of Soccer*, writes "In the preceding pages I have spoken repeatedly of the necessity to temper decisions with common sense and of the wisdom of not enforcing minute details of the laws in some instances when to do so will only harm the referee's image, as with the handling of a coach coming on the field to check a hurt player. My justification, within the laws, for such recommendations lies in law 5, IBD 8. It warrants our careful consideration."

Sellin then goes on to quote an important aspect of the spirit of the game. This paragraph was removed during the general rewrite of the laws in 1998 but is still a guiding principle for referees. Sellin quotes the IFAB decision.

"The *Laws of the Game* are intended to provide games should be played with as little interference as possible and in this view it is the duty of referees to penalize only deliberate breaches of the law. Constant whistling for trifling and doubtful breaches produces bad feeling and loss of temper on the part of the players and spoils the pleasure of spectators."

Sellin continues with, "This is a very important paragraph. It suffices as justification for the referee's seeing fit not to interrupt play for a goalkeeper's fifth step, an infinitesimal lifting of the foot during a throw-in or a goalkick taken from a foot outside the goal area. I would estimate that were one to stop play for every trifling infraction, the actual playing time of the game might be reduced to twenty-five or thirty minutes and some junior games would be reduced to little more than alternate throw-ins!"

Trapping the ball
Contact between the ball and the hand is perhaps the most mistakenly whistled foul. Particularly with parents new to the game (in youth recreational play) referees hear loud cries of, "Hand ball, ref." It becomes easier for the referee to whistle and award a kick rather than hear the flurry of cries. Parents on the offending team often accept the call after inadvertent contact because they clearly saw there was contact between the hand and the ball.

That remains the only foul that must be committed deliberately. There must be intent on the part of the player to handle the ball. Even if the player gains some degree of advantage because the ball drops nicely after unintentional contact, it is not an infraction.

Advice to Referees 12.10 has a rule of thumb for judging handling offenses: "It is handling if the player plays the ball, but not handling if the ball plays the player." That is a bit simplistic but it offers newer referees a starting point. Experience helps referees refine those decisions.

Advice to Referees 12.9 says deliberate handling "means that the player could have avoided the touch but chose not to, that the player's arms were not in a normal playing position at the time or that the player deliberately continued an initially accidental contact for the purpose of gaining an unfair advantage." Do not let the cries of parents, coaches and opponents sway your decisions.

Keepers handling the ball near the penalty area line
The position of the player does not matter. The only consideration you judge to determine if the goalkeeper commits an infraction is the position of the ball with respect to the line. When the ball wholly crosses outside the penalty area line, whether on the ground or in the air, and is then touched by the goalkeeper, it is a foul.

The assistant referee must also get an angle to view the play. Do not let the player's body block your view. Do not guess that the ball is wholly outside the penalty area — if you are not certain it is outside, allow play to continue.

Learning more about no-calls
Most referees do not take advantage of the time available to them to learn more about their craft. Halftime is the perfect opportunity to seek the advice of your partners and analyze the decisions you've just made — good and bad.

In *Fair or Foul: The Complete Guide to Soccer Officiating*, Paul and Larry Harris, have a section on "What to do at halftime." They say, "Law 7 states that halftime shall not exceed five [now 15, 10 in Federation] minutes, except by consent of the referee. If, due to special circumstances, the referee deems it necessary to extend the halftime period beyond five minutes, he will probably meet with little resistance, for this period usually lasts 10 to 15 minutes.

"Some experienced referees have the habit of announcing, upon the period's end, that 'Time is up, five minutes between halves.' They will then immediately start timing this interval and will reconvene the players four minutes later, allowing a minute for re-assembly and organization of the two teams. All of the above is advisable, for it establishes the referee's authority even during halftime and allows no extra time for rest.

"The referee should be seen only with his two neutral (assistants) at halftime. They shall not accept refreshment from either team, nor shall they be seen discussing the game with managers, players, coaches or spectators. This valuable time is to be spent exchanging mutual constructive criticisms on the progress of the game.

"Probably the single most important topic at halftime should be a discussion of players' behavior and play. If there are problems or anticipated problems, (the second half invariably presents more of a challenge than the first), they should be brought out. Warnings, cautions and ejections should be discussed in detail. Often referees are seen at halftime with seemingly little to discuss. Two topics should be in mind: (1) "What did we do in the first half?" and (2) "How are we going to do in the second half."

Harris and Harris offer these hints on what to do at halftime:

"1. Always retain the game ball at halftime, for you are responsible for the ball until game's end.

2. During the five minute interval, warm up again by running from one goal to the other as you re-inspect the nets, which may have become loose with halftime activities.

3. Never be afraid to ask a fellow referee at halftime if he is noticing things on the field that you are not seeing. If he is, it is his duty to report them to you.

4. If (an assistant) is doing his job, he should be complimented at halftime by the referee. If he is not, the referee should try to be constructive in his approach to him. The referee needs his support, for an uncooperative (assistant) can destroy the efforts of the best referee.

5. Be extra alert during the opening minutes of each half. That is the time when players will test your alertness and your strict enforcement of the rules of the game.

6. Never smoke within view of players or spectators."

Discussing calls

While the percentage is decreasing each year, there are still many carry-over coaches, coaches who grew up playing other sports and have converted to soccer now that their sons and daughters are playing in a local league. They feel it is their right to analyze and understand each referee decision. After all when they were playing basketball or baseball, the officials continued the stoppage in playing action to describe the call and offer an interpretation. The environment for soccer is different. Ours is a continuous action sport.

As the referee, you don't owe anyone an explanation of your decision. It is not your duty or function to explain the law interpretations to coaches, players or spectators. Certainly you should not hold up playing action to do such. However, if a calmly worded question can be answered by a sentence or two, and does not interrupt your concentration on more important game matters, offer the person a reasonable answer. Then focus on the game. Look at your assistants. Check your watch. Have a private word with a potentially troublesome player.

Gaming a referee

Some coaches are masters when it comes to gaming the referee. "Hey ref, what was that call?" "Sir, it was pushing." "That wasn't pushing. Can't you get it right?" The coach is trying to get the referee to think about past calls, hoping to raise (or lower) the bar to benefit his team on future decisions.

It can even start before the match. As the coach hands the referee the lineup card, she offers the thought, "Wow, this team is really rough. Did you hear they got two red cards in the last game they played? That sounds about right since they broke one of our girl's legs last year. They're just a nasty team." The gamesmanship has started before the opening whistle.

Do not let yourself be influenced by gamesmanship. Act strongly to prevent further comments. Say something neutral like, "We'll watch for rough play by both teams today." Move away from the coach and rejoin your partners.

Continue playing

Your first thought as soon as you saw the PlayPic was to shout, "High kicking." Join the thousands of parents who watch their sons and daughters every weekend. Agreed, the foot is high — almost seven feet off the ground.

However, the absence of an opponent nearby dictates that no call be made. You must not punish a skilled player for displaying the skills that are a part of the game. It does not matter that the cleats are exposed. ❸ is in no danger in that play. Do not whistle to stop play simply because you see a dangerous act. It must be a dangerous act, with an opponent nearby, that causes that opponent to cease active play for the ball. That is the infraction according to the law, rather than according to the parents.

Dangerous play

When players raise a foot much above waist level while playing the ball, many mistakenly call that "high kicking" and think in turn that high kicking is automatically a foul. Despite the potential for injury whenever feet and heads come close to each other, that is not always a foul even though it may be dangerous. Kicking high is not the only way feet and heads can come together. It also happens when a player attempts to head the ball below waist level. Whether it is a foot too high or a head too low, you must assess whether the dangerous action can be called as a foul. Being dangerous by itself is not enough.

Advice to Referees 12.13 lists three important criteria to help you determine if dangerous play should be whistled: the action must be dangerous to someone; it was committed by an opponent close by; and the dangerous nature of the action caused the opponent to cease active play for the ball or be other wise disadvantaged.

As **❺** realizes **⑧**'s leg is coming up, **❺** reacts by drawing her arm in to protect her body and retracts her head and neck to avoid injury. Had **⑧** not lifted her foot so high, **❺** would have headed the ball toward the goal or a teammate. **⑧**'s actions put **❺** and the dark team at a disadvantage, so you must stop play and award an indirect free kick.

That points out a rule difference between the various codes of play. Under the *Laws of the Game* and NCAA rules, if **❺** and **⑧** were teammates, there would not be a stoppage. Under Federation rules, that is an offense and the opposing team would be awarded an indirect free kick.

Legally shielding an opponent

The minor variations between PlayPics A and B and PlayPics C and D are slight and difficult for players and coaches to understand. Since the ball is within playing distance, about two feet from ⑨'s feet, ⑨'s actions are legal. ⑨ might well have both arms out to his side as his balance shifts from right to left to shield the ball. ⑨ may move his feet to turn in a circular motion around the ball, keeping his body between the ball and ❹.

There may be physical contact. In fact, there may be quite a lot of physical contact. ❹ may try to get a foot to the ball to toe-poke the ball away. Both players may bump torsos as they move and countermove to gain or keep an advantage. There may be some minor holding or pushing as you see ❹ doing in this PlayPic. Do not stop play until ❹'s actions put ⑨ at a disadvantage. There may also be some contact in the upper body, hopefully restricted to the shoulder-to-shoulder area. ❹ may even use the front of his chest and bump the soft fleshy portions of ⑨'s shoulder in the back. Most of that contact will be legal.

Look for the now-frustrated ❹ to become so angry after several seconds of being screened that he drops his shoulder and aims it straight for the spine of ⑨. Move closer to screening situations. Look for them near lines, as ⑨ tries to ensure the light-colored team gets a throw-in by shielding the ball as it runs out of play. Look for shielding situations near the end of a period as the winning team tries to hold on to a narrow margin of victory. A desperate ❹ will often kick very hard to steal the ball away from ⑨ if it means his team may advance to the next tournament round — not caring if ⑨'s legs are in the way or not.

Shielding is a legal action by the player with the ball. Shielding situations invite contact that is normally not a part of onfield play. You need to move closer to shielding duels to prevent unwanted actions. A word to let both participants know you are nearby is often helpful. "Easy, guys" or "Careful around the ankles" is enough of a clue that you are in the area.

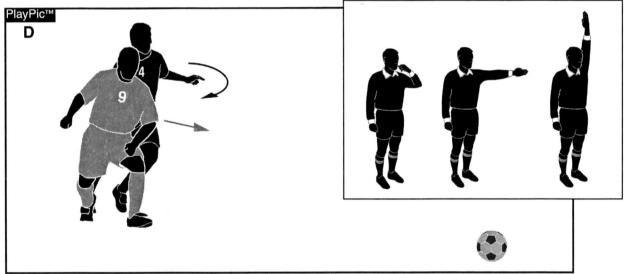

Impeding an opponent

In a scene replicated hundreds of times during a soccer match, opponents use their bodies to attempt to gain an advantage, keep possession of the ball and create time and space. In attempting to distinguish fair from foul, there are a few essential points you must observe.

Is the ball within playing distance? *Advice to Referees* 12.15 provides a guideline of two strides at the speed ⑨ is moving. In the PlayPic, ⑨ is almost five yards from the ball, clearly outside playing distance.

Is there physical contact? ⑨ moves back and forth, moving slowly to keep his body between the ball and the opponent. At that point, ⑨ is obstructing, interfering with and blocking the path of ❹. Once physical contact occurs, initiated by ⑨, you should consider the direct free kick offense of charging an opponent. *Advice to Referees* 12.22 allows you to consider an offense written into older versions of the *Laws of the Game*, charging an opponent away from the ball.

What you see in the PlayPic, with the ball five yards from the players, is an illegal act.

Continue playing

While the two PlayPics (above and on the facing page) are nearly identical, there are vital differences. ⑳ dropped his hips toward the ground. As ⑳ nears ⑪ and contests for the ball both feet are on the ground. The friction of sliding along the surface will stop his momentum before he contacts ⑪, giving ⑪ the possibility to jump over ⑳'s outstretched leg.

Those minor but important differences become a part of your foul recognition. Coaches and spectators don't have the years of experience it has taken you to develop the skills to read those subtle differences. They hear the whistle when their player mis-times a tackle and note the silence as a ball is cleanly stripped from their striker. Then they cry out that you are not being consistent. Be strong.

Kicking

As  throws his body into defense in a desperation slide tackle, the potential for serious injury exists. ②② started his tackle too late or too close to ①①. ②② has strong lateral momentum and will not contact the ground until he is under where ①① is standing now. The wide expanse of ②②'s body leaves ①① little escape. All ①① can hope to do is get airborne before contact to minimize injury. If ①①'s cleats are buried in the grass as ②② makes contact, the torsion on the ankles and knees is extreme.

That mis-timed tackle is at least reckless (unnatural movement designed to intimidate an opponent) and might be an example of a player using excessive force (placed the opponent in considerable danger of bodily harm). The key to watch for in determining excessive force is to watch ②②'s hips as he starts the tackle. If he throws the hips upward, into the opponent, he is after the opponent's body. If the hips drop toward the ground, where the ball is, he simply mis-timed the tackle while playing for the ball.

Referees no longer judge a player's intent. We don't know if ②② wanted to hurt ①① or just clumsily started the tackle one step too late. You simply make your judgement based on what you see the player do. Here, ②② was high and late and that is a foul. The determination that the foul was reckless or used excessive force leads to the display of a misconduct card.

Inevitably, players will exclaim, "But ref, I got the ball." *Advice to Referees* 12.8 is clear: "Making contact with the opponent after touching the ball while performing a tackle does not necessarily mean that a foul has not been committed. *The declaration by a player that he has in fact played the ball is irrelevant if, while tackling for the ball, the player carelessly, recklessly or with excessive force commits any of the prohibited actions.*"

Tackling the ball

Study the PlayPic. Is that dangerous play? Is that kicking? Could it be a no-call? From that one look, it is hard to tell. That's the reason you are advised to referee the defense. Too many referees watch the path of the ball, at all times. Look at the ball to determine its path and speed, but then focus your eyes ahead of the ball and pick up the defensive player that will be engaged in the next significant action. If all you see are attackers with open space, continue to look around and read the play to see where the next defensive action will take place. It may be a shot on goal, so see if the goalkeeper is rushing out. It may be a cross into the mixer, so look to see if the sweeper or stopper is holding an attacking midfielder.

Too often, you learned to think tackling the ball involves a slide tackle. Not true. If ⑧ gently inserts a leg between ❺'s legs, and does not make contact with ❺ before flicking the ball to one side or the other, he has tackled the ball. Although a rare case, if executed properly, do not whistle the play dead because of some belief that "the play looked bad." Certainly at some lower-skill levels, the players may not have the ability to execute that move without exposing their opponents to some danger. So, if in the opinion of the referee, it was a dangerous play, whistle for the indirect free kick.

As you move up in competitive levels, you will see more of those actions. Your foul-recognition skills must improve to keep pace with the level of play you officiate. Discuss those new actions with a trusted partner, mentor or instructor.

That PlayPic also indicates another possibility — some previous action prompted ⑧ to be upset at ❺ and ⑧ senses a perfect opportunity for retaliation. The action is not a gentle attempt to play the ball, but rather a hard-driven kick to ❺'s sensitive body parts. The foul is kicking, so award a direct free kick. Now you face a more difficult decision. Was the kicking motion an "unnatural movement designed to intimidate an opponent" (reckless) or did the kick "far exceed the use of force necessary to make a fair play for the ball and place his opponent in considerable danger of bodily harm" (excessive force)? The distinction determines the color card you display. If you focus on the ball as it travels toward ❺, you miss the preceding actions and lose sight of what ⑧ was trying to do. What was ⑧ looking at? How far had ⑧ traveled to get involved in the play: knowing how much momentum ⑧ built up is a factor in judging the seriousness of the action. Did you catch the earlier action between ❺ and ⑧ to know why that action took place? With all those details, you now have sufficient information to give the proper card.

Tackling the ball from behind

Read the play. Referee the defense. Anticipate the next significant playing action and move to get the proper angle. This book contains those phrases dozens of times. It all comes to bear on this single incident.

Literally, microseconds differentiates a foul from a clean tackle. It's clear from the PlayPic above that 21 is going to fall down. Was it a foul? Let's look at some essential elements and piece together the right answer.

The defender's leg is on the ground, same as the ball. The defender's hips are on the ground, meaning he didn't launch himself into 21's back. The defender's body is well clear of any contact with 21. Looks clean so far.

The biggest key is the path of the ball. 21 is running straight into the camera, straight ahead. If the ball were still running directly in front of 21, that would be a key that the defender did not make contact with the ball. But the ball has been pushed aside at a 45-degree angle. In a skillfully executed move, the defender tackled the ball cleanly from behind — legally. 21 may trip over the outstretched leg of the defender but that is not a foul.

You have an obligation to watch the entire play. Does the defender raise his left foot off the ground to ensure 21 crashes to the ground? Does 21 retaliate against the defender? With both of them on the ground, does the defender kick out at 21's legs? Too many referees watch the ball and can't answer those significant questions. You need to be able to answer those questions. If you can, your game control improves considerably because you are focusing on the things that are most important.

Contesting for the ball

Contesting for the ball

Many referees have difficulty determining fair charges, or deciding which player to call for the foul if there is contact.

PlayPic A shows two players relatively close together, within playing distance of the ball, both with an equal opportunity for the ball. As long as both players leave their arms near their sides, there is no foul and play can continue.

PlayPic B is a tougher decision for the referee. Here both players are leaning in toward their opponent. There will be shoulder-to-shoulder contact, without any pushing or holding with their arms. Again both players have an equal opportunity to play the ball. Let play continue as long as nothing is dangerous.

Unfair charge — jumping at an opponent

Fouls occur when one player is playing the ball and the opponent is playing the man. PlayPic C shows the dark-shirted player focused on the airborne ball, going straight up to play the ball. ❹ has his head down, focused on ❾'s torso and jumping into ❾ at an angle.

If ❾ is contacted before the ball gets there, his header will be misdirected, causing him a disadvantage. If ❾ is contacted after he heads the ball away, he still has his ribs and torso exposed to the onrushing opponent, potentially causing injury. In either case, it is a foul (jumping at an opponent), so award a direct free kick.

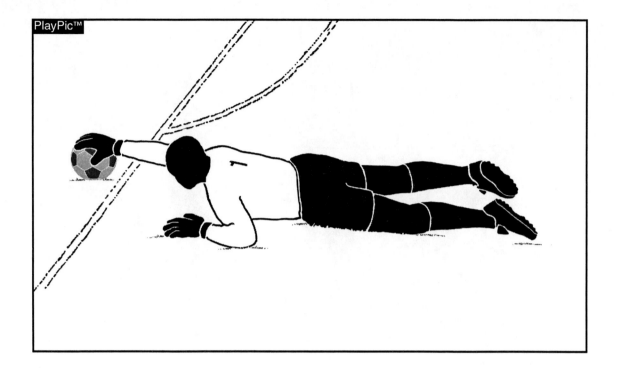

Goalkeeper's body outside penalty area

The position of the player does not matter. The only consideration you judge to determine if the goalkeeper commits an infraction is the position of the ball with respect to the line. Until the ball wholly crosses outside the penalty area line, in the air or on the ground, it is still inside the penalty area and can be handled by the goalkeeper. The fact that the goalkeeper is mostly outside the penalty area and handles the ball does not constitute a foul because the handling is inside the penalty area.

The assistant referee must also get an angle to view the play. Do not let the player's body block your view. Do not guess whether the ball is inside or outside the penalty area — be in a position to see it clearly and, if you are not certain it is outside, allow play to continue.

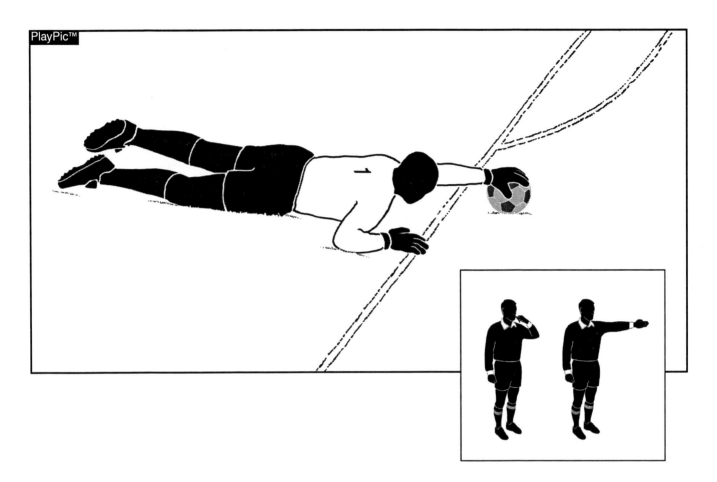

Goalkeeper within penalty area reaches outside to play a ball

The position of the player does not matter. The only consideration you judge to determine if the goalkeeper commits an infraction is the position of the ball with respect to the line. If the ball wholly crosses outside the penalty area line, whether on the ground or in the air, and is then touched by the goalkeeper, it is deliberately handling the ball. Award a direct free kick to the attacking team from outside the penalty area.

The fact that the goalkeeper is inside the penalty area does not allow him to play the ball. The assistant referee must also get an angle to view the play. Do not let the player's body block your view. Do not guess that the ball is wholly outside the penalty area — if you are not certain it is outside, allow play to continue.

Contact, no foul

Jumping

Advice to Referees 12.2 states, "Referees should not punish actions that are accidental or inadvertent." On the header above, there is going to be a clash of heads and possibly even an injury. We know it can happen, evidenced by U.S. striker Michelle Akers' collision with Norwegian defender Linda Medalen during the Feb. 14, 1999, exhibition match between the U.S. national team and the world all-stars. Akers broke several bones under her eye and needed 25 stitches to close the wound. Then, as above, both players focus intently on the ball. Both are aware another player is in the area but their concentration is on scoring the goal or defending. When both heads and the ball arrive in the same space at the same time, a wreck happens. Wrecks can lead to serious injury or the perception that referees are not concerned with player safety but such contact is an integral part of a well-played game.

Other situations where you see wrecks are when opposing players go to kick the ball in opposite directions. The legs come to the ball from both sides and if the timing is right (wrong?) the ball stays perfectly still but the torque applied to both player's legs causes them to spin wildly.

In those situations, you could be perfectly positioned, be within 10 yards of the play, apply all the preventive officiating at your disposal and injuries may still occur. They are wrecks, accidents and a common part of physical contact sports such as soccer. If needed, bring the coaches and trainers on the field to deal with players that are shaken up because of the wrecks. (*Note:* In matches played under National Federation rules, any players attended to on the field by a team representative must leave the field. The team may substitute or play short.)

The players you see in the PlayPic are legally jumping to play the ball. Both have gone airborne, both are trying to play the ball, both are focused on the ball, both have their arms raised for balance. That is fair play.

Jumping is not a foul. Jumping *at* an opponent in a careless or reckless manner is an unfair action.

Striking or attempting to strike

Airborne battles between opponents are exciting to watch. Players who are strong in the air are a valuable commodity to a team. Lightning quick goals can result from a single cross to a well-placed header to the back of the net.

Players who are less skilled in the air resort to various tactics to counter such opponents. In our PlayPic, ❺ goes up with an elbow into ㉑'s ribs. Even the attempt to strike is punishable by a direct free kick. If you deem the act reckless, award the direct free kick plus a caution. If the act uses excessive force, award the direct free kick plus a send off.

❺ is also demonstrating another tactic used by defenders to deny space and punish airborne players. See how his right leg is well forward of his body. ❺ is hoping that some contact with that leg is enough to throw off ㉑'s timing and cause the header to miss the target. As a minimum, ㉑ will not have sufficient space to land without contacting ❺'s leg, which will cause ㉑ to fall and contact the ground. There is the potential that after a couple of those, ㉑ may lose the resolve to go airborne if ❺ is in the area. Thus, the light-colored team loses a potent offensive weapon — because you did not do your job and protect the skills of an attacking player playing fairly.

Goalkeeper — diving at the ball

The attacker rushes in with the ball at his feet — only the keeper to beat. The keeper rushes out, past the goal area, past the penalty mark, crouches, tries to make the attacker commit and finally leaves his feet to make a diving save.

What excitement! That play is what the game is all about — trying to score goals and trying to prevent the ball from going in the back of the net. Whether the ball is gobbled up by the keeper or the attacker jumps for joy at the scoring of the game-winning goal, a roar goes up in the crowd, louder by one side than the other, all appreciative of the good play.

It is when things are not so clear that referees are called upon to make a decision. At one end of the spectrum is the PlayPic above. The keeper has committed to his right, made his dive, fully extended along the ground, arms outstretched and clearly not fouled the attacker.

Goalkeeper — jumping at the opponent

All too often, the scene looks more like the PlayPic above. Changing any one of a number of elements can create that picture. The attacker puts on a late burst of speed, the attacker changes the angle of the attack at the last moment, the keeper is wrong-footed and has to take an extra step to dive to the proper side, the keeper's reactions just aren't fast enough to cope with the attack — any of those elements can create the scene in the PlayPic.

In looking at the PlayPic, a moment frozen in time in a dynamic play, hopefully you agree it is careless and thus, a foul. Most will agree it is reckless and thus misconduct meriting a yellow card. The arguments start when you consider if that is excessive force, or using intentional violence. If you decide it is excessive force, then it is serious foul play (the ball is in play, the foul is against an opponent while challenging for the ball and the foul occurred on the field) and a sending off is called for.

What factors can you look for to help you decide? Players' age and competitive level. Weather conditions. Past meetings between those teams and their record of misconduct when playing each other. Comments made earlier in the game between the keeper and opponents. Score. For example, if the ball that is rolling into the goal makes the score 4-0, and the keeper figures by wiping out one opponent, the next time down they'll be less likely to take him on, it can be argued he used excessive force.

Trying to decide from one PlayPic is exceptionally difficult. You need to evaluate the whole play and be a part of the action from start to finish to know exactly what to do. This is what should run through your mind when you see that scene happen on a field: "I know I'm going to caution the keeper. What else has he done so far to help me decide if he should stay in the game?" It's a difficult choice you have to make. Many will say leave him in the game, he's only doing his job. Others contend his actions injured the opponent who must miss next week's game — maybe the keeper should miss next week's game also.

Strikers challenging goalkeepers

Here is one more situation where wrecks are frequent. Two players move in opposite directions with their focus on the ball. There is some awareness that opponents are nearby, but to take the time to look up and find the opponents means they beat you to the ball.

The goalkeeper has gotten low to protect the ball rolling along the ground. He has thrown his arms high into the air to prevent the chip shot. His legs are going out to his right to make his body as big as possible in defense. His head is up but his eyes focus on the ball.

⑫ must extend his body to reach the ball. He pokes it up into the keeper's chest but does not continue to swing his leg to present a danger to the keeper.

Their forward momentum may bring them together, possibly very forcefully. But neither player has committed a dangerous act or a careless act. If play must stop to attend to an injured player, the referee drops the ball at the spot where the ball was when play was stopped (unless it is in the goal area). In matches played under National Federation or NCAA rules, the referee may award an indirect free kick if one team was in clear possession; otherwise, drop the ball.

Goalkeepers expose themselves to dangers

Being a goalkeeper is a demanding function on a soccer field. PlayPics on pages 302 and 304 point out that goalkeepers are subject to their fair share of wrecks and injuries. They fling themselves at the feet of opponents in an effort to prevent the goal.

Defensive players quickly come to the aid of their goalkeepers and will intervene to battle opponents who attempt to harm the keeper. While there is no special privilege written into the *Laws of the Game*, the spirit of the game demands that you offer your utmost attention to incidents involving the keeper.

In the PlayPic above, you want to be sprinting into the goal area and be nearby when those players land on the ground. The goalkeeper has control and possession. Quickly penalize any action by ⑧ or ⑩ that causes ① to lose possession. In most instances, the contact pictured above would not be sufficient to stop play as both players are going for the ball. Perhaps a calming word or two from you would be in order.

Playing the ball

There are times when inevitable collisions happen between goalkeepers and attackers. In this fast-paced sport, split-second timing often determines a goal from a blocked shot or a shot that sails over the crossbar from the game-winning goal.

The properly positioned referee observes the attacker leap to head the ball. The attacker's knees and legs rotate back so there is no danger to the goalkeeper. Both players left the ground, with the attacker elevating much higher. Both player's eyes focus directly on the ball. Microseconds after the attacker heads the ball goalward, the goalkeeper makes contact with the attacker's head. Although it may stun ⑪ and there is a potential for serious injury, that is a clean play.

In the opinion of the referee, if that is viewed as a careless or reckless act, the offense would be striking. Two factors are essential to your not whistling a foul — both player's eyes are looking directly at the ball and the closeness of the ball when the contact took place. If the ball were three feet away when contact occurred, the decision should be different.

Ball in and out of play — player's position

The position of the player does not matter. The only consideration you judge to determine if a ball is in or out of play is the position of the ball with respect to the line. When the ball wholly crosses the goalline or touchline, whether on the ground or in the air, it is out of play.

The fact that ⑧ is entirely outside the field of play and plays the ball does not stop play. The assistant referee must get an angle to view the play. Do not let the player's body block your view.

Referees do not have the authority to allow an advantage situation when the ball wholly crosses over a boundary line. If the opponents were the last to touch that ball before ⑧ goes to play it, and it passes wholly over the line before ⑧ kicks it, the referee or assistant referee cannot rationalize that it would have gone to the light-shirted team anyway, so it's better to let play continue. If the ball passes wholly over the touchline, the restart must be a throw-in.

It is the action of the ball, not the referee's decision that stops play in this case. So, the fact that players may still be competing for the ball is irrelevant. Should there be some contact after the ball wholly crosses a boundary line, you have two choices. You may decide the contact was trifling or careless and ignore the contact. Or you may decide the contact was at least reckless and thus becomes misconduct. Display the appropriate card. The restart, however, must be a throw-in, goalkick or corner kick.

Referee decisions

• The position of the player does not matter. The only consideration you judge to determine if a ball is in or out of play is the position of the ball with respect to the line.

• Shielding is a legal action by the player with the ball. Shielding situations invite contact that is normally not a part of onfield play but may still be otherwise legal. You need to move closer to shielding duels to prevent unwanted actions.

• Look at the ball to determine its path and speed, but then focus your eyes ahead of the ball and pick up the defensive player that will be engaged in the next significant action. If all you see are attackers with open space, continue to look around and read the play to see where the next defensive action will take place.

• Deliberate handling "means that the player could have avoided the touch but chose not to, that the player's arms were not in a normal playing position at the time or that the player deliberately continued an initially accidental contact for the purpose of gaining an unfair advantage."

Quiz

Without referring back, you should be able to answer the following true-false questions.

1. Do not whistle to stop play simply because you see a dangerous act. It must be a dangerous act, with an opponent nearby, that causes that opponent to cease active play for the ball.

2. When players exclaim, "But ref, I got the ball," you should not whistle a foul against them.

3. It is not a foul when one player is playing the ball and the opponent is playing the man.

4. Handling the ball is the only foul that must be committed deliberately. There must be intent on the part of the player to handle the ball.

1 - *True*, 2 - *False*, 3 - *False*, 4 - *True*

Chapter 24

Misconduct

Law 5 details the duties and powers soccer referees have during matches. The powers are enormous. Complete control rests in the hands of the certified referee, no matter how young. Used unwisely, a 12-year-old referee can dismiss an entire bus load of adults from around the game site — and they have to leave. But there are many intermediate steps to deal with misconduct.

A common sense legal opinion

The following is extracted from *Sports Officiating: A Legal Guide* by Alan Goldberger, J.D. In his chapter "Check-up for Basketball Officials," Goldberger says, "Let me again caution you: This book is not an officiating manual, as I told you. I am the last one to tell you how to officiate. But, if your integrity is being questioned within earshot of others or an episode of name-calling occurs, again, under circumstances that others hear what is going on, if you do not penalize in those two instances, you may be hard pressed to justify your actions should an assault upon you occur during or after the game.

"For one of the first questions that somebody always asks at a league or conference disciplinary hearing when misconduct towards an official has been charged is, did you, Mr. Referee, penalize the coach or the player during the game for remarks or actions that preceded the alleged assault? If your answer is no, the league or review committee may well conclude that you, the official, precipitated the action against you. An unjust result? Sure. Unfortunately, it's the way things work. Remember that Heaven, and commissioners, help those who help themselves."

The learning point is to take action when the problems are small so they do not grow to the point where a disciplinary hearing is needed.

Stop sign

The stop sign has two uses. Stopping substitutes from entering the game too quickly and letting a coach or player know you've taken enough heat. For handling a confrontation, use the stop sign sparingly. It is simply a signal that demonstrates, "Coach, I've listened to enough." If you use it sparingly, the offender and others will know the offender has been warned. Then if the offender acts up again and is whistled for misconduct you have visual proof that the offender was warned.

There are two methods to display the stop sign. The first is to angle your body so one shoulder faces the offender, leave your arm down lower, just above waist level and angle your hand so the offender sees the heel of your hand.

The second is more confrontational and more powerful. You stand facing the offender, arm raised to shoulder height and face your complete palm toward the offender. Use whichever is appropriate to manage the situation. Don't pull the big gun until it's needed.

Cautions

There is a much folklore about issuing cautions. Some of it is good ("Get something for every caution" or "Treat your yellow cards like money — spend them wisely"). Some of it is bad ("Don't give a caution in the first few minutes because you'll wind up giving too many later in the game").

Use your personality. Before reaching into your pocket to get the card, run a series of thoughts through your mind. What effect will the card have on the game? What effect will it have on the player's behavior? Do I have other tools at my disposal that will yield the same result?

Canadian Emerson Mathurin was a FIFA referee and serves as a FIFA inspector. He wrote a chapter for *In The Eye Of The Whistle, II: The Refereeing at the 1990 World Cup*, which contained a statistical analysis of cards given out by referees. "Finally, the ratio of dismissals to cautions in the 52 matches was 1 to 10.6, and 1 to 8 in the knock-out rounds. Previous graphs and statistics have revealed that such high ratios have been achieved by more successful and experienced referees in Canada. What this seems to indicate is that a caution administered properly by a referee has a considerable influence, not only on the offending player but also upon the conduct of all players in the game. As Hoyle observed in his article, 'Man Management,' that was published in 1990 in *CanSoRef*, the official magazine of the Ontario Soccer Referees' Association, it is not the disciplinary card that counts, but rather the way in which the discipline is administered."

When events occur

Knowing when events are likely to occur helps you prepare. Statistically, the numbers that follow have been a part of the game for decades. Will events happen in your games in exactly this manner? Probably not. But over your career, these same patterns will emerge time and again.

This extract is from the same chapter by Mathurin: "The purpose of the study was to examine the effects of cautions and dismissals in the 1990 World Cup final tournament. In the 52 games played in the tournament, 170 cautions were issued, most of them for offenses of the type which FIFA had directed the referees to deal with firmly, and 16 players were dismissed, three-quarters of them for serious foul play or violent conduct. Examination of data revealed that in the 52 games taken as a whole, the 20- to 30-minute span was the most critical moment in the first half, in the sense that the greatest concentration of misconduct incidents occurred in that period. The greatest explosion of those incidents occurred in the 25- to 30-minute span in the first half, but 10 minutes earlier in the second half.

"One obvious lesson that referees can learn from events in the 1990 World Cup final tournament is that, in terms of match control, the last five minutes of play and the second half of overtime periods in knock-out competition are critical. Another obvious lesson is that a caution administered properly by the referee has a considerable influence not only on the offending player but also upon the conduct of all players in the game.

"Despite all the statistics that have been presented in this study one should never lose sight of the fact that referees cannot caution or dismiss a player until after the misconduct incident has occurred. What we have considered in our analysis is the time that referees dealt with misconduct and, by inference using subsequent events, how well such discipline was made to stick, that is, the recognition by and the impact upon players and their coaching staff. If we have one expectation from the exercise, it is that training officers (instructors) will emphasize and referees will realize that changes in the *Laws of the Game* are not necessary to control the game better to ensure 'Fair Play.' Only the ability and the willingness of referees to exercise their authority at the proper time and to 'bite the bullet' are needed. The *Laws of the Game* are published annually by FIFA for all to learn. It remains for players to respect them, and for referees to apply them by punishing those who fail to do so. In the final analysis, as was so evident in the 1990 World Cup final tournament, there simply is no room for compromise with brutality and cynicism."

Foul behind the referee's back
The NISOA mechanics for communicating with referees who do not observe a foul that occurs behind their back, or when play is blocked from view, parallel standard USSF mechanics.

"That usually requires the involvement of the trail assistant. It requires that the trail assistant exercise good judgment based on the game flow and player interaction. When the trail assistant observes the incident not seen by the referee, ask:

1. Can I handle the incident by talking to the players from my vantage point?

2. If I signal now to stop play, do I take away a goal-scoring advantage from the offended team?

3. Is the incident, and are the players, better handled at a later time by the referee at a normal stoppage?

In short, the assistant asks the same questions a referee asks when deciding whether or not to stop play

to penalize unfair player conduct."

Technical area
Unfortunately, too many instances of misconduct come from the technical area. This extract from the USL handbook details one league's requirements. Perhaps you local league could adopt parameters right for your local conditions.

"• Home and visitor's benches must be large enough to accommodate at least 10 persons per team.

• A clearly marked technical area should extend no more than one meter on either side of each bench and at least one meter away from the touchline.

• No more than 12 persons shall occupy the technical area and it shall be restricted to dressed, named substitute players, coach, assistant coach, trainers and medical staff.

• The coach and other permitted persons must remain within the confines of the technical area at all times during the game.

• Only one person has the authority to convey tactical instructions and he must return to his position on the bench immediately after giving these instructions.

• All occupants of the technical area must conduct themselves, at all times, in a responsible manner. All occupants are subject to the disciplinary control of the referee.

• Drinking water must be provided at the home, visitors' and officials' benches.

NOTE: Neither team owners, nor front office staff are allowed in the technical area."

Abandonments and terminations
Eric Sellin, in *The Inner Game of Soccer*, wrote "When I was beginning to officiate, I asked an experienced colleague at what point you abandon a game for any reason: rain, darkness, spectator interference. He replied that when it was the right time, I would know it. There is, in fact, no one else who can tell the referee when to stop play due to bad weather nor what constitutes a point of no return in crowd interference. That will be the official's decision based on a myriad of contributing factors. The input may even be heavily weighted psychologically from his viewpoint. He may be in no frame of mind to tolerate disreputable behavior for even the shortest amount of time, or he may wish to see that a game is played out."

PlayPic™

Diving

The potential payback for fooling the referee in the penalty area even once is tremendous — a penalty kick, leading to a goal 82 percent of the time. Is the striker willing to take the risk? Here's a typical scenario: He's tried eight times to beat the skillful man-marker and been unsuccessful each time. He sprints ahead, knocks the ball a little too far forward to get it before the keeper gets there. One last quick glance over the shoulder to confirm the referee is far enough away from play and the stage is set — he's been working on that move all week in practice.

The player's mindset: Start with the scream to get everyone's attention. Then kick one heel into the other heel so teammates get to shout, "But ref, didn't you hear the defender kick him?" Make sure my knees are the next body part to hit the ground — otherwise it hurts too much. As my hips sink into the ground, fling my arms wide for effect but quickly bring them in under my chest so my chest and face don't hit the ground too hard. Wait a tenth of a second before starting to roll around and begin the screaming for the second time.

Is that it? Is that the beloved whistle I worked so hard to hear? Yes, a long, loud blast of the whistle. Since I finished my job, I can now get up to celebrate with my teammates. What's this? The referee is headed directly to me, asking me my name. That isn't what I had planned.

Recognition. Good referees referee the defense. If the defender did nothing to cause the attacker to fall, did not carelessly or recklessly kick or trip the attacker, then there is no reason to whistle a foul. Top referees study videotape for hours and see team tendencies and national styles of play. They watch to detect subtle differences between players who fall after being fouled and those who drop of their own choosing. Most top referees will warn players once with eye contact, a subtle shake of the head or perhaps by saying, "Come on, this game is best played on your feet." If you decide to stop the game to issue a caution, stop the clock if playing under Federation or NCAA rules.

A common gesture has crept into refereeing, and some suggest the improper gesture is irritating or dismissive to the fallen player. Rather than raising a upturned palm for all to see (many referees do it five or six times in a row), maybe use eye contact and a look that lets the players know you understand what's going on — and you wish they would stop. Similarly, do not attempt to inject humor by holding up nine fingers as if judging a diving competition or holding your nose as if to say the dive stinks.

Throw-in — unfair distraction

The throw-in originated as a simple means to get the ball back into play once it crossed over a touchline. The rulemakers wanted to make it an awkward motion so the throwing team did not gain a huge advantage but simple enough so that almost everyone could do it properly after minimal training.

The beauty of soccer is when the ball is at the feet of the 20 field players. That's the most exciting portion of the game. Your job is to keep the ball in play for a majority of the time. Do not allow an opponent to delay a throw-in by unfairly distracting or impeding the thrower. If you or an assistant referee are close enough to do some preventive officiating before the distraction takes place, do it. If **㉓** is already waving his arms, yelling or gesticulating, caution **㉓** for unsporting behavior and show the yellow card. That is one of the mandatory cautions, as pointed out in *Advice to Referees* 15.7. Stop the clock if playing under Federation or NCAA rules.

There is much misunderstanding on that simple point. An opponent may stand anywhere on the field, even directly on the touchline in front of the thrower. But **㉓** needs to be there before the ball is thrown in. If **❼** legally moves two feet to create the space to throw the ball into play, **㉓** may not move two feet in the same direction to block the throw. Some referees ask a defender to move 10 yards away during a throw-in. You have no such authority. Be very wary of a defender who yells just as a thrower releases the ball, even if he is yelling directions to a teammate. That may happen once as a legitimate need to reposition a teammate but the second time it happens you should consider it a tactical move to distract. Caution the offending player.

Tackle from behind, which endangers the safety of an opponent

⑳ is about to suffer the worst of all possible fouls. He is about to feel ❺'s cleats in the unprotected flesh of his upper calf, with no awareness that the contact is about to occur. That is potentially a career-ending injury. At a minimum, there will be pain from the resulting contact. Nevertheless, with ⑳'s forward momentum, and the momentum added by ❺, he will fall heavily on his sternum and face. If he twists to avoid such a hard landing, he subjects himself to broken arms and collarbones. None of these is a pleasant prospect.

Stop the thuggery. Be absolutely certain it does not happen a second time in a game you are refereeing. It's bad enough that a player may contemplate doing it once, but if you show everyone that the consequences are severe, and that you are upholding the law as written, you will red card the first offender.

As a result, players respect you more. Even ❺'s teammates may have a kind word for you after sending him off for a foul of that nature. Your games will be more flowing. You will have more creative runs by skilled players. You find the average goals per game increases. Games are more fun if you take care of business and send off players who commit fouls of the sort pictured above.

Striking — using the ball as a weapon

It does not matter if it is a ball, shoe, rock, corner flagpost or equipment bag, if a player throws something at an opponent during play, it is a foul. Remember, attempting to strike is punished the same as striking, so even if the item misses its intended target, award a direct free kick to the opposing team. Then you must decide the seriousness of the incident to rule on misconduct. In most cases, you would decide the foul was at least reckless, so give a card.

In the PlayPic above, we have the special situation of a goalkeeper within his penalty area striking a player outside the penalty area. International Board decision 1 to law 12 spells out the punishment as a penalty kick. *Advice to Referees* 12.6 states the "restart is located where the offense originated."

You must read play to determine that the emotional temperature has reached a point where such action is about to take place. Actions of this sort do not take place in a vacuum. It's probable that opponents had words, someone made threats or heavy contact occurred before the goalkeeper heaves the ball at an opponent's head. Read those signs and use preventive refereeing to keep the keeper's temper under control.

Sometimes you cannot read the signs within your game because the emotions are a carry over from a previous meeting between the teams or players. Doctoral research by prominent Washington state referee Cindy Moore concludes that behavior is more prevalent among female players.

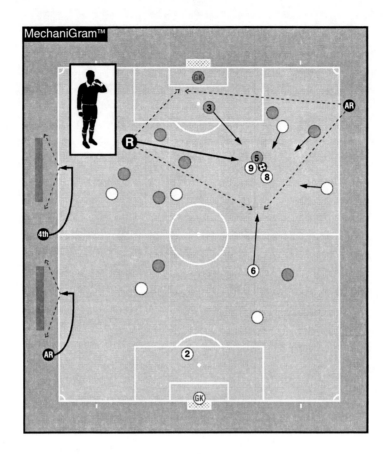

Trouble on the field — prevent bench problems

Action on the field:

Three players on the field get tangled up, two fall to the ground as a third looks over them. Soon they are standing in a small, confrontational cluster. Other players from both teams move toward the three players.

Referee Responsibilities

Sprint to the trouble spot with a loud blast of your whistle. Use your strong voice to let players know you are coming, then as you near the melee, begin to use soothing tones to restore calm and order.

Using a loud phrase such as, "I've got him. Leave him to me," as you run in, followed by, "I'll take care of this," in a quieter tone will calm most tempers. Quickly react by having other players stay away, either using a hand gesture or your voice.

Assistant Referee Responsibilities

If you are the assistant nearest the field trouble, use wide vision to take in as much as you can around you. Record what you see on your game data wallet so you can present facts to the referee.

If you are the bench-side assistant and the trouble is on the other side of the field, hustle into a spot between the bench and the trouble. Turn and face the bench area and use your personality and voice to keep coaches, trainers and substitutes in their technical area. Continually glance over your shoulder to see if the referee wants your assistance. If a fourth official is available, signal that the fourth official should take the other bench. If people leave the technical area and move to the trouble spot, record their number or description on your game data wallet so you can present facts to the referee.

Dissent

There are two main types of dissent — emotional and calculated. ❼ reacts angrily to the referee calling a direct free kick against his team, jumps up, runs to the referee and for a few seconds shouts comments directly into the referee's ear. That is crossing the line and should be carded. Some dissent is spontaneous, emotional dissent which lasts from two to 10 seconds, the player realizes the futility of the argument and settles back into the game.

You can shorten the duration of some emotional dissent by getting the ball into play quickly — the player faces the choice of standing there to argue with you or scurrying off to play defense. You can further cut down on emotional dissent by whistling, signaling the direction for the restart and quickly moving to your next position. The player will be arguing with a person who is now 25 yards away.

Soccer is an emotional sport. Allow some level of emotional dissent. Use your personality to diffuse some of the dissent. If humor is part of your management style, use a line or two to calm the player. Support the spirit of the game but maintain the authority of the officiating team.

Calculated dissent takes on a harsher tone. It may be continuous. It may be both verbal and via hand gestures. Like a cancer, there is a danger of calculated dissent becoming more widespread. Sage referees have offered the advice to deal with calculated dissent in the same manner as it is presented. If ❼ wanders by you and quietly says, "Referee, that last call was horrible. You're an idiot." you might also quietly respond, "Thank you, ❼. That's enough." If more people heard the dissenting comment, you might want to take the opportunity to have a public word with ❼ as the players ready the ball for play. In that way, others are aware you are dealing with the dissent.

If the player directs dissent toward an official in a very loud voice, or with accompanying gestures seen by all in attendance, you must use stiffer actions. An example is a goalkeeper who runs 40 yards out of his penalty area, screaming the whole way, and confronts an assistant referee after a goal. If you do not deal with such actions sternly, it diminishes the authority of the officiating team and that affects game control. Such an action deserves a caution.

Also consider players who "talk over the referee's head." That is calculated dissent. "Hey Mike, don't you think this referee is terrible? Isn't he worse than the guy we had last weekend, the one the coach scratched? Referee cards must be coming in Cracker Jack boxes now." When you approach the players making those comments, they inevitably say, "But I wasn't talking to you, ref. I was talking to my teammate." If you think you can stop the comments with a word or two, or with other tools at your disposal, do so. If the team persists in making those comments, caution an offender. In an effort to put a stop to such misconduct, if the referees of that team's next two games call you to find out about the team, let them know of the team's tendencies.

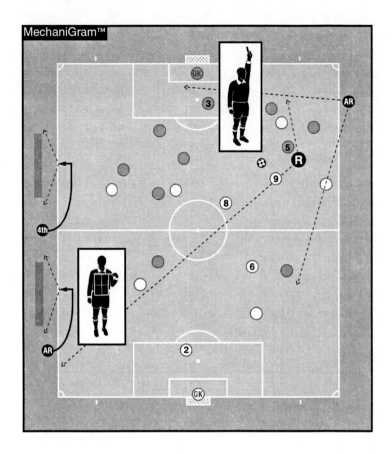

Trouble on the field — referee taking action

Action on the field:
Several players tangle up and at least one of them commits misconduct. A larger group of players heads in that direction, but prompt action by the referee prevents further misconduct. The referee asks all other players to move away, except for ⑤ and ⑨.

Referee Responsibilities
Once the larger group moves away, orient yourself so you can see the majority of the players. Stop the clock if playing under Federation or NCAA rules. Isolate the two players from each other, angled on either side of you. Record information in your game data wallet (time, team, players' numbers and your code to help you remember the reason for the misconduct). Federation rule 5 tells you to inform the coach, scorer and other officials why the player is being cautioned or sent off. Speak with one or both assistants if you need more information.

Assistant Referee Responsibilities
Stand ready to offer additional information as requested by the referee. If you observed misconduct (behavior worthy of a yellow or red card, given the circumstances in this particular game), briefly inform the referee of the player's team, number and reason for the misconduct. Everyone will shout at you for more information or to dispute your facts. Now is a good time to speak only with the referee. Be brief but factual.

Wig-wag to request a foul or point out misconduct

Law 6 provides for assistant referees to indicate "when misconduct or any other incident has occurred out of the view of the referee."

Commonly, assistants use the signal above to indicate a foul. The same signal is to be used if the assistant spots misconduct and needs to alert the referee. During the pregame discussion, the referee should mention whether assistants should talk to players about low-level misconduct. "If you have any magic words to make the players behave a bit better, use them. Let them know we're a team. If your words don't work, let me know and I'll come use my tools."

If you call the referee over, be ready with jersey color, jersey number and color of card to display. Some referees have been taught to cover their badge with their free hand, while giving the signal above, to indicate the misconduct element. Mention that in your pregame discussion.

Displaying misconduct cards — the quick card

Some physical contact fouls, such as jumping at, spitting at, kicking or striking quickly escalate the temperature of the game. A player's psychological temperature is an important gauge as to how well you are performing as a referee. Some incidents need a douse of cold water to lower the temperature quickly.

In the PlayPic, ㉒ jumped at the goalkeeper under the pretext of heading the ball. As soon as contact occurred, ㉒ extended his forearm well away from his body, effectively pushing the goalkeeper to the ground. By the time ① regained his feet and ❷ ran to the area to protect his goalkeeper, the referee sprinted in, displayed the card high for all to see and is admonishing ❷ to leave the opponent alone. The referee will quickly draw ㉒ away from the incident, in that case possibly off the field behind the goalposts, ask the defense to set up for the free kick, gather and record the required information from ㉒, move into position near the dropping zone and signal for the restart. If done smartly, from the instant of the foul until the ball is in play, it might take as long as 35 seconds.

Do not issue all cards that quickly. The recommended method is to whistle and signal the foul, draw the player off to the side away from the other players, gather and record the information and then display the card, but that can change depending on circumstances.

That aggressive physical foul, particularly because it was directed toward an airborne, exposed goalkeeper, does not allow you that time. You need to step in and take charge. You need to restore calm quickly. You need

the goalkeeper to know justice will be served. As soon as he sees the card, he should have nothing more to say. Teammates will argue for the red card if you only show the yellow, but it will be a half-hearted argument. They saw how quickly you got to the spot of the foul, how quickly you decided to card and your firm dealing with the offender. ㉒'s teammates may squawk a bit about how it was only a bump and certainly not deserving of a card but again, because the card is already in the air they know their chances of changing your mind are miniscule. Their arguments quickly fade.

Contrast the quick card with a potential scenario. The goalkeeper winds up on his butt and the ball winds up in the net. The referee walks toward the goalkeeper thinking about what to do. By the time ① regains his feet there are already six players in the goal area with more coming from every angle. While trying to remain calm, 19 screaming players surround the referee, the sidelines have erupted and everyone is screaming at the referee and the assistant. It may take minutes to restore order. There may have been several cards handed out. From that skirmish, players may have picked out opponents and feel they "owe them one," which will make game control very challenging. That second referee did not do well with a moment of truth, a make-or-break incident in a game.

The default mechanic described in the *Guide to Procedures* is to issue the card slowly, after recording the necessary information. The *Guide to Procedures* also notes the possibility that a quick card might be needed.

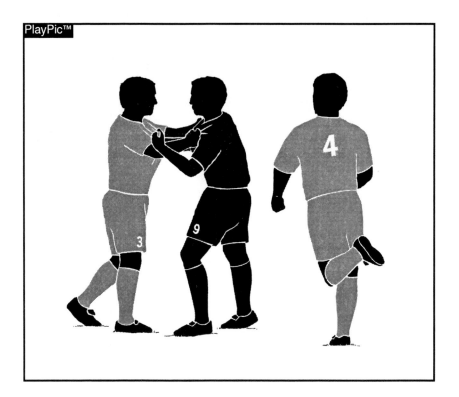

Misconduct — the third player in

Most referees have seen players squabble in the heat of the moment. The action gets a little rough, there is some contact that ❾ thought was a foul but wasn't whistled, so ❾ says something uncomplimentary. ❸ takes offense to those words and they play patty-cakes. English referee instructors use the term, "Handbags at 10 paces." In any case, neither player is guilty of serious foul play or violent conduct at that point. You can run over there, have a few words and quickly restore order between the two combatants.

The problem is the third player into the scuffle. A different mentality takes over when the third player arrives. Coaches and teammates want to restore the equality in a situation that is quickly becoming unequal. When ❹ rushes in, several of ❾'s teammates want to rush over there to make sure ❾ is OK. What was two quickly becomes a dozen. While you were capable of handling two players, a dozen shouting players in a tight pack becomes a handful. Inevitably, someone in that pack is going to say something silly, an opponent will take offense and throw a punch. If that happens, deal with it.

But try not to let it happen in the first place. Get there quickly. Your physical presence is the biggest deterrent to the third player joining in the festivities. Make some noise. Either with your whistle or your voice, make some noise to let everyone know you don't want that third player involved. Direct ❹ to back away — you'll sort everything out without his help.

What usually happens with two players is they throw their arms around a little, the referee comes over to break it up and everyone plays on happily. Even if it escalates into something worse, you still have a game of soccer, now being played 10 against 10. But when you have a dozen players congregate into a small area with punches thrown and obscenities shouted, you have to give serious consideration to terminating the game because of the unsafe playing atmosphere.

All those bad things happen starting with the third player. If you can keep the third player out of the fracas, you promote game control. You meet your moment of truth head-on, and win.

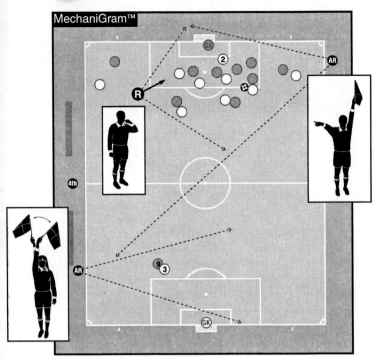

Foul behind the referee's back — informing the referee

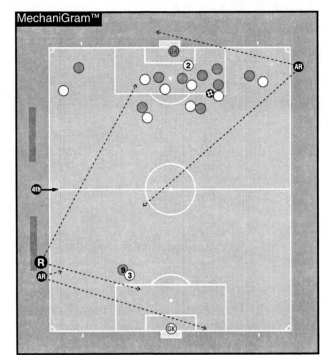

Foul behind the referee's back —more details

Action on the field:

Two players, well away from action around the ball, escalate from a verbal argument into a physical confrontation. Both ⑨ and ③ take closed-fist swings at one another. The striking by ⑨ connects while ③ narrowly misses with a punch to the head.

Referee Responsibilities

You are watching play around the ball. Apparently for no reason, the lead assistant raises a flag. As you look quizzically at the assistant, the lead assistant points to your trail assistant, standing with the flag raised vertically. Once you make eye contact with the trail assistant, she gives the flag a slight wave. Whistle to stop play. Run to her and turn so you are oriented to face as many players as possible.

Assistant Referee Responsibilities

As the lead assistant, you focus on play and ②, who is in an offside position. Out of the corner of your eye, you catch the trail assistant with her flag raised. You raise your flag vertically and direct the referee's attention to the trail assistant.

The trail assistant remains with the flag held vertically until making eye contact with the referee and then gives a slight wave of the flag.

Action on the field:

Two players, well away from action around the ball, escalate into a physical confrontation. The referee is notified and runs to the trail assistant referee.

Referee Responsibilities

You run to the trail assistant and turn so you are oriented to face as many players as possible, standing side-by-side with your assistant. You listen as she reports the events as she saw them. Ask any follow-up questions until you are sure of your course of action. Stop the clock if playing under Federation or NCAA rules.

Assistant Referee Responsibilities

The trail assistant needs to convey critical information accurately and quickly. The referee must take action based on that information, often with serious consequences. In this scenario, the conversation might be, " ⑨ , striking … violent conduct. ③ , attempting to strike, violent conduct. Restart is a direct free kick to dark since ③ was the first to push. Since the foul was here, the restart is just outside this penalty area." Respond to any follow-up questions asked by the referee.

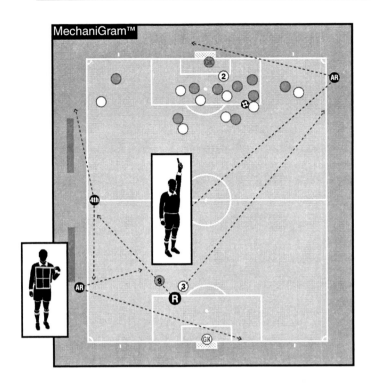

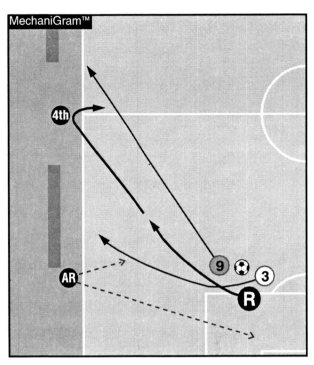

Foul behind the referee's back — displaying the cards

Foul behind the referee's back — get the game started

Action on the field:
Two players, well away from action around the ball, escalate into a physical confrontation. Both **9** and **3** take closed-fist swings at one another. The striking by **9** connects while **3** narrowly misses with a punch to the head. The referee sends off both players.

Referee Responsibilities
Once you are sure of your course of action, display red cards to both players and inform them they are being sent off (Federation = disqualified; NCAA = ejected). Do not allow play to restart until both players are off the field.

Assistant Referee Responsibilities
The trail assistant must understand that some criticism is expected. Coaches may attempt to argue that the other player started it or mention that **3** should not be sent off since the punch did not actually strike the opponent. Expect that criticism and it becomes easier to understand. If someone directs offensive, insulting or abusive comments to you, inform the referee of the facts.

Action on the field:
The trail assistant told the referee **3** was the first to push **9**.

Referee Responsibilities
It is best if you walk between the players as they walk to their respective benches. Listen for taunting comments as **9** passes in front of the white bench. If you need to inform the fourth official or official scorer of the reason for the send offs, do so from close range. Return to the location where the first foul occurred and restart with a direct free kick in favor of the dark team since **3** was the first to foul.

Assistant Referee Responsibilities
The trail assistant must carefully watch the field players for other trouble spots. Two send offs are unusual and both teams may have reason to believe their player could not possibly have done the horrible acts they were accused of by the referees. There will be some level of dissent. Scan the entire field, occasionally taking in the other assistant referee. Move laterally to stay even with the second-to-last defender.

Improper mechanic — too close when issuing a card

Many referees are former players. Many referees still have strong competitive feelings and become offended when a player makes an overly aggressive physical play against an opponent. That becomes apparent when the referee displays the card.

Here ❹ recklessly tripped ⑪ and the referee has run 20 yards to give the caution. Due to his emotional state, the referee has gotten far too close to ❹ and invaded his personal space. That can lead to huge problems, particularly if there is contact.

There is an art to displaying a card properly. Body language and emotional states are very important. Yes, it is acceptable and effective to show some displeasure in your body language, if that's what it takes to sell the card and prevent recurrence.

Another improper action is to call the player to come to you, as if calling an animal. Ask the player to stop, to meet you halfway or to meet you somewhere else away from all other players. For an adult player, stop about two arm lengths away and rotate your body so you can see beyond the player's shoulders toward the largest number of other players. Record the necessary information: team, number, name, time and your shorthand code to remember the incident. Make eye contact with the player and display the card directly over your own head.

Various cultures read body language differently. Many of you have seen televised matches of South American games and seen Latin referees dramatically display the card with their whole body, ending with a snap and a flair as the card reaches its highest point. Culturally, that is appropriate. If you were to referee in their land and sloppily display a card at a 45-degree angle with you arm half bent, the players would read that as, "He doesn't really mean to give that card so whatever behavior earned that card is acceptable."

In an official memo dated Oct. 14, 1998, Display of Cards for Misconduct, Alfred Kleinaitis confirmed USSF policy when he said, "A card should not be displayed in an obviously dramatic fashion, using unusual hand or arm movements, held for an unnecessarily long time or otherwise displayed in a demeaning or aggressive manner. The recommendation in the *Guide to Procedures* is that a card should be displayed 'by holding it straight overhead' — that means over the head of the referee, not the head of the player."

Students of body language would have you set your heels firmly, one foot slightly in front of the other. Just as you raise the card to its fullest height, lean forward an inch or two — not a perceptible amount — and expand your chest. That's one example of getting big, something that is appropriate when issuing a card.

Second yellow card leading to send off

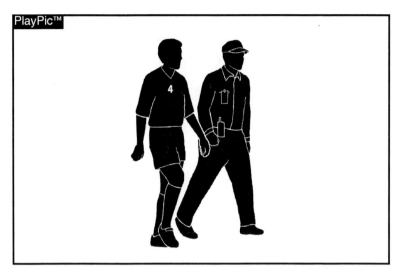

Security dealing with a player sent off

If a player persists in misconduct after having already received a yellow card, you must send that player from the field of play.

You must inform the player, coach and spectators of the reason for the sending off — was the misconduct bad enough to deserve a direct red card or was it a second yellow? Although it is not your immediate concern, the league or tournament might levy different punishment based on your decision.

If you decide the offense merits a caution, and it is that player's second caution of the game, the 1993 IFAB minutes detail the correct procedure: "The referee is required to show first the yellow card and immediately afterwards the red card (thus making it obvious that the player is being sent off because of a second cautionable offense and not because of an offense requiring immediate expulsion)."

For matches played under the National Federation code of rules, there is a different mechanic and a different punishment. For coaches or players who persist in misconduct and earn a second yellow card, you signal their disqualification by holding both the yellow and red card aloft together. That is commonly referred to as the "soft red." If the offender is a player, that team may replace the player. Coaches must leave the vicinity of the playing area immediately.

In a 1999 rule change, the NCAA states that the only card shown to a collegiate player after the first yellow card of a game is a red card.

Most referees don't work in stadiums and have a security staff to handle problems. Here ❹ was shown the red card and the security staff quickly came to the halfway line on the bench side of the field. Security should watch as the player collects his spare shoes, warmup suit and water bottle and then escort the player (now an outside agent) out of the playing area.

Sometimes the coach, assistant coach, trainer or statistician must depart. *Advice to Referees* 5.10 has further information on how to dismiss them from the playing field.

What should you do at your field? You must know what actions to take based on the rules you are playing under. The biggest concern you have is that the sent off (disqualified under Federation and ejected under NCAA) player not unduly influence the game or present safety problems to anyone at the game site. If you have those concerns, temporarily suspend the game and solve that problem.

Playing under Federation rules, the disqualified player is under the direct supervision of the head coach. Unless you feel absolutely compelled for safety reasons, do not send the player from the team bench area. In that rare case, force the head coach to assign an assistant coach to accompany the student-athlete. For legal purposes, you might record a note regarding the incident at the time you make that decision. If you disqualify a coach, the coach "shall leave the vicinity of the playing area immediately and is prohibited from any further contact, direct or indirect, with the team during the remainder of the game." Traditionally, you may hear referees refer to that as "sight and sound."

Under NCAA rules, ejected players are restricted to the team area. Coaches "ejected from the game, shall leave the premises of the field of play. …"

In USSF youth matches, use common sense. You do not want to be responsible for sending a youth player "sight and sound" away from a soccer field only to have that youth commit or be the target of violence. If the youth communicates a threat you believe to be viable, disrupts the match with unseemly comments or other actions that require removal, ensure the coach assigns an adult to supervise the youth for the duration of the match.

This material was extracted from a packet of material prepared by Pat Smith, USSF national instructor and national assessor. Smith prepared the handout for a USL clinic in Chicago on April 11, 1999. More than 90 referees were in attendance to hear what Smith had to say. While there are no right answers, these hard-hitting questions make you analyze when and how you display misconduct cards.

After taking the quiz, share the results with a trusted mentor or senior referee to see if you can spot patterns in game control based on your answers.

To test your ability to determine the appropriateness of your cards, answer these questions:

1. The laws stipulate that certain offenses committed by players must be cautioned. Do you agree with that policy?

Yes/No

2. Whether you agree with the policy or not, do you follow it to the letter?

Yes/No

3. Do you always caution a player who uses abusive language to you, an opponent or a colleague?

Yes/No

4. Do you issue a yellow card every time a player encroaches on a free kick?

Yes/No

5. How many warnings do you give players before you caution them?
A. One
B. Two
C. Three
D. Four

6. Do you feel that yellow cards help you to control a game?

Yes/No

7. When issuing a yellow card do you:
A. Just show the players the card?
B. Tell them they are being cautioned?
C. Give them the reason for the caution?
D. All of the above?

8. Do you:
A. Write the needed information before you pull the card?
B. Display your card and then write the needed information?

9. When an offense is committed that you might caution for, what do you consider a more important factor:
A. Impulsive action?
B. Intentional action?

10. What would you consider persistently infringing the laws?
A. Two fouls by the same player in three minutes.
B. Four fouls by the same player in one half.
C. Six fouls by the same player in 70 minutes.
D. Constant complaining to the referee over the officials' decisions.
E. All of the above.

11. Would you caution all manners of dissent?

Yes/No

Misconduct

• Top referees study videotape for hours and see team tendencies and national styles of play. They watch to detect subtle differences between players who fall after being fouled and those who drop of their own choosing. Most top referees will warn players once with eye contact, a subtle shake of the head or perhaps by saying, "Come on, this game is best played on your feet."

• Do not allow an opponent to delay a throw-in by unfairly distracting or impeding the thrower. If you or an assistant referee are close enough to do some preventive officiating before the distraction takes place, do it.

• Attempting to strike is punished the same as striking, so even if thrown equipment misses its intended target, award a direct free kick to the opposing team. Then you must decide the seriousness of the incident to rule on misconduct. In most cases, you would decide the foul was at least reckless, so give a card.

• If you are the bench-side assistant, hustle into a spot between the bench and the trouble. Turn and face the bench area and use your personality and voice to keep coaches, trainers and substitutes in their technical area.

Quiz

Without referring back, you should be able to answer the following true-false questions.

1. It is proper to raise an upturned palm for all to see (many referees do it five or six times in a row), to encourage a player up off the ground.

2. An opponent may not stand anywhere on the field, even directly on the touchline in front of the thrower. In fact, some referees order a defender to move 10 yards away during a throw-in.

3. Referees are being unprofessional if they attempt to inject humor into a tense situation.

1 - False, 2 - False, 3 - False

Chapter 25

Postgame

A cartoon shows a toddler sitting on the toilet under the caption, "The job's not over until the paperwork is done." The same is true for soccer referees. After NCAA games, referees are required to sign the official boxscore form. Professional division matches have several forms that must be completed and signed within 15 minutes so the teams can report to the league. Most tournaments have field marshals bring you a game result form so tournament staff can determine which teams advance.

Reflect on your performance

Did you do a good job? You don't need a coach, fan or assessor to tell you how you did. You should have a gut reaction about your performance. Did you make any technical errors in applying the *Laws of the Game*? When you saw two opponents 30 yards from the ball punch each other, did you send them off for serious foul play? That would be a technical error, for one of the elements of serious foul play was missing — against an opponent while contesting for the ball.

Common sense

Reflect on those incidents and decisions when you purposefully stretched the laws to suit the spirit of the game. Perhaps you were doing a game which had become lopsided. In the final minutes, with the score already 7-0, a player from the losing side intentionally stood directly over the ball after you awarded a free kick. While the laws allow for you to caution that player for failing to respect the required distance at a restart, you judged that the spirit of the game was served when you simply asked the player to step away without displaying the card. In hindsight, did you make the proper choices?

What is the standard?

Denis Howell, a Football League referee for almost 20 years, said in *Soccer Refereeing*, "I know of no other role in sport that has such an exacting apprenticeship, for there is so much to learn. So much prospect of trouble. So much sheer delight. A world a week to conquer.

"No wonder the mortality rate in the early years is so great. It is estimated that about half of all those who pass the Football Association examination pack up in one season, and half of the rest in two. For it is in those early days, on the local park and works' pitches, that one meets sheer abuse face to face — often for the first time in one's life. It is there one has one's parentage called to account and meets that most enthusiastic of all football fans, the local team secretary."

Did you deal appropriately with the coaches? The players? Think about those player management situations and how well you handled each one. Did you try a phrase mentioned in this book and find that it worked well? Did you experiment with a bit of humor and find that you relieved tensions with a joke rather than a yellow card?

Time management

Referees have the option of extending the half's final whistle well beyond the 45-minute mark (or whatever the game duration). Make sure that both teams are aware of your adding time to cover time wasted.

No one likes to see a senior referee having to run away from players after blowing the game's final whistle. Players can become furious at the referee for not adding time. Sometimes, the losing team needs a scapegoat to justify losing to their rival.

Choose a timely moment and nail the right player with a caution for timewasting. Do that around halfway through the second half. Repeat it with another timewasting player, if necessary.

In a humorous anecdote, in a hot game between a Miami team and a Tampa team, the referee actually took off his watch and gave it to the losing Miami-area soccer mom. He asked her to let him know when the time was over. He turned to the winning Tampa-area team that was wasting time and declared himself as a clock-less referee, "Let's play, guys. I love this game. We'll be here until midnight." They got the point and properly played the game. Of course, the spare watch in his pocket was the official game time but it sent a valuable message that the players heeded.

Seeking help

This chapter has a series of questions you may ask yourself to analyze your game. There are several tools, commonly used by assessors, that you can try. Analyze the data and see what it tells you about the game. Were you aware of those things during the game? If not, you probably need to become aware of them before you advance or upgrade. Work with mentors, senior referees, instructor and assessors. They have your best interests at heart. They want to see you improve. They want you at your best, for then soccer is served well when you use your skills.

Good luck in your games ahead.

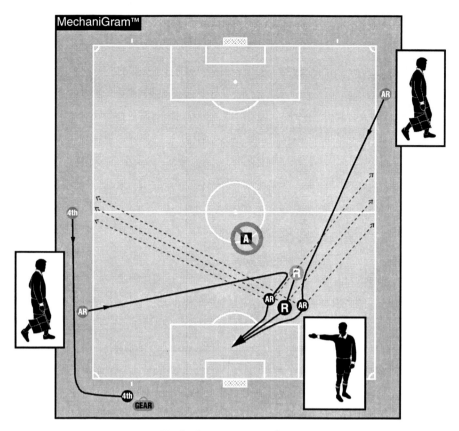

End of game procedures

Action on the field:
The full amount of time (including time lost) has been played and the referee whistles to end the period of play. One team scored more goals than the other.

Referee Responsibilities
Signal by pointing to the center circle with one extended arm. Collect the game ball, walk to a convenient meeting point for your partners and observe the teams departing the field. Depart the field as a team.

Many referees feel compelled to get very close to the team handshakes, inviting unwanted comments from those who choose to make them, such as at location A. Many referees also feel compelled to store their personal belongings between the team benches. An alternative recommendation is to store your kit along one of the goallines where the assistant referee runs the diagonal. Initiate the postgame debrief to garner valuable information from your partners.

Assistant Referee Responsibilities
Collect the game ball if nearby. Furl your flag while sprinting or jogging to join the referee. Observe the teams departing the field. Participate in the postgame debrief to garner valuable information from your partners.

The *NISOA Assistant Referee Duties & Responsibilities* says, "Finally, at the end of the period, both assistant referees (with flags furled) and the referee meet at the center of the field or at a place close to the far touchline to observe postgame formalities between both teams. All wait until the players are off the field or moved to the side. Then the referee and the assistant referees shall perform postgame duties and leave the field together as a team. They should not discuss any calls with coaches, players or fans."

WISCONSIN SOCCER ASSOCIATION
SUPPLEMENTAL REFEREE REPORT: FOR SEND OFFS ONLY
<u>This report must be mailed within 24 hours</u>
Submit a separate report for each person sent off from a game.
All reports are to be sent to the league commissioner.
Referee assault or abuse must also be reported to the State Referee Administrator on a separate form.

Game date ____ / ____ / ____   Location (city/field): _____   League: _____

Scheduled start time: _____   Actual start time: _____   Age group: _____

Home team: _____   Visitor: _____

First half score: ____ / ____   Second half score: ____ / ____   Final score: ____ / ____

Player's number: ____   Player's name: _____   Team name: _____

REASON FOR SEND OFF *(circle one number only)*

1. Serious foul play.

2. Violent conduct.

3. Spits at an opponent or any other person.

4. Denied an opponent a goal or obvious goal scoring opportunity by deliberately handling the ball.

5. Denied an obvious goal scoring opportunity to an opponent moving towards the player's goal.

6. Offensive, insulting or abusive language.

7. Received a second caution in the same match.

EXPLANATION *(give full details of the incident):* _____

_____

_____

_____

_____

_____

_____

_____

_____

_____

_____

_____

_____

_____

(Use additional pages if needed)

Referee name: _____   Phone number: (____) _____
Assistant #1 name: _____   Phone number: (____) _____
Assistant #2 name: _____   Phone number: (____) _____

Misconduct form — blank

The referee "provides the appropriate authorities with a match report which includes information on any disciplinary action taken against players, and/or team officials and any other incidents which occurred before, during or after the match." There is your edict — quoted from law 5.

Some leagues have dropped the requirement for a formal report on each cautioned player. They simply ask referees to note the player's number on the back of the score-reporting form.

Unbelievably, some tournaments are telling referees to dispense with formally reporting send offs. Do not fall victim to that lax attitude. If a player committed an action that led to a send off, report that action to the authorities. If there was a serious injury, especially if medical services were called to the scene, make a report of what you witnessed. Most states or leagues have simple check-off forms such as the one above to assist you in what to report.

WISCONSIN SOCCER ASSOCIATION
SUPPLEMENTAL REFEREE REPORT: FOR SEND OFFS ONLY
This report must be mailed within 24 hours

Submit a separate report for each person sent off from a game.

All reports are to be sent to the league commissioner.

Referee assault or abuse must also be reported to the State Referee Administrator on a separate form.

Game date __8__ / __8__ / __99__ Location (city/field): ___Tampa/Central___ League: __Premier__

Scheduled start time: ___12:00___ Actual start time: ___12:01___ Age group: __BU-18__

Home team: ___Rowdies___ Visitor: ___FCK1___

First half score: __0__ / __0__ Second half score: __0__ / __1__ Final score: __0__ / __1__

Player's number: __4__ Player's name: ___Tom Smith___ Team name: ___Rowdies___

REASON FOR SEND OFF *(circle one number only)*

1. Serious foul play.

2. Violent conduct. *(circled)*

3. Spits at an opponent or any other person.

4. Denied an opponent a goal or obvious goal scoring opportunity by deliberately handling the ball.

5. Denied an obvious goal scoring opportunity to an opponent moving towards the player's goal.

6. Offensive, insulting or abusive language.

7. Received a second caution in the same match.

EXPLANATION *(give full details of the incident):* _____

    In the 68th minute of play, SMITH was sent off for violent conduct.

    With the ball 40 yards away, SMITH struck opponent #9 with a closed fist twice.

    I was 20 yards from the incident.

(Use additional pages if needed)

Referee name: ___Bill Jones___ Phone number: (_813_) _555-1234_

Assistant #1 name: ___Mike White___ Phone number: (_813_) _555-2345_

Assistant #2 name: ___Sue Grey___ Phone number: (_813_) _555-3456_

Misconduct form — completed

Record the who, what, where, when and why. In the case of a preprinted form as shown, simply follow the directions on the form.

If you do not have occasion to complete those forms regularly, ask an experienced referee to assist you. State facts. Quote the reason for the caution or send off directly from the laws or rulebook.

Do not offer opinions as to what you think should happen to the offender. Do not state opinions such as, "That is the worst behavior I've ever seen from a coach. He ought to be suspended from the league forever." The disciplinary committee acting on your report will discount your emotional outburst and give less weight to the important facts because of your unprofessional remarks.

A common mistake among referees completing those forms the first few times — they confuse the issue. They say they issued a red card and then write that it was for a yellow card offense — "I threw number 6 out for dissent."

MLS postgame analysis

Thanks to USSF manager for professional referee assignments and assessments Herb Silva, *Referee* is able to show you the form that MLS referees complete after each game. Silva, MLS director of game operations Dr. Joe Machnik and USSF director of officials Esse Baharmast receive copies of those completed forms from each referee by Tuesday following the game. Each Tuesday night, the MLS referees from the past weekend, the MLS referees for the upcoming weekend plus Silva, Machnik and Baharmast conduct a conference call to discuss officiating matters. You can read the highlights from those conference calls by logging on to http://www.ussoccer-data.com/pubtopic.htm. Click on the "Get Topic List" and look for "MLS Conference Call Notes."

You can analyze your own games. Evaluate all your games — critical incidents such as penalty kicks, cautions, send offs and injuries. Equally important, be sure to look at the positive aspects of your good games; hustle, positioning, use of assistant referees.

Taking the time to analyze your game and writing down a few essential points will help you spot trends. If you've had 10 cautions for dissent in the last five games perhaps there is something in your game management style that causes players to unload on you. Having concrete data, you can discuss that with a mentor or experienced referee who may help you pinpoint the problem and offer suggestions.

Over the long term, watch your

United States Soccer Federation
GAME #
GAME OFFICIALS SELF EVALUATION FORM
DATE
VISITOR   **@ HOME**

FIRST NAME   LAST NAME   POSITION
                        REF. ID.   STATE
                        GRADE

THE DEGREE OF DIFFICULTY OF THE GAME WAS
DESCRIBE A MINIMUM OF THREE INCIDENTS OR EVENTS INFLUENCING THE COURSE OF THE GAME

PROVIDE REASONS WHICH LED TO MAKING SPECIFIC DECISIONS AND MAN MANAGEMENT TECHNIQUES
USED

GIVE A RESPONSE TO THE POST GAME DISCUSSION WITH THE MATCH INSPECTOR. POINTS TO
REMEMBER/ALTERNATIVE TECHNIQUES

DETAIL WHAT YOUR OVERALL STRENGTHS AND WEAKNESSES WERE DURING THE GAME.
STRENGTHS:

WEAKNESSES:

RECOMMENDATIONS TO NEXT REFEREE (i.e. tactics employed, gamesmanship, problem players, style of play)

RATE YOURSELF BASED ON WHAT YOU THOUGHT YOUR PERFORMANCE WARRANTED ON THE DAY AND
AFTER POST GAME EVALUATION.
RATING ON THE DAY OF GAME   RATING AFTER POST GAME EVALUATION
NAME: DATE:

---

averages; 1.2 cautions per game, a send off every 16 adult games and 4.3 penalty kicks per 10 games. Analyze your numbers every 100 games. Is there a sudden dramatic shift in your averages? Perhaps you've moved up a level of competition. Perhaps you're getting older and further from play and everything is not as clear.

Referee self-analysis after a game

The questions are extracted from a handout given out by the legendary Pat Smith, USSF national instructor and national assessor from Florida, at the USL clinic in Chicago on April 11, 1999. Smith's style is a no-bull, straight-ahead, let's-talk-plain-English look at the game — the sort of style you should be looking at when you self-analyze your own game.

After each game, ask yourself these questions:

Did I enforce the laws?

Did I protect the players?

Did I deal with violent play correctly?

Did I punish cheating?

Did I deal correctly with dissent?

Did I acknowledge my assistant referees at all times, even when not accepting their information?

• If the answer to all of those questions is yes, then you deserve a passing assessment.

• If you were not satisfied with the way you dealt with those problems, then perhaps you don't deserve a passing grade — it may be as simple as that.

Soccer Assessment Worksheet

_____
Name of referee

_____
Date of game

_____
Home team

_____
Visiting team

_____ Colors _____

_____ Final score _____

15 _____ | _____
30 _____ | _____
45 _____ | _____

60 _____ | _____
75 _____ | _____
90 _____ | _____

OT _____ | _____

Foul = number only   Goal = number inside "G"   Caution = number with circle   Send off = number with "X"

Remarks or assessors analysis:

_____
(Assessor)

_____
(signature)

Assessor's tool — foul chart

Many times referees can learn from tools used by assessors. Assessors in older age group games often use the simple foul chart shown here. However, it does not take a skilled assessor to track fouls.

Mothers, brothers, friends and fellow referees can chart who committed the fouls, who suffered the foul and the time of the incident. After the game, whoever completed the chart can give it to you for analysis.

Soccer Assessment Worksheet

T. Jones
Name of referee

10 Aug 99
Date of game

United
Home team

Kickers
Visiting team

Red ___ Colors ___ Green

1 ___ Final score ___ 2

15 $^6/_{12}$ $^9/_8$ $^8/_{12}$ $^{GK}/_4$ | $^2/_{11}$ $^8/_7$ Ⓖ ^{IFK} $^4/_9$

30 $^6/_{12}$ $^9/_{12}$ $^4/_{12}$ $^{11}/_{GK}$ | $^6/_{GK}$ Ⓖ

45 $^8/_{12}$ $^5/_9$ $^3/_{10}$ | $^{12}/_8$ $^7/_{10}$

60 $^7/_{12}$ | $^{12}/_7$ ⊗

75 $^9/_4$ | $^7/_H$ ⑥/₃

90 $^3/_{10}$ $^6/_{11}$ Ⓖ | $^2/_{11}$

OT ___

Foul = number only   Goal = number inside "G"   Caution = number with circle   Send off = number with "X"

Remarks or assessors analysis:

I. M. Right
(Assessor)

(signature)

Assessor's tool — postgame analysis

Look at the sample foul chart above and see if you can spot any trends or any errors made by the referee.

Did you catch it? The visitor's number 12 got hammered. The home team got away with seven fouls against an individual who scored two goals against them.

Finally, number 12's frustration got the better of him and he committed an act for which he was sent off, only his second foul of the game. Perhaps number 12 would have felt more protected if you cautioned one or two of the home team players. Perhaps an early caution, before the 30th minute, may have prevented the later fouls.

Have someone track a foul chart for you on an upcoming game. Are you catching the persistent infringers? Are you protecting the skilled players? Are you aware of the trends in the game?

MechaniGram™

Critical Incidents

① _____

② _____

③ _____

④ _____

Referee's name
_____

Date of game
_____

Team names & direction

↑ _____

↓ _____

1st or 2nd half
(circle one)

Age group

B

G

Men

Women

Analysis: _____

_____

_____

_____

_____ Assessor: _____

Assessor's tool — scatter chart

Some assessors like to chart where referees run for a short period during the game. Most often, a 10-15 minute period allows sufficient data to analyze the running patterns. However, it does not take a skilled assessor to track you.

Mothers, brothers, friends and fellow referees can chart where you ran for a 10-minute period, any significant incidents and where you were at the time of the incident. After the game, whoever completed the chart can give it to you for analysis.

What are some of the significant incidents you might record? Cautions issued, penalty kicks, when a player loudly screams, "You're terrible, referee," and goals scored.

MechaniGram™

Critical Incidents

① Red scores in 8th minute 1-0

② Caution to number 9 in 14th minute

③ Green scores in 12th minute 1-1

④ _____

T. Jones
Referee's name

10 Aug 99
Date of game

Team names & direction

↑ *United*

↓ *Kickers*

1st or 2nd half
(circle one)

7 - 17
Age group

U-18

G

Men

Women

Analysis: Covered field well; not afraid to use extreme positions over both goallines. Wide diagonal. Did you realize you cheated toward your more inexperienced assistant on the west touchline? Close at critical incidents: goal, caution, and penalty kick. Cleared through the center of the field quickly with a wide diagonal. Nice job.

Assessor: _____

Assessor's tool — strong performance

The young, fit referee in the MechaniGram above covered the field nicely. She was inside the penalty area when the first goal was scored, within 15 yards when the half's only caution was issued and had a perfect angle to see the foul occurred inside the penalty area.

Have someone track you on an upcoming game. Did you properly position yourself for restarts? Are you near the skilled players as they are fouled? Are you aware of the trends in the game?

MechaniGram™

Critical Incidents

① Red scores in 8th minute 1-0

② Caution to number 9 in 14th minute

③ Green scores in 12th minute 1-1

④ _____

T. Jones
Referee's name

10 Aug 99
Date of game

Team names & direction

↑ United

↓ Kickers

1st or 2nd half
(circle one)

7 -17

Age group
B U·18

G

Men

Women

Analysis: ___Inadequate coverage — notably at critical incidents. Almost 40 yards away at first goal scored. Reckless foul on 9 in 14th minute — caution issued. Told 4th official about caution from 25 yards away, led to "booking" the coach because he overheard negative comments about the foul. Again, 40 yards away at second goal.___

Assessor: _____

Assessor's tool — less than optimum

Sometimes when assessors analyze the run charts, serious problems spring to life. It's easier to point out why a referee is having problems. There is some tangible evidence to shock those referees who think they are stellar performers into seeing the facts.

Refereeing is not all about fitness. There is more to refereeing than simply running hard. But fitness is one aspect of positioning. Positioning is a major factor of game control.

There are many reasons why referees are not able to stay with the pace of the game: their fifth game in a row in a tournament setting, an injury that occurred earlier in that game, chronic problems, advancing age or poor conditioning. Some are understandable, some are not. The referee whose path we view in the MechaniGram above needs to analyze game performance and step down several age levels or get into a conditioning program. Or maybe just an attitude adjustment. Maybe the fitness is there. Maybe the referee feels the game does not deserve full effort. It does! The critical incidents are the same ones as shown for the fit referee.

Postgame review

After the game, it's a good idea to review what happened during the game. The postgame review is another important part of the learning process.

The first order of business immediately after the game is to relax. Officiating can be stressful and postgame relaxation helps get you back to normal. The second order of business is to finish the paperwork for the game.

At a reasonable time after the game, review the game with your partners. Some like to review before taking a shower and relaxing. Others like to wait until the postgame dinner. Do whatever is convenient and comfortable for you and your partners.

When reviewing the game, talk about:

Points of emphasis
Were the pregame points of emphasis handled effectively? Many times, rough play is emphasized. Did you control the game effectively? Were off-ball fouls called appropriately? If the points of emphasis were not handled properly, discuss remedies for your next game.

Tempo
Did you let the game come to you or did you assert yourself when you didn't need to? Did the game develop a flow? If not, is there anything you could have done to keep the game moving? Did you get the ball back in play quickly without rushing?

Bench decorum
How did you handle the benches? Did you let the coaches go too far? Were you approachable?

Strange plays, rulings
Discuss and review any strange plays or rulings. If necessary, confirm your ruling with the rulebook and casebook. Make sure you have the rule down so you can apply it correctly if it happens again.

Solicit constructive criticism
One of the ways to improve is to get opinions and advice from others. Your partners are a great source. Always ask if there's anything that you could have done differently or better.

After asking, accept the constructive criticism. Don't be one of those referees that asks, "How did I do?" expecting a shower of praise. If you don't want to know the truth, don't ask. Take the criticism offered, analyze the comments and apply the changes if you feel they are appropriate.

Be ready to offer a critique when asked. It's frustrating for an official who wants to learn to invite criticism only to hear, "You did a good job." There must be something that needs improving! You ought to be able to give your partners at least three things to think about after every game.

Write a journal
Consider keeping a journal during your season. Write down strange plays, your feelings about your performance, notes about your partners, things you did well and things you can improve on. The journal is a great way to look back during and after the season to see if there are patterns. If the same things keep appearing in your journal, you know there are things that need to be addressed.

Reviewing the journal is also a great way to start thinking about officiating before next season.

Postgame

• Many referees feel compelled to get very close to the team handshakes, inviting unwanted comments from those who choose to make them.

• Initiate the postgame debrief to garner valuable information from your partners.

• If a player committed an action that led to a send off, report that action to the authorities. If there was a serious injury, especially if medical services were called to the scene, make a report of what you witnessed.

• Taking the time to analyze your game and writing down a few essential points will help you spot trends.

Quiz

Without referring back, you should be able to answer the following true-false questions.

1. In completing postgame reports, you may state opinions such as, "That is the worst behavior I've ever seen from a coach. He ought to be suspended from the league forever."

2. Evaluate all your games — critical incidents such as penalty kicks, cautions, send offs and injuries.

3. One of the ways to improve is to get opinions and advice from others. Your partners are a great source.

1 - False, 2 - True, 3 - True

Chapter 26

Appendix

RESTART CHART

	Kickoff	Throw-in	Goalkick	Corner kick	Indirect free kick	Direct free kick	Penalty kick	Dropped ball
Distance opponents must be from ball	10 yards	No specific distance; may not interfere	Outside penalty area	10 yards, with exception of quick kick	10 yards, or own goalline between posts, or outside penalty area, except on quick kick	10 yards or outside penalty area, with exception of quick kick	10 yards, outside penalty area, and penalty arc and penalty behind penalty mark	No distance required
When ball is in play	When ball moves forward	When ball enters field	When ball leaves penalty area into the field of play	When ball moves	When ball moves, with exception of defender's kick in own penalty area (special circumstances in law 8)	When ball moves, with exception of defender's kick in own penalty area (special circumstances in law 8)	When ball moves forward	When ball touches ground
Can a goal be scored directly?	Yes	No	Yes, but only against opponent	Yes, but only against opponent	No	Yes, but only against opponent	Yes	Only after ball hits ground
Can the player who performs the restart play the ball twice in succession?	No	No	No	No	No	No	No	Yes (The referee performs the restart)

To: **Chair, State Referee Committee**
               State Referee Administrators
               State Youth Referee Administrators
               State Directors of Referee Instruction
               National Instructors

From: **Alfred Kleinaitis**
               Manager of Referee Development & Education

Re: **Misconduct by Attackers at a Free Kick**

Date: **January 26, 1999**

At the taking of a free kick, referees often focus their attention on the defenders and are alert for misconduct which defenders might commit in these circumstances. Such misconduct usually involves failing to respect the required distance and actions designed to delay the restart of play. Such attention is proper and should remain an important element in the referee's mechanics for handling free kick restarts.

If defenders form a wall at the proper distance and one or more attackers are involved in this formation, the referee must be alert for specific dangers and must adopt appropriate positioning in order to watch for possible misconduct by these attackers. Increasingly in recent years, some teams have adopted a strategy in which an attacker joins the wall (either at an end on inside) and, at the moment of taking the free kick, pulls or pushes a defender in the wall so as to open a space thorough which the ball might pass.

It is expected that referees will recognize the opportunity for a foul and/or misconduct to be committed by an attacker under these circumstances and will act appropriately to deal with it. What is of even greater importance, however, is the need to develop an approach to positioning at free kicks which will enable the referee to see such behavior (which frequently involves holding or locking arms behind the backs of the players). Experienced referees will also realize that proper positioning often serves to prevent actions of this sort from occurring in the first place.

To: Instructors Conducting Professional League Regional Referee Clinics
Youth and Amateur Tournament Instructors

From: Alfred Kleinaitis
Manager of Referee Development and Education

Re: Guide to Sending Off Offenses
Script for Sending Off Offenses Video
Script for Offside Videos

Date: April 23, 1998

GUIDE FOR INSTRUCTORS USING THE TAPE "SENDING OFF OFFENSES"

The United States Soccer Federation, in conjunction with Major League Soccer, recently put together a videotape with certain incidents that should have been dealt with by a sending-off. The title of the video is "Sending Off Offenses."

This tape is in no way intended to suggest that the behavior shown by the players is the norm for professional players in particular or for soccer players in general. However, these incidents, whether they be real or imaginary, do nothing to enhance the image of soccer in the United States of America and will not be an encouragement to soccer lovers to attend these games.

For this tape to be effective for the audience, it should be narrated so that the viewers learn not only that such conduct is unacceptable, but also why this conduct is unacceptable.

To be an effective manager, it is important to understand the why's of a player's behavior. The better the manager understands the why's, the better he is prepared to deal with the what's. There are five criteria that must be firmly attached to these offenses to make the argument for dismissal stronger. They are:
- Retaliation
- Especially tackle from behind
- Violent and excessive force
- No attempt to play the ball
- One or both feet directed towards an opponent above the ground
  with cleats/studs exposed

Players care about their teammates and they feel personally involved when the perception is that their teammate has been unfairly treated by an opponent and that an insufficient penalty has been assessed. The attitude is: "If you hurt my teammate, you hurt me." In consequence, this becomes the catalyst for retaliation.

U.S. Soccer House   1801-1811 S. Prairie Avenue   Chicago, Illinois 60616
Telephone (312) 808-1300   Telefax (312) 808-1301   E-mail SOCFED @ aol.com

342   *Soccer Officials Guidebook*

In this tape, there are certain incidents that lend themselves to this rationale by players. Referees must recognize the potential for retaliation immediately and deal with it quickly, correctly and firmly.

There is no place for brutality in soccer and there can never be a justification for it to occur.

Each of these fouls that fall within the criteria offered above are career-ending to the player. There can be no thought of "yellow card" or "admonishment" for the type of foul exhibited in this tape. The guilty player must be dismissed instantly, with no thoughts given to possible repercussions.

Referees have been given a mandate: "If you must err, then err on the side of a red card."

The message is clear, very clear: "Do it!"

In this video there are certain situations that have no "tactical importance" as regards the location of the foul. Many fouls occur in the center circle. It could be argued that there is no reason at all tactically for this foul, except possible frustration at the opponent. There is a foul quite close to the corner flag which the tape shows as quite brutal in scope. Referees should not be affected by players' pleadings that they "played the ball." It is important to note that the player who was fouled in this incident had scored two goals in this game.

Referees must recognize the "enforcer" and the "hatchet man." What is their role? Who is the "star"? Is he the target of the brutality? There are incidents in which there are attempts to intimidate the Etcheverrys, the Valderramas and the Donadonis. This must be pointed out in the narration of the video.

There is the player who continually plays "close to the vest," but seems to collect yellow cards for his transgressions. He must be recognized and known by his tackles.

Referees should not have to "think" too long about the seriousness of these fouls. The longer a referee stands about deciding what to do, the greater the possibility of being intimidated, physically harassed or of violent dissent.

While referees should not go into any game with preconceived ideas about players, realistically they should always be prepared. "The good referee is never surprised." If the message to the players is loud and clear, that you will punish transgressors to the fullest extent of the law, and that you are totally consistent in your application, then perhaps you won't have to go to the well too many times to prove it. Conversely, you must not be reckless in your recognition and punishment of these "sending-off offenses," real or imaginary.

If you do the job expected of you by all concerned in regard to violent play, then players will feel secure in the knowledge that they are being protected and that they are free to exhibit their skills and provide entertainment to soccer lovers. They will not have to live in fear the whole time they are playing.

cc: H. Silva, USSF
        J. Machnik, MLS
        E. Proctor, USL

To: Chair, State Referee Committee
           State Referee Administrators
           State Youth Referee Administrators
           State Directors of Referee Instruction
           National Instructors

From: Alfred Kleinaitis
           Manager of Referee Development & Education

Re: Instructions to Ball Persons

Date: January 26, 1999

FIFA has requested that national associations implement various means of speeding the return of the ball into play. Among the recommendations are having up to six balls available around the perimeter of the field and providing ball persons whose responsibility it is to provide the ball to a player for the restart and to retrieve the ball which was struck into touch.

Ball persons serve both teams equally and act only under the general instructions of the referee. Accordingly, the referee, or, at his direction, the fourth official should set time aside to brief ball persons on their duties and responsibilities.

In general, such instructions should be given simply and precisely, taking into account the age and experience of the ball persons. They should be reminded of the following requirements:

♦   they may not favor either team or any player
♦   they must refrain from commenting for or against either team, any player, or any specific action on the field
♦   providing an available ball takes precedence over retrieving a ball
♦   they must take every opportunity to prevent an extra ball from entering the field

It is generally expected that a ball person will not enter the field, even to retrieve an extra ball. However, the ball person should be instructed that reaching into the field or stepping into the field briefly will be permitted if this enables the extra ball to be quickly removed and if neither active play or any players are in the vicinity of the extra ball.

The referee, assistant referees, and fourth official need to be aware of the presence on the field of an extra ball which cannot be quickly removed by the ball persons and which could lead to confusion. If, in the opinion of the referee, an extra ball moves into the area of active play, or if this area shifts in the direction of an extra ball, he may stop play, order the extra ball removed, and restart play with a dropped ball where the ball was when play was stopped (subject to the special requirements of Law 8).

The spirit of the game suggests that referees should be sensitive to selecting an appropriate time for stopping play under these circumstances so that a team having possession of the ball at the time is not penalized unduly. In fact, where an extra ball entering the field is associated with a restart (throw-in, free kick, etc.) the referee should stop play in such a way as to require a retake of the restart.

U.S. Soccer House   1801-1811 S. Prairie Avenue   Chicago, Illinois 60616
Telephone (312) 808-1300   Telefax (312) 808-1301   E-Mail SOCFED @ aol.com